THE GRAND NATIONAL

THE CHRISTENING OF THE BROOK BY CAPTAIN BECHER

The Grand National

1839—1931

By

DAVID HOADLEY MUNROE

With Forewords by

LORD WAVERTREE
AND E. A. C. TOPHAM
Clerk of the Course and Official Handicapper, Aintree

ILLUSTRATED

LONDON
WILLIAM HEINEMANN LTD.

FIRST PUBLISHED 1931

PRINTED IN GREAT BRITAIN
AT THE WINDMILL PRESS

Contents

PART ONE

PART TWO

Illustrations

PART ONE

Illustrations—Continued

FOREWORD

BY LORD WAVERTREE

IT is surprising that no history of the Grand National has been written for a quarter of a century. Yet this is the case, for Finch Mason's *Heroes and Heroines of the Grand National* was published in 1907, and since then no such book has been written. Thus there should be plenty of room in most sporting libraries for Mr. David Munroe's story of the race, which brings it up-to-date, to the very moment when Grakle passed the winning post last March. The description of each race will naturally make delightful reading for those who are interested in the history of the Grand National, and particularly for those who like to recall the races they have actually seen at Aintree. While for those who have owned, trained, or ridden horses the volume will be irresistible.

My own record in the Grand National is one win with twenty-seven horses. Perhaps I have been unlucky—most owners think they are! But the story of my own horses in the National, if briefly told, will not come amiss here, since it gives an insight into the things which happen to most owners, and will give a clear idea of the hopes and disappointments that the game holds in store for some of us.

In 1896 I came to the conclusion that The Soarer was the horse to buy with which to win the National. I bought him from my old friend David Campbell of the 9th Lancers. At Hurst Park The Midshipmite fell and The Soarer fell over him, although Mr. Campbell, who was riding, said he would have won. Thus he was allowed to start at 40 to 1 at Aintree, and as the result of his victory the 9th Lancers were full of money.

The horse improved beyond all belief between his victory and the next National. When he won he was a scarecrow of a horse, but the following year he was a beautiful animal, full of quality, with his wide Skylark quarters and hind legs which strode over his forefeet as he walked—a true indication of great stamina. David Campbell telegraphed to me from India claiming the right to ride him again, in which I concurred. It had, however, been my intention to ride him myself as the weight would give me a comfortable saddle, and he went with me in his gallops over fences better than anyone else, and as I had ridden a great number of winners myself I felt quite able to do him justice. The improvement in the horse was so wonderful that Mr. Campbell, to whom I left the management, was frightened to take any risk by running him previously. The consequence was that when he started for the National in 1897 he was mad fresh, and I could see him with my glasses, jumping over fences, in front of the others, with considerably more vigour than was necessary. This continued until he reached Valentine's Brook, where there is a distinct drop, and here a still more almighty jump brought him to his knees. But he got up and continued the race on his own; and I could see him jumping fences in front of the field until he reached the water jump, when I noticed that something had upset him. He increased his speed and put his head up in the air, took off a good length in front of the water jump, and landed a good length over it—the most enormous jump I have ever witnessed. He seemed to have his eyes closed as he galloped straight on to the paddock and apparently did not see the white rails, which he snapped like a carrot. Then he charged into the wooden palings which separated the paddock from the course and crashed through them! He was cut in many places, and eventually had to be operated upon in his skull, which had been fractured. This operation I had conducted on behalf of the veterinary surgeon by a F.R.C.S., who was very interested in the case. The hole in his skull, which was just below the centre of his forehead, never healed up, and although he ran again in 1898, ridden by Arthur Nightingall, he ran very badly, as he was shivering with fright and trembling like a leaf. I was not able to run him again.

Soon afterwards I discovered that in Wellesley I owned a very good horse. He was one of a batch I had bought from Mr. Murphy of Breemount, who at that time owned all the best jumping blood in Ireland. He was a magnificent-looking animal by Gallinule out of a daughter of Mavourneen, and he was trained by Willie Moore. He astounded us as a four-year-old by beating both Manifesto and Drogheda in a trial, and we eventually tried him again at equal weights two miles over fences with North Sea, the champion two-mile steeplechase horse in England at that time, together with my own horse Specs, who was the champion two-mile selling plater, with a 6-stone boy on his back. He won so easily that the others were pulled up, and there was no question that we had discovered a great horse. Unfortunately for me he was killed when he was sent to run in the National Hunt Juvenile Steeplechase, when he got on to the railway line and broke his leg. I also owned his brother, a year younger, who was even a better horse to look at, and he caught Newmarket fever and died, a three-year-old.

In 1919 I was able to run a five-year-old called All White, which I had bred myself. I fully expected that he would win the race, with his wonderful breeding and stamina. Unfortunately for me my jockey, Chadwick, was ill and could not ride, and the only jockey I could find to ride the weight, 9 stone 10, was a French jockey called T. Williams, and I had to put him up at the last moment. The second time round there were very few horses left in the race. All White had jumped Becher's Brook for the second time, when, although almost leading the jockey pulled him up and stood still for some time, and then started him again and followed the others, who by this time were nearly out of sight. But my horse finished the course and was fifth. I asked the jockey why he had pulled him up and he said that he was sick from having eaten his lunch, but that he went on again as soon as he had finished. That was hard luck for me, for I think he would have won.

The next year I ran him again and he was ridden by my own jockey, Chadwick. After jumping the fifth fence he slipped up on the wet ground on the flat. The going that year was very bad, and the day was so thick that we could not see the horses from the Stand.

The following year, 1921, he was again ridden by Chadwick, carrying more weight, 10 stone 13 lbs. After jumping the water jump a long way in front of the other horses, he was striding along with his ears pricked and the race well in hand. It was a very windy day and all the luncheon papers of the crowd had blown into a drift in front of the open ditch on the left hand side, and very foolishly his pilot did not pull out into the middle of the course to avoid it, but actually rode his horse where the paper drift was lying in front of the open ditch. He took an almighty leap over the paper, ditch and fence, and shot his jockey on to the ground on the landing side. But Chadwick had stuck to the reins, and putting them back over the horse's head and vaulting into the saddle, he followed on a long way behind and finished third to Shaun Spadah and The Bore, who were both beaten horses. I consider that also was bad luck.

I ran him the following year, 1922, again ridden by Chadwick. Sergeant Murphy carried him out at the canal fence and Chadwick did not persevere, but stood and watched the fun. Sergeant Murphy actually finished fourth after refusing the fence again, losing his bridle and having it put on again; so All White surely could have beaten him if the jockey had ridden him at the fence again! I could not run him the next year, as he was lame. The following year he was carried out again at the canal turn, ridden by Tighe, and in 1925, although far from fit from being stopped in his work, he was started and ridden by Mason, who took the outside the whole way round, and he fell at the last fence but one. I ran him again in 1927, but the horse was not sound and was pulled up.

It is a very difficult thing to find a horse capable of winning the Grand National Steeplechase; and if you find the horse it is difficult to bring him fit and well to the post, and when you have done that it is very hard to find a good jockey.

The foregoing remarks are an epitome of my attempts to win the race, and I only tell it at the author's request to give some idea of the difficulties with which most owners who have National ambitions have to contend.

Dear Mr. Munroe,

I have read your MSS. with great interest, and I think it is a most valuable contribution to the history of the Grand National, and to that of steeplechasing. It has brought the history of the Grand National right up to the present time, and gives a really true and entertaining account of the race. I feel sure that the book will arouse a great deal of interest, and that it will be very useful as a source of information.

[*Signed*]   E. A. C. TOPHAM

November 10, 1930

B

AUTHOR'S NOTE

THIS book was inspired by the fact that the only previous history of the Grand National which has ever been written made its appearance some twenty-five years ago. My first Grand National left me with a very definite curiosity about the past history of the race, but a minimum of investigation showed that this curiosity must go unsatisfied unless I was prepared to undertake some real research in various places. There were plenty of books which discussed incidents in individual races, and a few which gave segments of actual history; but for some incredible reason only one had been devoted entirely to the Grand National, and that one ended with the events of a generation ago. The original research was made with only the vaguest ideas of writing a book, but fear and trepidation were at length banished by the interest of the thing, and I determined to make an attempt at bringing National history up to date in as complete a manner as I could.

The hunt for material started in the British Museum, and in the course of a few months I read all the books obtainable that had anything to do with the Grand National or with anyone connected with it. Next came a study of the files of old newspapers, and on top of this I had the good fortune to talk with a number of people who had the sort of first-hand information about past races that I lacked. It was comparatively simple to estimate the value of this last type of information, but in the case of that gained from the printed page it was a different matter.

The hardest problems which cropped up were those caused

by the differences of opinion which appear in different books. When a statement has once appeared in print, it is likely to do so again, and the writer is faced with the job of tracing that statement back to its originator, and of deciding whether that originator was in a position to know exactly what he was talking about. The size of The Lamb, that great little steeplechaser who won the Nationals of 1868 and 1871, is a case in point. Various heights have been attributed to him, and he is sometimes described as being only fourteen hands two inches, but I have taken the opinion of an author who knew "Mr. Thomas"—he rode The Lamb in his second victory—and who states definitely that the horse was exactly four inches higher than that. And yet this same author is led astray on certain other questions where his authority is less unimpeachable, and where other people were in a position to have more exact knowledge.

Another writer, who flourished more recently, is horrified because certain of the obstacles in the early days of the race are spoken of as "hurdles," and because the banks which abounded at the same period are mentioned as being sometimes less than two feet high. The facts are that many of the early fences *were* nothing more than hurdles, and that some of the early banks were very small indeed; it must be remembered that not only the Aintree course, but even the race itself, have changed out of all recognition since the Grand National was first run nearly a hundred years ago. I am thoroughly aware that in some ways this book will disagree with certain accepted ideas, but to such criticism I can only reply, in all humility, that such changes as I have made seem to me justified by the information at my disposal.

I should like to take this opportunity of thanking Lord Wavertree for his very great kindness in writing a foreword to the book. As Mr. Hall Walker he was one of those lucky owners who have won the greatest steeplechase in the world at their first attempt, and his victory with The Soarer in 1896 was gained in an era of exceptionally good horses. Lord Wavertree's name is of course very well known under both rules of racing, and I feel deeply honoured that he allows it to appear on the title-page of this effort of mine.

My sincerest thanks are due also to Lord Lonsdale, to whom I am indebted for the information about Captain Machell. Mr. E. A. C. Topham, the Clerk of the Aintree Course and the Handicapper for the Grand National, gave kind advice and assistance; in addition to that, he was good enough to write me a letter as an introductory note for this book, and I wish to express my thanks and appreciation. Further assistance came from Messrs. Weatherby and Sons, in whose offices are centred the Official Stud Book and the Registry for all racing. The map of the early Grand National course is reproduced by their kindness from *Steeplechases Past* for 1848, and I owe a particular debt to the Stud Book Department for much of the material which appears in the chaper on breeding.

Others whose help has been invaluable are Captain and Mrs. J. W. Bridges, Mr. A. Henry Higginson, M.F.H., and Mr. Morley Kennerley, and I should like to thank them, and the Hon. Mrs. Aubrey Hastings, who allowed me to spend a day at her stables at Wroughton, where I saw and learned much that was interesting. Mr. Louis Bruguière generously let me photograph two of his old prints which appear in this book, and which describe much better than words the informality of early steeplechasing. The frontispiece, which shows a famous incident in the first year of the race, is reproduced by the courtesy of Messrs. Arthur Ackermann and Sons, of London, from an old print in their possession.

Books from which I have drawn material are *Heroes and Heroines of the Grand National*, by Finch Mason; *Men and Horses I Have Known*, by the Hon. George Lambton; *Racing and Steeplechasing* (Badminton Library), by the Earl of Suffolk, Arthur Coventry and Alfred E. T. Watson; *My Racing Adventures*, by Arthur Nightingall; *Triumphs and Tragedies of the Turf*, by Campbell Russell; *Memories of Men and Horses*, and *My Kingdom for a Horse*, both by William Allison; *A Trainer to Two Kings*, by Richard Marsh; *Arthur Yates, Trainer and Gentleman Rider*, by Arthur Yates; *The Influence of Racing and the Thoroughbred Upon Light Horse Breeding*, by William Scarth Dixon; *The Points of the Horse*, by Capt. M. H. Hayes; *A History of Steeplechasing*, by William C. A. Blew; *Letters from an Old Sportsman to a Young One*, by A. Henry Higginson; *In My Opinion*, edited by Major E. W. Lyons; *Thoroughbred Types*, edited by Charles D. Lanier.

Finally, I should like to thank the editors of *The Sportsman* for their kindness in permitting me to use extracts from an article which I wrote for them some two years ago, and Messrs. David Allen and Co., of Liverpool, for assisting me at a very difficult point in the research.

Lee-on-Solent, Hants.

    September, 1931.

PART ONE

CHAPTER ONE

The Blue Riband of Steeplechasing

SOME years ago the late Lord Marcus Beresford, who was at that time Manager of the Royal Stud at Sandringham, received a visit from a sartorially perfect delegation of Frenchmen who had come to England to buy blood stock. Among the horses they examined was Perrier, a remarkably handsome and well-bred colt, but one who had done nothing very wonderful on the race course. A grave array of top hats and frock coats surrounded the horse while Lord Marcus waxed cheerfully enthusiastic, as horsemen do on these occasions; he mentioned Perrier's beauty and good breeding, and in a burst of inspired eloquence, stated that he undoubtedly should have won the Derby.

"Why didn't he win the Derby?" asked one of the Frenchmen.

"Because," said Lord Marcus, who was seldom at a loss for words, "at a critical moment in the race he was passed by six or seven other horses!"

If Lord Marcus could so engagingly coin a brand new alibi to explain away a racing defeat on the flat, one wonders what shining child of his imagination might have sprung from the Grand National Steeplechase, a race in which his opportunities would have been gloriously unlimited. From the very nature of steeplechasing, it is a sport in which any number of things may happen to a horse, and this fact is nowhere more evident than at Aintree, where the Grand National is run. For many years the "National" has been the blue riband of steeplechasing, and a horse who has won it is assured of a place among the immortals of the Turf, whatever he may have done or failed to do in the past. It is probably the hardest test of stamina in the racing world, but just how hard it is no one can really appreciate until he has seen the thirty great fences, and watched a huge field of good horses race over them for the distance of nearly four and a half miles.

When you go to the National you are generally persuaded by your own curiosity, or by that of a more energetic companion, to go down to have a look at the fences, and possibly to walk part of the course. You stroll up to one of the fences and are amazed to find that even by standing on tip-toe you can hardly see over the top. You straightway go to wondering how a horse can be expected to get over such a huge obstacle, and how the jockey feels when he sees it looming up before him. When you see the course stretching away into the distance, one great fence after another, and realize that each fence is much like the one you have just examined, you suddenly feel that there is no other race course in the world like this one, and you go back to a place in the stands with a heightened sense of excitement and anticipation.

All about you is noise and bustle, talk of this horse and that; people mill back and forth below you in the enclosure, and the strident voices of the bookmakers rise up from their posts on the rail. At length the sport begins with two flat races, but hovering in the back of your mind is the thought of those great jumps, and the events on the flat seem somehow tame and uninteresting. After they are done with, many people get up and go out to the paddock to see the National horses saddled, but the wise man hugs his seat, for in a few minutes the stand is filled to overflowing, and many who have left never get back again. Someone says: "There they are!" and necks are craned to watch the horses as they come out through a little gate to the right. If you were lucky enough to be there in 1929, you watched the scene in brilliant sunshine, and saw, as well, the largest number of horses, by more than twenty, that has ever taken part in the race.

A long line of horses files by, their jockeys clothed in brightly coloured silks. One by one they pass in parade until the count has reached sixty-six. Up to the left of the stands they turn and come back, some cantering quietly, others pulling hard on their way to the bend in the course where the starter lines them up. For a wonder this huge cavalcade is quiet and well-behaved; a few break and dance about, but are quickly brought into line, the flag falls, and with a roll of thunder they are off into the country. There has been much speculation as to what will happen when this mighty wave of horses breaks over the first fence. Your heart beats quickly—and, amazingly, they are all over! Only two down at the next jump, but at the third someone refuses, and there is a mass of milling horses and kaleidoscopic colours. But don't watch the falls; the favourite is out in front, the brilliant chestnut is striding away into a terrific lead, and perched above those swinging shoulders is a jockey in pink with black and white striped sleeves. Round the bend at the Canal Turn he leads them, and comes running easily back toward the stands, sails over the Water Jump, and is away into the country again. Behind him come those that are left, but only twenty-two in all—double that number are out somewhere on the course, and will wander slowly home, to bear after their names that ambiguous phrase "did not finish."

The favourite is still leading at the Canal Turn in the second round, but at Valentine's Brook he spreads a plate, and as he does so another chestnut, a big powerful horse with a tangerine jacket on his back, bursts from the second group, and sets sail for the leader. The favourite is tiring under his big weight, and that loose shoe is bothering him, and the other creeps up. Only two more fences, and then the run in! The tangerine sweeps by, clears the last fence, and gallops home in front—and the Grand National has been won by a rank outsider, a 100—1 shot!

The Grand National is run during the last week in March, and may be said to act as the grand climax of the season's steeple-chasing, in spite of the fact that a certain amount of racing over fences continues on into the month of April. The races run through the winter on the Park Courses—by which is meant any steeplechase course other than Aintree—in conjunction with several which are held at Aintree itself, are interesting not only in themselves, but because they form a series of training grounds for the National. Of the especially notable races at Aintree, two are run the day after the National; they are the Champion, contested over one circuit of the course, and the Foxhunters', an absolute facsimile of the National as to distance, jumps, and weight carried and differing from the National only in that it is for gentleman riders. The other Aintree steeplechase of particular importance is the Grand Sefton, which comes in November; like the Champion, it is run over part of the National course, and as the National comes only about four months later, the winner of the Grand Sefton receives a lot of attention, for he has shown that he can jump the Aintree fences.

From the time racing begins on the Park Courses in the autumn, until the start of the National in March, the search for the ultimate winner of the great race goes on. All through the winter

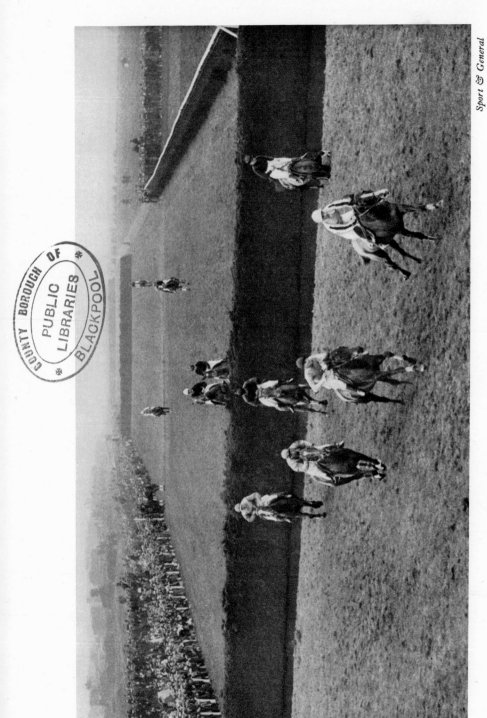

Sport & General

EASTER HERO LEADING AT BECHER'S IN 1929.

there are races in different parts of England, and during the first half of March the "preliminaries" come to a head at Gatwick, Hurst Park, and Cheltenham. The distances of these March races are much the same as that of the National, but the mere fact of victory in the National Trial at Gatwick or Hurst, or in the Gold Cup at Cheltenham, is no criterion of future success at Aintree, despite the fact that horses who do well in them are generally the popular fancies there. Every year a lot of these popular fancies go out into the Aintree country in fine fettle, only to return chastened and sober, and to remind their backers again that at Aintree past performances must be discounted, and that the National is a law unto itself. Like any other race, the National is won by the horse that comes in first; but it is primarily a jumping race, and it is often said that any horse that can jump the fences and stay the course is a potential winner, regardless of his speed. When Count Kinsky rode his own mare, Zoedone, to victory in 1883, a veteran trainer gave him the following advice before the start:

"Ride just as if you were out hunting the first time round. After that, and not before, you may begin to look about you and see what the others are doing."

In other words, jump the fences, and let everything else go hang until halfway through the race; and this advice would be difficult to improve on. George Stevens, who won the National more times than any other jockey, always hung way behind in the early stages of the race, so much so that on one occasion the owner of Stevens' mount rushed to the rail as Stevens came by at the finish of the first round, and shouted at him to get on. The jockey may have felt that he was riding this race and the owner was not, but get on he did, and won very comfortably, which he would very probably have done in any event.

The Grand National was run for the first time ninety-two years ago, when Queen Victoria was young and steeplechase jockeys rode across country with an eye on the spire of a distant church; and it has increased in popularity ever since. The owners of National horses come from every rank in society, from farmers to royalty; and success is not necessarily founded on great wealth, for many a horse has started life in some humble capacity and been bought for next to nothing at all, only to blossom forth into a Grand National winner. The Derby may be "the greatest race in the world," but for many hunting men and others who like to see horses race over fences, the National is The Race of the year, and like Arthur Nightingall, the great jockey who won it three times, they "love to hear the word Aintree pronounced, even in a hushed whisper . . ."

CHAPTER TWO

The Grand Liverpool, and the Stone Wall Years

TO people who are accustomed to the orderliness of modern steeplechase courses, with their fields of level grass divided by neat artificial jumps carrying a gaily coloured flag at each end, it is perhaps difficult to convey an idea of what the Aintree course looked like in 1839 when the Grand National was first run. Steeplechases were inspired by the good old hell-for-leather match races, run across any naturally-fenced country that happened to be available, and in which the winner proved to his own and everyone else's satisfaction that he could get his horse from one spot to another faster than the other fellow.

A certain slim formality appeared when the number of runners increased to a dozen or more, the jumps were perhaps changed and stiffened, and flags were placed here and there to insure that all the riders followed roughly the same course; but the type of country was very little different. The greater part of the course was without a rail on either side but was more or less circular, and this was the most noticeable departure from the old point-to-point. At Aintree a few of the fields were grass, but a great many of them were heavy plough; and they varied from year to year as different things were planted in each field by the farmer who worked it. For the first forty-six years of the race there was no rail on the inside, and on several occasions there were only two fields of grass in the whole course.

In the early days there was a grand stand, but it was not large, and many of the spectators were mounted and followed along as best they could on the inside of the course, cutting across to meet the runners at the finish, and often conducting miniature steeplechases of their own. The rest of the spectators were spread out wherever their fancies indicated: on the tops of fences, in trees, and on the tops of the big coaches which were drawn up near the start and the finish, both of them being, roughly, in the same place. The whole scene was one of considerable confusion—men and horses scampering in every direction, back and forth across the course, scurrying to get out of the way as the horses approached—and there was no particular organization or strict application of rules.

Steeplechasing from the beginning was thoroughly popular with sportsmen in general, but it was frowned upon by the established authorities of flat racing, who regarded it as a sort of bawdy, illegitimate connection: charming lady to play about with, and all that sort of thing, but really not the kind one could introduce to one's people!

The sudden and continued prominence of the Grand Liverpool Steeplechase, as it was called at this time, was probably due to the fact that it was the first jumping race with a really desirable prize to be won. Twelve hundred pounds was the purse in 1839, and though that does not sound impressive compared to the great value of the race at the present time, money was worth more in those days, and it was a very respectable sum for a sport that was still in its infancy. The Grand Liverpool's predecessor at Aintree was a selling steeplechase which was first run in 1836. It had no great monetary value, and is noteworthy only because the victor that year was the famous Captain Becher on The Iron Duke.

The conditions of the Grand Liverpool in 1839 were as follows:

"A sweepstake of 20 sovs. each, 5 sovs. forfeit, with 100 added; 12 stone each; gentlemen riders; four miles across country; the second horse to save his stake, and the winner to pay 10 sovs. toward expenses; no rider to open a gate or ride through a gateway; or more than 100 yards along any road, footpath or driftway. (55 subscribers.)"

"Four miles across country . . ." The distance was actually a little more than this, and there were twenty-nine jumps in all, fifteen to be negotiated in the first round, and fourteen in the second. Most of them were little two-foot banks with gorse on their tops and a smallish ditch one side or the other, but there was an occasional post and rail thrown in for good measure, and three of the fences were quite stiff enough to fill any horse and rider with respect. The first of these was Brook No. 1, now known as Becher's Brook. Originally a natural brook with a tiny trickle of water, it had been dammed up to a width of about eight feet, and a yard back on the take-off side was a strong timber fence some three and a half feet high. By a diabolical intervention of nature the approach to this brook and to the other one, which will be described presently, was through the heaviest plough on the course, which served to slow a horse up just when he needed his speed most. Becher's Brook, therefore, if not as formidable as it is now, was a very respectable sort of fence, and its difficulty was increased by the landing side being a yard lower than the take-off. Brook No. 2, however,—later known as Valentine's Brook—was a regular rasper. Out of the plough arose a two-foot bank which acted as a guard rail for a wide deep ditch. On the far side of the ditch was a three-foot timber fence, with a considerable drop

c

beyond it, and the distance from the bank to the top of the fence was at least nine feet. There seems to be a variety of opinion among writers on the Grand National as to whether or not there was a third brook in the Aintree course in 1839. The official map, reproduced here by the courtesy of Messrs. Weatherby & Sons, proves conclusively that there were only two brooks—exclusive of the Water Jump, which was non-existent in 1839—and all the contemporary accounts and descriptions of the course mention only two brooks. Finch Mason, in his *Heroes and Heroines of the Grand National*, introduces a third brook somewhere in between Becher's and Valentine's, but the map does not uphold him any more than the written evidence.

After Valentine's there was nothing very frightening until near the finish of the first round of the course, where a pile of loose stones had been raised to a height of four feet eight inches. This wall was not the formal, carefully laid affair that the painters of the race would lead us to believe. There are very few existing prints of early Grand Nationals, but these invariably show the wall as a very neat sort of thing. The explanation of this error probably lies in the fact that in 1843 the wall was as neat and formal as anyone could have wished, and that the painters preferred to portray it in that fashion. The wall was not jumped in the second round; instead, the field swung out to surmount a stiff post and rail of something over four feet, and though this was not as formidable as the wall, it was quite hard enough for horses that were finishing a long race through deep and exhausting mud. This particular post and rail was banished in 1844, but various similar fences were put up at other points, usually in front of some fence that seemed too easy, during the first five or six years

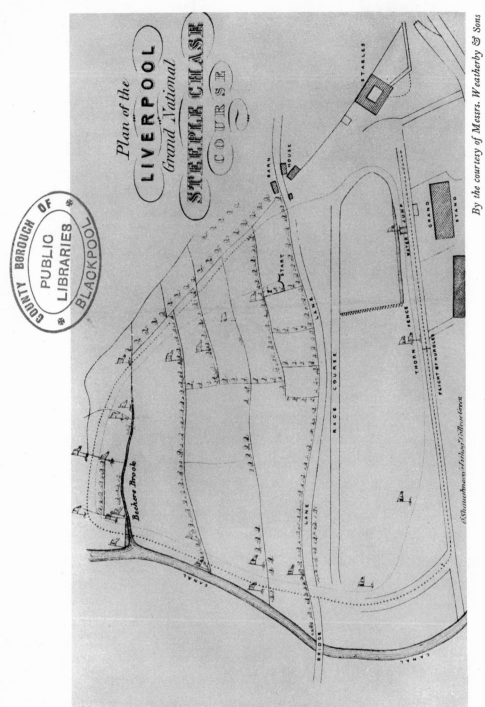

Plan of the
LIVERPOOL
Grand National
STEEPLE CHASE
COURSE

By the courtesy of Messrs. Weatherby & Sons

THE GRAND NATIONAL COURSE IN 1848.

of the race. An irate journalist complained on one occasion that the Aintree fences "are so small that one needs a microscope to discover them," and such comment was generally followed by fevered erections of posts and rails.

"No rider to open a gate or ride through a gateway, or more than 100 yards along any road, footpath or driftway." The fact that such a prohibition was necessary in the conditions shows how very much the course resembled that of an old-fashioned point-to-point. Very few of the fences were level along the top, and a jockey might wander round the country more or less at will, as long as he passed the flags on the correct side and obeyed the above ruling. A fence might be jumped at any spot for a hundred yards or more of its length, and the lower places were as popular as the gaps are in the hunting field.

This possibility of choice in where to jump gave a jockey a brilliant idea on one occasion. When he walked the course the day before the race, he carefully marked with small pieces of paper what seemed to him the most jumpable places in each fence. Fortunately for his peace of mind he did not observe a competitor who followed him around and as carefully moved the tiny sign-posts to the highest and hairiest places he could find; but on the running of the race he soon found he had started something he could not finish, and followed the paper trail to an early fall!

The race in the first year had seventeen starters and included most of the good steeplechase horses of the period. A contingent of bellicose Irishmen had come over to support two of the Irish horses entered, which belonged to Mr. Ferguson. Their names were Rust and Daxon, and they were big powerful animals, much the most impressive looking of the horses in the paddock before the race. They were the early favourites, along with a well-known English mare, The Nun; and many fancied Charity, who had been trained over the stone walls of Gloucestershire, and should therefore experience no difficulty at the Wall. As "the off" time drew near, however, Mr. John Elmore's Lottery, to be ridden by the famous Jem Mason, came on in the betting, and, to the impotent rage of the Irish who lacked only numerical power to make their horses start at odds on, was soon installed as favourite at 5—1. The tiny village of Aintree was the scene of many pugilistic encounters that day late in February; the tavern did a rushing business to a chorus of blows and recriminations, and peace was by no means restored when Lord Sefton, the "umpire," lined the horses up at the start.

An Irish cheer arose when Daxon strode out in the lead with Captain Becher on Conrad in close attendance. The first few fences were taken at a rushing speed by this pair. At Brook No. 1, the powerful Irish horse hit the fence, but floundered over, and went on, leaving Captain Becher to make history. Conrad lacked the mighty shoulders of Daxon, and the fence stopped him with a bang, but the Captain continued, and presently found himself on his hands and knees with a perfect view of a cavalry charge. A moment of thought, and he dived like a mermaid into the deepest part of the brook; the field thundered over his head, spurred on by the voice of Becher deploring the lamentable coldness of water deprived of the concomitant brandy!

The Irish hopes were soon blasted, however, for Daxon fell, was remounted, and then fell again, this time for good, while his compatriot Rust suffered an even worse fortune. He was going quite well until he came to the lane near the end of the first round. At this point, however, his prowess upset some of those who had bet on other horses, and they saw to it that he did not emerge from the lane until the rest of the field was thoroughly "gone away." Charity confounded her admirers by being the only horse to come down at the Wall. In the words of a contemporary bard, who celebrated the race in verse: "But Charity in horse and man too often is asleep, sirs . . ." And the field, rather thinned out by now, struggled away for the second round. The Nun collapsed at Brook No. 2, and by her side Dictator caught his knees in the fence, toppled over, burst a blood vessel, and died in a few minutes. Lottery was now very obviously the best; he sailed into the straight going easily, jumped thirty-three feet over the last fence, and won in a canter from Sir George Mostyn's Seventy Four, with Paulina a poor third.

The Irish were more belligerent than ever by this time, and immediately protested the race on the grounds that the made fences were unfair. They were met with the rather natural reply that they should have thought of that before the race, and that, in any event, the fences were as fair for one as for another. To which we might add that the time of 14 minutes 53 seconds gave all and sundry plenty of opportunity to show what they could do several times over. The above-mentioned bard remarks that "the lightning speed of Lottery despises all control." Though this seems a product of excessive admiration, the fact was that the English horses knew more about galloping over fly fences than animals which had been schooled to crawl up and down Irish banks, and it was not until 1847 that the Irish realised this with sufficient thoroughness to send over a horse who jumped flying fences fast enough to win.

The time was undoubtedly slow, but the going was very bad, and Lottery proved himself a good horse in faster run races during the next few years. It is amazing how he seems to have dominated the imaginations of the other owners, and through them, of the framers of the conditions of the race. The following year Mr. Power on Valentine saw fit to bet that he would be first over the Stone Wall. He brought the field along at a terrific rate, accomplished his endeavour, and in spite of it managed to finish a bad third behind Jerry and Arthur in a race that was run in 12 minutes 1 second. Valentine's pace had told on many of the field, however, and Lottery and three others knocked down themselves and a good portion of the Wall. This does not look very impressive for Lottery, but so completely did he imbue the spectators with the belief that he would have won but for this mishap that heads were put together in an effort to destroy his chances for 1841. When the conditions appeared for that year, the winner of the Cheltenham Steeplechase was obliged to carry eighteen pounds extra—this in a race at equal weights of 12 stone each! Lottery was the Cheltenham winner, so the penalty was clearly aimed at him. Even with this crushing weight he ran very respectably until the terrific impost told, and Mason pulled him up. The winner of this race was Charity, the Gloucestershire failure of 1839, who defeated the two greys, Cigar and Peter Simple, in a tremendous finish, and inscribed herself in the records as the first mare to win the National.

In 1842 Lottery was again penalized eighteen pounds for having won the Cheltenham race two years before, and was again pulled up when the weight told. The next year he was fourteen years old, and no one feared him any longer; he carried only five

THE STONE WALL IN 1839.

By the courtesy of Messrs. Arthur Ackermann & Son

pounds extra, and finished seventh in his last appearance at Aintree. He was not a handsome horse, for his back was very long and his quarters strangely short, but muscle stuck out all over him, and he could gallop as well as jump. He had won a flat race at Beverley as a five-year-old; after that had changed hands for one hundred and twenty pounds at Horncastle Fair, and was hunted a season with Mr. Anderson's Staghounds before his steeplechasing career began. Mr. John Elmore, his owner, was a great figure in the steeplechasing of those days, and had many good horses in his stable at one time or another. He was a horseman of the old school and trained and worked his horses in the hard, old-fashioned manner; but they seemed to come out of it all right in the long run, and certainly won races. He lamed Lottery a few days after he bought him by jumping him over iron railings, garden chairs, and anything else that happened to be around, but the horse eventually became sound again, and was a familiar figure in the hunting field long after his racing days were over.

Mr. Elmore had good luck in the National, for in 1842, the second year that Lottery was handicapped out of the race, he won it with Gaylad, his second string, to the confusion and annoyance of the other owners.

The gentleman rider rule seems to have been purely a gesture, for not more than four or five of the riders in 1839 were anything like amateurs. Captain Becher was one of the few, and in spite of his ignominious dive to fame, was a very excellent horseman. He was a protégé of Thomas Coleman, the "father of steeplechasing," and when he returned from the Peninsular War with a courtesy title conferred on him by the Duke of Buckingham, he settled down to a cross country career in earnest. He had a beard which was said appreciably to increase his weight, was a man of great physical strength and hardiness, and must have been somewhat the type of the famous John Mytton, who rode bears into dining rooms, cured himself of the drunken hiccoughs by setting his shirt on fire, and never carried a pocket handkerchief for the simple and sufficient reason that he never needed to blow his nose! Captain Becher had the singular faculty of doing something noteworthy in steeplechase inauguration. In the St. Albans Steeplechase of 1830, probably the first race in England in which a real "field" of jumpers competed, he finished second on Tatler by a brilliant feat of riding; in 1836 he won the first steeplechase at Aintree on The Iron Duke; and in the first Grand National he parted company with his horse in so skilful a manner that his name has come ringing down the years!

The Stone Wall which destroyed Lottery's chance of winning the National twice was curiously attractive to the Liverpool authorities. After the 1840 fiasco it was taken down, and when Charity won she had merely to spread herself over a ten-foot water jump with a thick thorn fence on the take-off side. But the attraction of having a splendid scrimmage and pile-up right in front of the stand was overwhelming, and in 1843 the Wall came back, this time with a layer of turf along the top, and the wall itself made of masonry. The result must have been eminently satisfactory, for Tinderbox smashed through the Wall, Teetotum plunged himself and his owner-rider's beautiful curls on top of them, and Lottery added to the show by clearing the mix-up with a tremendous leap. Tinderbox was badly hurt, however, and the wall was definitely banned, to give place to a post-and-rail which remained until the erection of the Water Jump in 1847.

By the courtesy of Messrs. Arthur Ackermann & Son

THE FINISH IN 1839.

CHAPTER THREE

1843 to 1871, and the Grand National Hunt Committee

THERE were two important changes during the next few years, in addition to those already mentioned. In 1843 the race became a handicap, and its name was changed to "The Liverpool and National Steeplechase," which name gave place four years later to that of "The Grand National Handicap Steeplechase." Top weight was twelve stone eight pounds; the lightest weight carried by any starter was eleven stone, and winners from date of declaration were obliged to carry five pounds penalty. The powerful, erratic Peter Simple thus shouldered thirteen stone one in '43; but if he had not bolted all over the place in his customary fashion, he would probably have bettered his position of third in spite of the weight. The winners for a long time were from the bottom or the middle of the handicap, and it was not until 1893 that Cloister's great victory destroyed the conviction that no horse could win under twelve stone or more.

The year after the race became a handicap, Tom Tug, the favourite, furnished entertainment by running away and half scaring his jockey to death. He eventually came in third and Discount won; but Tom Tug would probably have done so if his jockey had not spent most of his time with "his hands in his mouth and his spurs in the reins." Matthew, the first Irish winner, fluctuated amazingly in the betting because a lady in a mesmeric state had seen him win, and the public could not make up its mind whether or not to be superstitious. The two previous

winners, Cure-all and Pioneer, were so unheard of as to be unquoted by the bookmakers; the latter appeared in the paddock
with a long shaggy coat and protruding bones, but he won in
10.47 over a distance that had been inadvertently increased to
nearly five miles, and almost broke the heart of his owner, who
had been careful not to bet on him.

1849 was a year of confusion and tragedy. While the horses
were assembled at the post, Lord Sefton called the jockeys back to
him for a conference. Some of them obeyed, others did not, and
in the midst of this uncertainty some unidentified person gave the
starting signal, and they were off. The start could not have been
worse, and horses were strung out all over the course. The well-
backed Kilfane promptly fell, and was jumped on by Sparta so
hard that his thigh was broken and he had to be destroyed.
Further on Equinox came down, breaking his back; four other
horses piled up on top of him, and at the next fence, Curate,
second the year before, broke *his* back.

The curious point is that all these accidents occurred at tiny
jumps, little banks about eighteen inches high. It has been suggested that they were so much the colour of the plough from
which they arose that the horses did not notice them, but it seems
more probable that they were such objects of scorn to horses who
had just jumped fences like Becher's and Valentine's that they
were careless about them. Any hunting man knows that a tired
horse is much more likely to fall over an easy jump than over one
that forced him to pull himself together and make an effort; and
there is no doubt that the roll of casualties in the early days of big
and little fences was much greater than that of modern Aintree
with its more uniform jumps.

The tragedy of this race is somewhat relieved by an incident which is alleged to have taken place near the finish. Captain D'Arcy on The Knight of Gwynne had been offered some great sum if he won, and in addition had bet heavily on himself. As they came into the straight, only Cunningham on Peter Simple was ahead of him, and D'Arcy is supposed to have shouted an offer of a thousand pounds, soon after increasing it to four thousand, if Cunningham would pull his mount and let him win. One gains the impression that they argued violently all the way up the straight, but D'Arcy seems to have had no luck, for Peter Simple won comfortably. Incidentally, this is not the same Peter Simple referred to before, who was a grey horse by Arbutus. Cunningham's mount was a bay son of Patron, and though not very fast, was a great jumper and stayer and had marvellous action through heavy going. He won again in 1853 in deep mud which was just to his liking, and he received a fine ride from Tom Olliver, who thus won his third National, as he had ridden Vanguard in '43, and Gaylad the year before.

It has been said on various occasions that almost all National horses have been sold at some time or another in their careers for next to nothing at all, and that if they have not, their sires or dams have. Like most generalizations this is only about one-quarter true, but it is true that many winners at Aintree have either had or inherited a humble or unusual past. Mr. John Osborne, riding on the Shrewsbury coach one day, took a fancy to the near leader, a mare called English Lass, and bought her for fifty guineas. He hunted her for a while with the Meath, where she performed creditably enough, and then bred her to Ishmael, by whom she had a bay colt named Abd-el-Kader.

In 1850 Abd-el-Kader, a compact little horse about fifteen hands two inches high, appeared at Aintree, and attracted no attention in the paddock before the race. He was unquoted in the betting but went into the lead at Becher's the second time round, was never headed from there on, and won from thirty others in 9.57 ½, the fastest time on record. The next year he did it again, and the time was only a second and a half slower. Aspersions have been cast upon the authenticity of Abd-el-Kader's times, because they were so much faster than previous races; but Miss Mowbray won in 9.58½ a year later, and no one seems to have questioned that. She was another that received no attention from the book-makers, and most of the racing men in England had turned up their noses at her at one time or another; she was considered a good enough hunter, but certainly not worth the hundred guineas which was her price. At length she distinguished herself in a very fast run with the Oakley; several people decided that she was not so bad after all, and dashed off to see her owner. Mr. Mason got there first, with a hundred guineas in his hand, and the mare was his. She won a flat race and then a steeplechase at Leamington, but neither of them was of vast importance, and she was started in the National just on the off chance. The race was run in good going at a terrific pace—gallant little Abd-el-Kader had gone up fourteen pounds in the handicap since the year before, and the weight was too much for him—but Miss Mowbray justified her entry by winning from Maurice Daley and Sir Peter Laurie after a great struggle down the straight. The next year she was second to Peter Simple, and ran so well in spite of the heavy going, which she did not like, that she was a strong favourite in 1854 for a long time before the race. Lottery's old jockey, Jem Mason, was to come out of retirement to ride her, and the public confidence in her was so great that the bookmakers are reputed to have lost their nerve. Whether or not some of the less respectable of the knights of the book and pencil were responsible was never proved, but in spite of every precaution, she was "got at" the day before the race; though as such things go, she was treated very leniently, and merely incapacitated temporarily by the application of a blister. Abd-el-Kader was also scratched at the last moment, as he had hurt himself on the way to Aintree, and with two of the best horses out of it, Bourton won the race. Miss Mowbray was favourite again the next year and started all right, but she dropped her toes into the bank on landing over Becher's, and the good mare rolled over with a broken neck and back. Her jockey was knocked out cold and lay in a heap until another horse obligingly kicked him in the head and brought him to again!

The period of 1855 to about 1860 is that of the lowest ebb in Grand National history. The fields were about average from the point of view of numbers, and there were some good horses and jockeys—George Stevens began riding about this time—but there were too many second-rate people connected with the sport of steeplechasing in general. The increase of popularity had been accompanied by infamy, and courses where there was racing over fences had become rendezvous for all the undesirable elements in England. The sport's position as the disreputable poor relation prevented any adequate check being put upon the activities of these people, and steeplechases were good pickings for those with ingenious underground ideas of how to make money. There was no governing body to make and enforce rules, and the stewards of the various courses were powerless when it came to taking any effective action. All they could do was to suspend a jockey for foul riding or an owner or trainer for questionable practices, but as there was no alliance between the different courses, suspension could only be for the remainder of the meeting, and when that meeting lasted only a day or two, suspension was nothing very terrible for the one who had been "set down." And no matter what villainy a man had perpetrated in steeplechasing, he was completely *persona grata* in flat racing, for the Jockey Club was not interested in disputes arising from the former sport. Foul riding was difficult to detect in both sports, for the matter of that. Race courses were overrun with gangs of rowdies, and a patrol judge was in for a bad time if he objected to anything which took place away from the stands; so a foul which occurred beyond the view of the stewards was very likely to go unpunished. As an old veteran jockey remarked to a novice suspected of having done something doubtful in full view of the stands: "Don't drop your anchor in the harbour, lad; drop it out at sea!"

Fortunately some of the most influential people connected with steeplechasing were not content to let the situation continue until it became utterly impossible. Mr. W. G. Craven, a well-known owner, and a member of the Jockey Club, took the lead with Mr. B. J. Angell and Mr. E. C. Burton, and laid siege to the Jockey Club as a whole. It was obvious that no matter how strong an organization they might build up among the stewards of steeple-chase courses, they could not be really effective without an alliance with the parent body of racing. There was a good deal of opposition, but Lord Coventry and Lord Suffolk joined the petitioners. Then came the Duke of Beaufort and Lord Westmorland, and when Mr. George Payne added his influence, the opposition broke down. In the autumn of 1866 the Grand National Hunt Committee was formed.

The efforts of these gentlemen had accomplished a good deal in an informal way even before this committee came into existence, but steeplechasing now had an organization with which to clean its own house, and which would be backed by the Jockey Club to a certain extent. There is no doubt that this regulation of the sport completely destroyed a number of small and very pleasant meetings of the unofficial sort, such as the old Thirsk meeting, but it is equally certain that without such a regulating body steeplechasing would have died a natural death within a comparatively short time. Under the rules of the Grand National Hunt Committee, any horse or man who competed in unrecognized meetings—*i.e.*, meetings not run under the rules and supervision of the committee—was banned from all recognized meetings of either steeplechasing or flat racing, and the same thing applied to anyone "warned off" for questionable practices. Steeplechasing had at last been put upon a solid footing and equipped with a definite and powerful arm with which to enforce the rulings necessary to its continued existence.

The Grand National Hunt Committee remained in force until the end of the year 1883, when it was dissolved to make way for a new committee under the same name. This new committee was promptly formed, was much more closely allied to the Jockey Club, and therefore just so much more powerful. The first draft of the new body appeared in "The Racing Calendar" for February, 1884, and contained thirty names famous in the racing world. Future elections to the committee were to be by ballot of the whole committee, and five members were to be elected each year to serve as stewards for that year. The relation between the two sports is made obvious by the fact that nine out of the thirty were members of the Jockey Club as well as of the G.N.H.C.

In spite of the troubles and changes which were present in steeplechasing at this time, the great popularity of the sport kept it in a flourishing condition to outward appearances, and the Grand National probably suffered least, as is usually the case with the big and important races, for the crooked element generally prefer the obscurity of the smaller events. Some of the fields were not up to the standard quality—George Stevens brought Freetrader, his first winner, home in front of a bunch of very mediocre horses in 1856—but several famous jockeys and conspicuous owners competed during these years. In 1856 the Aintree Spring Meeting was extended to two days, with the National run on the second, and the year after there occurred an incident which caused a very definite advance in the flagging of the course.

A horse called Emigrant, who had been sold for various sums in the course of his career—one transaction being the aftermath of a game of cards—belonged to a pair of well-known bookmakers named Hodgman and Green. Charles Boyce rode him with an injured arm strapped to his side above the elbow, and was faced with the necessity of getting him first over the Water Jump, as Hodgman had backed him to be leading at that point. The going was very bad, and in some parts the horses had to struggle through a veritable morass. Emigrant and Westminster rose for the Water in unison, but the former jumped so quickly that he landed nearly a length to the good, and the bet was safe. In the course of the first round, however, Boyce had decided that the bad going near the Canal was an utterly senseless hazard; when

From a print in the possession of Mr. Louis Bruguière

EARLY STEEPLECHASING.

he arrived at the worst of it the second time, he hopped his horse over a fence at the side, galloped along on the harder ground beside the towpath, and eventually won. He had a perfect right to do this, according to the conditions of the race, and taking due regard for the laying out of the course, but it undoubtedly made a difference to the result, as the rest of the horses were exhausted after floundering through the mud. The following year flags were put up at various points to prevent any repetition of such a performance.

Nothing very remarkable happened during the next two years except that in 1858 the weather was so horrible that the race had to be postponed for three days, and when it was run only a few people turned up to watch it. The horses had to combat a wind which knocked over a drinking booth, and probably the only horse or man who derived any pleasure from the whole perform-ance was the rider of the winner, William Archer, father of the famous Fred of that name. His mount, Little Charley, had tried the National four times but had been a signal failure until stimu-lated by a course covered with slush, when he won quite easily.

The weather was excellent the next year, but the horses were less so, and Half Caste won a rather unexciting race from the French horse Jean du Quesne. In fifth place behind them, how-ever, was a mare called Anatis, whose victory in 1860 was one of the most curious in National history. She had such dickey legs that her trainer dared not school her much over jumps, and from the National of 1859 until she started at Aintree the following Spring, she had not even looked at a jump. Strangely enough she was favourite at 7—2, possibly because she was ridden by the famous "Mr. Thomas," whose real name was Mr. Pickernell; but

D

whatever the reason, her rotten legs carried her safely round the course and home in first place. Captain Townley was second on The Huntsman, a subsequent winner, and when he saw that Anatis had the legs of him in the straight, shouted jokingly: "Tommy, you little devil, is a thousand any good to you?" But as Townley remarked afterwards: "Tommy was too busy to reply!" And he was, for Anatis was a nerve-racking ride for anyone. Probably no other eminent race has ever had a full fledged parson among its jockeys, but Mr. Ekard on Bridegroom was such a one, and it is said that if his name had been spelled backwards the trail would have led to a well-known sporting family in the Midlands.

George Stevens had been piling up riding experience ever since his win on Freetrader, and in 1861 he made up his mind that Jealousy was going to win. He turned down thirteen other mounts which were offered him, only to be disappointed, for the owner who had first call on his services refused his consent, and Stevens was obliged to stand on the rail and watch Jealousy come home in front. The year after that The Huntsman won in 9.30 in a race that was marred by the unfortunate death of the jockey, James Wynne, who was killed when his horse fell and rolled on him at the gorse hurdle before the Water Jump. The Huntsman's year was the last before the course was lengthened, so that his time compared to those of later horses is not as startling as it would otherwise seem.

In 1863 and 1864 the race was won by two sisters owned by the late Lord Coventry, and both horses were ridden by Stevens. Lord Coventry was then a very young man and just at the beginning of a distinguished career. For many years he was a leading figure in many fields of sport. He lived to be more than ninety years old. I remember seeing him at meets of the Croome Hounds in Worcestershire, a pack which he founded in 1867; he was a very old man then, but was often out in a motor car, and was keenly interested to the very end.

The first of the sisters was Emblem. Neither she nor Emblematic, the second winner, were very impressive to look at, and the strenuous training methods of Weever made them look even lighter than they were. Emblem seemed all shoulders and quarters, with no middle at all, but she won without much difficulty, and was probably a better horse than the other, although Emblematic was third in '65, when Emblem failed to place.

1865 was the first year in which was shattered the theory that nothing but an old and experienced steeplechaser could win the National. Alcibiade was only a five-year-old, and though he had won some unimportant flat races, he had never jumped a fence in public, so that his starting price of 100—7 was surprisingly short. He carried a big weight for such a young horse, and it would probably have been too much for him without the brilliant riding of Captain Coventry, who got him home first after a desperate finish with Captain Tempest on Hall Court. Alcibiade thus took his place as the first five-year-old to win the National.

Salamander turned in a surprise victory the next year, and proved himself a bargain horse by so doing. Mr. Studd bought him out of a hovel in Ireland in the course of a trip taken in the hope of picking up a good hunter or two, and had no idea that Salamander was anything out of the ordinary. The horse looked like an exhausted scarecrow at first, and though food and good care worked wonders, it was considered rather laughable to run him in the National, and he started at 40—1. Mr. Goodman, who had ridden Miss Mowbray to her unexpected win fourteen years before, came out of retirement to ride him but was filled with anything but confidence, and the horse was practically unbacked, despite the inviting odds. Thirty-one horses started, and there was much interference. L'Africaine, supposedly the best steeplechaser in existence, was knocked over, but Salamander won in a canter and beat Cortolvin, who was first the next year under eleven stone thirteen, the highest weight carried to victory since the race became a handicap. Salamander's win was astonishing to his connections and to the public in general, but it was something more than that to a certain hot-headed gentleman in the stands. Hall Court was a popular choice by reason of his second the previous year, and when Salamander came into the straight with a big lead, this enthusiastic spectator confused his colours with those of Hall Court, and shouted: "Hall Court wins for a monkey!" The bet was promptly snapped up by someone better informed, and the first speaker was out of pocket to the tune of five hundred pounds!

In 1868 that brilliant horse, The Lamb, whose great heart and terrific agility made up for the fact that he was little more than fifteen hands high, appeared in the National for the first time. He was ridden by one of the best jockeys who ever rode in a steeplechase, namely Mr. George Ede, whose *nom de course* of "Mr. Edwards" was a synonym for horsemanship and presence of mind, and he and the compact little grey stallion were a hard combination to beat. Approaching the Water Jump, The Lamb was attended on either side by a loose horse, and a stride away from the take-off both suddenly crowded in on him. Mr. Ede calmly hit one horse with his whip, shifted the whip to the other hand, slashed at the other horse, and then jumped the fence with perfect efficiency. The whole operation was carried out quickly, smoothly, and neatly, as if he had been sitting in an armchair instead of on a jumping horse, and happening as it did in front of the stands, astonished and delighted the spectators. The Lamb went on to win the race from the very good Pearl Diver, but if Mr. Ede had not outridden Tomlinson in a whirlwind finish, the placing might have been reversed. This was Mr. Ede's only victory in the National, for unfortunately he was killed on the last day of the Aintree meeting two years later, when Mr. Carew's Chippenham fell and rolled on him in full view of the stands.

After The Lamb's first victory George Stevens got into his stride again, this time with a horse called The Colonel. He was a very handsome horse, despite the stigma of the word half-bred, and he won the race in 1869 in most convincing fashion, after hanging back through the early stages in the regular Stevens manner. A year later Survey looked like a winner, coming into the straight, but unfortunately he twisted a plate just as Stevens started to bring The Colonel up; the finish was a two horse affair, with The Colonel finally beating The Doctor by a head after a great battle. The fences were not very high this year, the going was good, and the horses were above the average, so that of the twenty-three starters, only one fell, five were pulled up, and the unusual number of seventeen completed the course.

The subsequent career of The Colonel is interesting. After his second triumph at Aintree he was sold to Baron Oppenheim and taken to Germany, where he failed to distinguish himself. He ran again in the National—in 1871—and carried top weight into

fourth place, and then went back to the Continent for good.
It is said that he later became the charger of the King of
Prussia, afterwards William I of Germany, but this story seems
to be somewhat legendary. Whether or not this is true, however, he was eventually used at the stud at Beberbeck, and
through his daughters became the grandsire of the good stallions
Optimus and Obelisk.

The clairvoyantly prophesied victory of Matthew, the first
Irish winner, was quite outdone, in the matter of signs and por-
tents, by The Lamb's second win. In December of 1870 Mr.
Pickernell received the following letter from Lord Poulett, who
owned the Lamb.

Army and Navy Club
Thursday Night
15 December, 1870

My dear Tommy,

Let me know for certain whether you can ride for me at Liverpool on The Lamb. I dreamt *twice* last night I saw the race run.
The first dream, he was last and finished among the carriages.
The second dream, I should think an hour afterwards, I saw the
Liverpool run. He won by four lengths, and you rode him. I saw
the cerise and blue sleeves, and you, as plain as I write this. Now,
let me know as soon as you can, and say nothing to anyone.

Yours Sincerely
POULETT

Nor was this all. As a race train arrived in Liverpool the day
before the National, a little white lamb hopped out of a truck and
legged it off down the track as fast as it could go. Even the pres-

ence of The Colonel and George Stevens could not compete with this, particularly as The Colonel was shouldering 12 stone 8, and The Lamb started at 5—1. He was as agile as ever; at the Canal Turn, two horses fell in a heap right in front of him as he landed over the fence, but The Lamb hopped them cheerfully, and went on to win amidst scenes of great enthusiasm. Lord Poulett led him in, and on the way to the unsaddling enclosure, The Lamb lost most of the hairs in his tail, and Lord Poulett his watch, as souvenirs of the victory!

There were a great many good horses running at this period, and it is remarkable that several of them were prevented from winning the National by pure bad luck, most of it quite unconnected with the regular hazards of the race. In 1872 Schiedam, Harvester, and Scarrington, ridden by three famous jockeys, Mr. Richardson, Mr. Yates, and Robert I'Anson, were fighting it out through the straight, when something happened to every one of them. Schiedam was almost knocked down by the fallen Primrose—a mare who was supposed never to fall—Harvester had his foot nearly torn off by a stud on one of his own shoes, and Scarrington twisted a plate and cut his leg badly, though I'Anson managed to keep him going long enough to take second place behind the weedy and second-rate mare, Casse Tête. Opportunity knocked but once in the cases of Mr. Yates and I'Anson: they never had other chances as good as this one, and both retired at the end of their careers with victories to their credits in almost every great steeplechase except the National. Mr. Richardson was more fortunate, and has a large place in history as the rider of two winners.

CHAPTER FOUR

Captain Machell, and the National from
1873 to 1885

THE year 1873 marks the first success in the National of
Captain Machell, one of the most famous and interesting
personalities in the history of British racing. As a subaltern he
was very well known for his exceptional athletic ability, and one
of his most remarkable races was with "Deerfoot," who was
considered the greatest runner of the period until Captain
Machell beat him. On another occasion he knocked from his
pedestal the champion walker, a certain market gardener from
London. He and Machell were matched to walk from Newmarket to London for a purse of one thousand pounds; the
gardener was defeated, and with the fruits of the victory Captain
Machell bought one of the first horses he ever owned.

When Captain Machell retired from the Army, the late Lord
Lonsdale and Lord Calthorpe took Beaufort House and stables
near Newmarket, and engaged him to manage the stable. This
was his first important connection with the turf, and it was
under the aegis of these two gentlemen, and, to a lesser extent, of
Mr. Henry Chaplin, later Lord Chaplin, that he rose to his great
position in the racing world. It has often been said that the
betting side of racing appealed to him more than any other, and
he certainly betted very heavily; but contrary to the general
belief, he did not make a fortune out of betting, and as a matter of
fact lost somewhat more than he made in that way. The allega-
tion that he was primarily interested in betting is belied by the

fact that he was an unusually good judge of a horse, and of "form," and that he did make a good deal of money selling horses. With his fine eye for a horse, he would buy one out of a selling race, bring out its latent ability, race it a few times, and then dispose of it at a profit. A fine example of how he could spot a really good horse at a glance is furnished by the notorious rogue Pan, whom Captain Machell saw galloping in the distance one day. He realized his capabilities immediately, and was quite disappointed when he found the horse was not for sale. It was probably the only time in Pan's history when he was not for sale, for he was believed in by practically no one at the time, with the possible exception of his owner; but he eventually justified Captain Machell's opinion by running second in the Grand National, and what he might have done with an honest disposition was never discovered.

Nothing could convince the touts that Captain Machell was not a scheming trickster whose one idea in life was to keep them from knowing how good his horses were, but this was unquestionably a case of evil lying in the eye of the beholder. His cleverness in turning a seemingly mediocre horse into a very good one apparently greatly distressed the touts, but as he was a man of the highest integrity, and invariably told the truth about his horses, it was certainly no fault of his if certain people chose to believe he was not doing so.

Captain Machell owned some very good horses under both rules of racing at one time or another, and his record at Aintree includes three National winners. The first of these was Disturbance, who was hunted in the days before he became a racehorse by the Hon. Hugh Lowther, now the Earl of Lonsdale. Mr.

Lowther had a good deal to do with Disturbance's schooling, but the horse was ridden in the National of 1873 by Mr. Maunsell Richardson. There were some good horses running that year, and the greatest danger to Disturbance was Mr. Chaplin's Rhysworth, a big fine-looking horse who had finished fourth in the Derby of 1869. Rhysworth excelled Disturbance in size and looks, at the last fence he was in the lead, and for a few moments it looked as though the pupil would confound his two masters—Captain Machell and Mr. Richardson had given Rhysworth all his early schooling over fences—but Disturbance was a stayer, and the Derby horse was not the sort to give his best in a ding-dong battle up the straight. He quit when he found Disturbance was sticking with him, and Mr. Richardson cantered in six lengths ahead. The winning jockey was the hero of the day, and a banquet was given for him shortly after the race. On the top of the menu were printed the words: "Disturbance, but no Row!" —a command which is said to have been completely disregarded in the course of a hilarious evening!

The next year Captain Machell had three starters. Disturbance was one of them, and his two new horses were Reugny and Defence. A great deal has been written about a disagreement that Captain Machell and Mr. Richardson are supposed to have had as a prelude to this National, but Lord Lonsdale, who was living with Captain Machell at the time, assures me that nothing of the sort occurred. Some ten days before Reugny, Disturbance, and Defence were "tried," Mr. Richardson was given the choice of which horse he would ride in the National, and he chose Reugny, whom Lord Lonsdale believes was always better than Disturbance. Mr. Richardson thought Disturbance was the

From a print in the possession of Mr. Louis Bruguière

EARLY STEEPLECHASING.

better horse, but he had trained Reugny himself, and was therefore anxious to ride him. There was no question of an argument as to which horse Mr. Richardson should ride, or of Captain Machell being annoyed because his bets had gone wrong, and, as it turned out, the race was one of the most successful Captain Machell ever had from the betting point of view.

Mr. Richardson's choice proved to be the right one, and riding his usual excellent race, he brought Ruegny from behind to snatch the victory from the very good Chimney Sweep. Disturbance came in sixth, but Defence fell, and it is probable that he was not at his best until a year or two later. When Captain Machell bought these three horses for twelve hundred pounds few people thought them anything out of the ordinary, but after two of them had won the Grand National, opinions rather naturally changed, and shortly after Reugny's victory, Mr. Gerard Leigh gladly paid ten times that sum for them. Unfortunately neither Reugny nor Disturbance were ever much good from that time on. Probably this was the result of a little injudicious schooling at the hands of their new owner, before they were sent to Mr. Arthur Yates to be trained. Defence turned out very well, however, and was just running into his best form when Mr. Leigh died, and the horse's engagements were automatically cancelled.

In 1875 Mr. Pickernell rode in his eighteenth National. As many other good jockeys did in their day, he found the strain of years beginning to tell on him at about this time, and was inclined to take an occasional drink before a race in the way of "jumping powder." This year, indeed, he must have taken rather more than an occasional one, for he confided to a friend afterwards that when the flag fell at the start he was very doubtful of the direction in which he was supposed to go! Fortunately he chose correctly and once started was as good as ever. His mount was Pathfinder, who had been hunted by the famous Quorn huntsman, Tom Firr. Pathfinder found the going too much for him, and at Becher's the second time round was so exhausted that Mr. Pickernell almost decided to pull him up, and would have done so if it had been his horse. But as Pathfinder was not his, he resolved to struggle on as far as he could, and was soon astonished to feel the horse getting stronger and fresher beneath him at every stride. By the time the last fence was passed his mount was tiring again, but was still game and so managed to struggle past the post a length ahead of Dainty, and thus won a race in which he had almost been pulled up.

Captain Machell's Laburnum failed to distinguish himself in Pathfinder's National, and the following year he pinned his hopes to Chandos and Regal. The former was about the best hurdler in England, but Lord Lonsdale, who rode him in most of his work, says that he was a very curious horse to ride, and had a habit of dipping his head so that he became unbalanced. He was the public choice at 100—30, but Captain Machell rightly anticipated that he would have trouble at the drop fence, and was careful to include Regal, his other starter, in all his bets on the favourite. Regal's starting price was 25—1, but when Chandos fell and was out of it, Regal went to the fore and won very cleverly from Congress, who was ridden by the brilliant gentleman rider Mr. Wilson. "Mr. Rolly" on Zero came a terrible cropper and almost broke his neck, but when Sir James Paget, the famous surgeon arrived at the spot after a feverish dash across the course, he was amazed to find that the vertebra had slipped back into place of its own accord. If the vertebra had not thus astonished the medical profession, the course of history would have been somewhat changed, for hidden beneath the *nom de course* of Mr. "Rolly" was the Earl of Minto, who later became Viceroy of India.

Reugny with Mr. Wilson in the saddle was a good favourite in 1877, Chimney Sweep and Regal were well backed, and Congress's second the previous year brought him many followers. The last-named suffered an eleventh hour change of jockeys, when Mr. Lowther, who was engaged to ride him, unfortunately broke his shoulder, and was obliged to let Joe Cannon take the mount for him. The betting situation, however, was rather remarkable, in that the horse whom many people suspected might be the best in the race was not especially popular. The public knew that Austerlitz was a really good horse, but were less sure of the abilities of his owner-rider, Mr. Fred Hobson. The stable connections shared the feeling of the public that Mr. Hobson could not get the best out of the horse and did their best to get the mount for Robert I'Anson. They hinted politely that it was bad enough for a man who held on to his saddle when jumping to ride an experienced steeplechaser, but that it was pure folly for a mere five-year-old like Austerlitz to be handicapped in such a way. Mr. Hobson was quite modest about his strength in the saddle, and was inclined to agree with his critics, but Mr. Yates urged him to go ahead and ride, and Austerlitz finally started with his owner up at the odds of 15—1. Mr. Hobson certainly did "pull leather" at one fence after another, and he was criticised by some for making too much pace, but he rode such a good finish that Congress had to be satisfied with another second place, and behind him came no less a person than Mr. Pickernell on the Liberator, a very good horse who won in '79 with Mr. Garret Moore up.

Many horsemen have "sold the wrong horse," and probably few famous breeders of thoroughbreds can look back on their sales of yearlings and others without wishing they had kept one certain horse instead of another. Sceptre, the greatest mare that ever lived, never carried the colours of the present Duke of Westminster, although she was bred by the late Duke. In America, Mr. Belmont lost the fruits of a lifetime of breeding when he sold Man o' War as a yearling. But few mistaken sales have reacted as quickly, and with as much poetic justice, as Linde's disposal of Seaman. The famous Irish trainer had three first-rate steeplechasers in his stable at the Curragh; he had complete confidence in Cyrus and Mohican, but knew that Seaman was fundamentally unsound in spite of his very real ability. When Lord Manners made him an offer for Seaman in the autumn of '81, Linde sold him without a qualm, for he felt certain the horse would not stand the sort of preparation necessary for the National.

Seaman was put in the hands of Jewitt, who trained him along very lenient lines and sent him to Aintree in March of '82, about three-quarters fit. Lord Manners took the mount himself, Mr. Tommy Beasley rode Cyrus, and his brother Harry was up on Mohican, who started favourite. Everything seemed perfect for the Linde stable, for Lord Manners had never ridden in a race before, the weather was awful, and the going still worse, none of which were likely to help a partially trained horse. Half-way through the second round, however, Mohican fell, and Cyrus and Seaman came into the straight together, a long way ahead of the rest. Mr. Beasley sat down and rode, Cyrus began to draw away, and it was assumed to be all over bar the shouting, when suddenly Lord Manners made his run! Seaman came up inch by inch then faltered badly at the last hurdle, where he broke down in the suspensory ligament of a hind leg. But he was game, and his inexperienced jockey proceeded to outride the great Mr. Beasley, winning by a short head in a slashing rainstorm.

Lord Manner's performance could not have been more remarkable, for he not only beat one of the best jockeys in the National's history, but did it on a horse who was not really fit, and who broke down so completely at the last fence that he never ran in a race again. It is impossible to imagine what glories Lord Manners might have gone on to if he had taken steeplechase riding seriously. He rode in one more race a short while afterwards, and won it, whereupon he retired with the extraordinary record of two victories in the same number of attempts—one of them the Grand National!

The next year saw a field of only ten starters, the smallest in the history of the race. Third behind Seaman and Cyrus had come the staying mare, Zoedone. Count Charles Kinsky, the popular Austrian, had decided that she was the horse for him, only to be disappointed at the amount of money Mr. Clayton wanted for her. He had regretfully given up the idea, when he won a thousand pounds on Corrie Roy in the Cesarewitch. He promptly bought Zoedone for eight hundred pounds, with a two hundred pound contingency if she won the National. The mare was slow, but she could jump and had plenty of stamina, and the fact that the fences were a bit larger than usual was all in her favour. The trainer's instructions to Count Kinsky are given in the first chapter; unlike many riding orders they were obeyed absolutely literally, and Zoedone outstayed the field, drew away in the straight, and won by a comfortable margin.

There is a sort of unwritten law at Aintree that a National winner must be an old steeplechaser with long experience over all sorts of fences and that he must have fallen a time or two in the big race to be worth any consideration at all. It is a pretty good generality as such things go, but Alcibiade had shaken it to its foundations in 1865, and Voluptuary shattered it again nineteen years later. He had won some good races as a three-year-old, and had even enjoyed the distinction of leading the field at one point in the Derby of '81, which was won by the American horse, Iroquois; but this somehow does not seem much of a recommendation for Aintree honours, particularly as he had never run in a steeplechase. The public was at a loss whether or not to back him. On the one hand was his inexperience, and on the other the fact that he was to be ridden by Mr. E. P. Wilson, who apparently had the greatest confidence in him. He finally started at 10—1, and ran very well to win from Frigate and Roquefort, both excellent horses who won the race subsequently.

The later career of Voluptuary is fairly well known. He ran without distinction in several other Nationals and was then sold to Mr. Leonard Boyne, the actor, who promptly put him in training for the drama. "The Prodigal Daughter" had a long run at Drury Lane, and every night the old National horse leaped the Water Jump in the middle of the stage, while his unfortunate jockey delighted the gallery by a spectacular dive into the brook.

Roquefort, who ran third behind Voluptuary, was a long-backed stayer of great merit but uncertain disposition, and no one could prophesy how he would run on a given occasion. It is not true, as is often stated, that he was bought, "out of a cart," but the belief can be traced to the fact that he was on sale at Tattersall's as a three-year-old among a bunch of carriage horses when Mr. Arthur Yates bought him. He won some good races for Mr. Yates, but his wayward temper caused him to have few friends, and Mr. Yates sold him before his first appearance at Aintree He changed hands twice more before the National of 1885; but in that race he was ridden by the same Mr. Wilson who had done so well with Voluptuary, and for whom Roquefort ran as he had never run before, and forced Frigate to be satisfied with second place again. Roquefort was a splendid jumper, and did his job thoroughly as long as there were fences in front of him, but the moment the run-in was reached he lost interest, and wanted nothing but to get off the course. As his age increased this quality grew more pronounced, and his jockey could never tell when he might run out to the left. He ran in several more Nationals, but without Mr. Wilson in the saddle he could do no good; he followed Voluptuary into the hands of Mr. Boyne, and eventually appeared on the stage in America.

An unfortunate phase of Roquefort's year was the poisoning of Zoedone. She was favourite and was coupled in the betting with Bendigo, who had just won the Lincolnshire Handicap; so if she lived up to expectations in the National the bookmakers were going to be badly hit by the "Spring Double." Whoever the conspirators were, they waited until the last minute, and as Count Kinsky rode out on to the course he noticed a spot of blood on the mare's nose. The veterinary's examination after

E

the race proved the presence of poison, which must have been injected by someone in the crowd. Kinsky said afterwards that she seemed utterly "dead" under him as they lined up for the start and at no time acted like herself. She jumped in very slovenly fashion and got round the first time only by a miracle; at the fence before Becher's in the second lap she sprang straight up in the air and then toppled over the jump in a heap. She was on her feet again in a few moments, but the damage had been done thoroughly, and she was never any good from that time on. The bookmakers were accused as usual, but the thing had been staged so cleverly that there was no possibility of finding the culprit.

CHAPTER FIVE

Developments of the Aintree Course—
The Significance of Times

THE year 1885 is one of great importance in the National's history, for it marks a very definite signpost in the development of the Aintree Course. Changes of one sort and another had been going on right from the beginning, and the lengthening of the race in 1863 has already been noted; but most of the changes were so gradual as to be barely noticeable at the time they were made, and it is only when one looks back over a period of years that one sees how great the difference is. In 1863 it was notable that the course was practically all fallow, wheat or seeds, and various commentators on the first forty years of the race speak of the heavy plough before such-and-such a fence in a way that shows it to have been quite the ordinary thing. In 1885, however, the whole course was grass for the first time, and was railed in on the inside from start to finish. Plough reappeared occasionally after this but in smaller quantities, and since the early years of the twentieth century there has been nothing but grass.

Another change which took place about this time was the institution of the preliminary hurdle. A flight of hurdles was erected fairly near the stands, and this had to be jumped by the horses on their way down to the start as a sort of "warming up." Just how useful this practice was cannot be estimated; certainly the hurdle was knocked over by a good many horses who straightway ran very decently in the race itself. The preliminary hurdle was used for about twenty years, and finally eliminated in the year 1907.

The fences had undergone changes also; year by year they had been varied and sometimes shifted, but while their number remained much the same their height was gradually increased, and in 1885 the course was beginning to look much as we know it now. There have been changes since then: most of the smaller fences have been stiffened, and the three last hurdles have been removed from the run in, which is now a flat of four hundred and ninety-four yards. But the continuous grass and inside rail of 1885 marked the final disappearance of the race's point-to-point character, and the beginning of the modern race course.

It will be of interest perhaps to give at this point a description of the fences in 1885, and thus to show the changes that have been made since the course was first laid out in 1839.

The distance was four miles eight hundred and fifty-six yards, which it is at present. In the first round there were fifteen jumps, the last of which was the Water, and the course was the same in the second round until Fence No. 27—No. 12 in the first circuit —was passed, when the horses swung out and finished over three gorse hurdles, which have since been removed, thus avoiding the Water Jump, the big Open Ditch, and the hurdle preceding it. Below is a description of the fences:—

Fence No. 1 & No. 16—Small gorse hurdle.

No. 2 & No. 17—Thorn fence, 5 feet high, with a 3 foot rail on take-off side.

No. 3 & No. 18—Thorn fence, 4 feet 6 inches high, 2 foot guard rail in front of ditch, 6 feet 8 inches wide and 3 feet deep. All of this on take-off side.

W. A. Rouch

The Preliminary Hurdle.   Manifesto on left.

Fence No. 4 and No. 19—Rail and fence, both 2 feet 6 inches high, about 18 inches apart.

No. 5 & No. 20—Hurdle, 3 feet 6 inches high, bushed with gorse.

No. 6 & No. 21—Becher's Brook. Thick Thorn fence, 4 feet 6 inches high, with 2 foot 6 inch guard rail. On landing side a natural brook 9 feet 6 inches wide and 6 feet deep.

No. 7 & No. 22—Thorn fence, 5 feet 6 inches high, with 2 foot 6 inch guard rail in front of it.

No. 8 & No. 23—The Canal Turn. The jump was placed at the spot where the course made a ninety degree turn so that the horses had to make a sharp turn left immediately on landing. Thorn fence, 5 feet high, with a 2 foot guard rail in front of a 6 foot ditch on take-off side.

No. 9 & No. 24—Valentine's Brook. Thorn fence, 5 feet high, with a 2 foot guard rail in front, and a 5 foot brook on landing side.

No. 10 & No. 25—Gorse hurdle, 3 feet 6 inches high.

No. 11 & No. 26—Thorn fence, 4 feet 6 inches high, 2 foot rail guarding a ditch 6 feet wide and 3 feet deep on take-off side.

No. 12 & No. 27—Thorn fence, 5 feet high, with a 2 foot guard rail, and a 5 foot ditch on landing side.

No. 13—Gorse hurdle, 3 feet 6 inches high.

No. 14—Thorn fence, 4 feet 6 inches high and 2 feet wide, with a 2 foot rail guarding a 6 foot ditch on take-off side.

Fence No. 15—The Water Jump, 12 feet 3 inches of water which
was 2 feet deep, with a perpendicular thorn fence,
2 feet high and 1 foot thick on take-off side.

Nos. 28, 29, 30—Gorse hurdles, 3 feet 6 inches high.

The course was obviously stiffer, as far as the jumps were concerned, than it had been in 1839, for there were only twelve comparatively easy jumps out of the thirty, as opposed to the numer-
ous small ones of the early years. It must be appreciated that the
thorn fences were "made fences" in one sense of the word, but
that they were nevertheless alive and growing, and that any vari-
ation from year to year was caused by the trimmers doing their
work too thoroughly or not thoroughly enough. The stiffening
of the fences was accompanied by an increase of grass and conse-
quent better going, which maintained the balance and made the
course more of a racing test.

Up to a certain point these changes in the course may be said
to have affected very largely the type of horse that ran in the
National; but by about 1870 the hunting field aspect of Aintree
had given way to that of a race course, and the stamp of horse
required for steeplechasing had become standardized. The old-
fashioned half-bred hunter had, with a few exceptions, disap-
peared from the National and from first-class steeplechasing in
general, and with the thoroughbred once in favour, he was
gone to stay. This does not mean that hunters vanished from the
National, or that they ever will, but that the hunter good enough
for the race must be a faster and therefore better bred horse.
With the increased popularity of the sport, horses were bred with
the advance intention of training them over fences, and steeple-

chasing no longer depended to such an extent on animals who had been tried on the flat and found wanting.

It is obvious, of course, that many steeplechasers have been, and are now, cast-offs from the flat, but the breeding of steeple-chasers became a careful, exact science instead of a casual happy-go-lucky affair. Summing up, the National type of horse was largely influenced by the development of the course until about 1870; after that it depended more upon the development of the thoroughbred horse itself.

The remark has been made that the National is a race in which, comparatively speaking, jumping is more important than gallop-ing; but it must not be inferred from this that the pace is by any means slow—merely that the fences are so stiff that no amount of speed can offset the lack of real jumping ability. It is not gen-erally realized, however, just how fast the horses do go in this race, and it may be of interest to compare the speed of the National with that of the Derby, which of course draws the best class of flat race horses in England, and which is naturally run at a rattling good pace.

The Epsom Course, over which the Derby is run, is a mile and a half long. The first quarter mile is uphill—and if there is any-one who believes that that hill after the start is not steeper than it looks, let him go out and walk it—and from that point there is a descending turn at Tattenham Corner, a long run on the flat, and a very slight incline up to the finish. Averaging the times of races run since the War, the Derby has been run in 2 minutes 38 seconds by three-year-olds carrying 9 stone—fillies carry less weight, but the vast majority of the starters are always colts. In other words, the Derby winners have run at an average speed of a mile in 1 minute 45 seconds.   (The world's record for the mile is 1 minute 34⅘ seconds, set by the American horse, Roamer, at Saratoga, in August of 1918.)

Two circuits of the Aintree course, over which the National is contested, amounts to 4 miles 856 yards. The course is perfectly flat all the way, but there are thirty stiff jumps. The average time for the same period of years is 9 minutes 55 seconds; the average age of winners is a little more than eight years, and the average weight they have carried is a little over 11 stone. Thus the National winners have moved at a rate of a mile in 2 minutes 9 seconds, 24 seconds slower than the Derby winners. Figuring it out at weight for age, it is clear that the National horses go nearly as fast as those in the Derby—and they keep on doing it for nearly four miles and a half instead of a third of that distance, and jump thirty fences while they are at it.

The subject of the time taken to run the National is naturally one of interest, but it is possible to attach too much significance to this side of the race, for it has already been pointed out that the jockeys are usually more intent on getting over the fences than on anything else. The presence of a rapid, impetuous horse who cannot be rated off the pace, will often make a field of comparatively poor horses cover the distance in faster time than that made by better horses who lack such a leader, and the question of the weather and the going is another thing to be considered. It is impossible to estimate what time would have been made in the various races in snowstorms, or in the 1911 affair of mud and rain, which was won by Glenside, if the conditions had been different; and even over a period of years the times cannot be taken as meaning very much, for it has been seen how the course was changed and lengthened, and the fences put in and taken out from time to time.

Significant or not, however, the subject is interesting enough to merit discussion. One is inclined to argue that the average of 12 minutes for the first ten years of the National obviously denotes the presence of the old-fashioned hunter, but the argument receives a jolt when the average of the next ten years drops down to considerably under 10 minutes, for the hunters did not depart from the race in a huff, automatically and in unison, in the year 1850! The period of the sixties is of no use in this tabulation, for the course was lengthened and otherwise changed at that time, but the average from 1871 to 1880 is 10.17. The next like period is roughly the same, but 1891—1900 shows a great improvement, and is 9.56. A great many good horses ran during this period, and it is even the opinion of many excellent judges that they have never been equalled. Certainly no one can tell how fast Cloister might have gone in '93 if he had been pushed, for as it was he broke all existing records after leading from the start, won in a canter by forty lengths, and carried top weight into the bargain. From the end of this period until 1910 the average was 10 minutes, and from then until 1920 it was little more, though this was the War period, with three of the races run at Gatwick, and as such has no value in this computation. The last ten years gives us the best average since the changes of the sixties, and the time of 9.51 forms a basis of argument for those who champion the modern thoroughbred as being superior to his prototype of twenty or thirty years ago.

There are many people connected with horse racing who believe that the horses, jockeys, and indeed almost everything else of

the old times are superior to those of the present day, and there
is no way of proving them wrong. Certainly no National horse
has showed himself to be any better than Cloister and Manifesto,
and in flat racing Ormonde and Persimmon are still names to
conjure with. However, it is amusing to note that a writer in the
Seventies speaks of "these decadent times," and deprecates the
horses and jockeys of that period as compared with the good old
days—in spite of living in an era that produced classic winners
like Galopin and Doncaster, and such jockeys as Fordham and
Archer!

CHAPTER SIX

Breeding and Blood Lines in the National

THE question of improvement—or the lack of it—in National horses, brings us inevitably to the subject of breeding and blood lines. A really complete discussion of the breeding of all the horses who have run in the National would fill this book, indeed many books, and my intention here is merely to show the origin of the horses who ran in the early days, and to trace the trend which breeding has taken since then by mention of significant names in the pedigrees of outstanding horses.

It is a truism of flat-race breeding that only winners get winners but that the best horses are often out of mares with no very distinguished past on the race course. The perfect example of this is shown by Persimmon and Diamond Jubilee, the two horses who won the Derby for King Edward when he was still Prince of Wales. They were full brothers, by the unbeaten St. Simon, out of Perdita II. This mare was only a rather good plater, but reproduced the quality of her ancestry—she was by Hampton-Hermione—and was the foundation of the Royal Stud at Sandringham. The question of National horses siring subsequent winners arises practically not at all, for during the past sixty years the great majority have been geldings, and only four entire horses have won the race since 1876. In the early years we find that The Sea, unplaced in 1840, was the sire of Freetrader, who won sixteen years later, and Arthur, second in 1840, was the sire of The Lamb's dam. It is interesting that The Sea was by Whalebone, whose son, Sir Hercules, sired Arthur.

These are isolated instances, however, and have few parallels in later years. It must be admitted that most Aintree winners have been sired by good horses, and that their dams have usually been mares with either racing or Stud Book successes to their credit; but on the other hand there is no important race in the world which has been won by so many animals of obscure or surprising origin as the Grand National. A point which bears out the truism mentioned above is that although eleven mares have won the National—the most recent was Shannon Lass, in 1902—not one of them has produced a horse good enough to get into the first three at Aintree.

Most of the National horses during the early years were half-breds, in the Stud Book sense that any horse with common blood, regardless of how small an amount, is a half-breed. Search in the pedigrees of these early horses is often unproductive, for there were many horses bearing the same names, and those of the dams were usually not even mentioned. When the Grand National Hunt Committee was formed, great efforts were made to obtain some order out of this chaos, but how difficult it was may be judged by the following paragraph in Messrs. Weatherby & Sons' first "Steeplechase Calendar":

"In preparing . . . this first volume of 'Steeplechases Past,' considerable pains have been taken to obtain pedigrees, and information to enable us to distinguish or identify in the index horses of the same name. This has often been found difficult. . . ."

As a result, the sires of many of the horses who ran in the early years of the National are not known with any degree of accuracy, and the names of their dams are usually conspicuously absent. The sires were probably for the most part thoroughbred horses, but the type and quality of many of the dams can only be guessed at. They were probably some sort of very good half-bred animal, and about the only reasonable certainty is that they did not have in their veins the blood of horses bred purely for draught purposes. The great lumbering-draught horse, with immense limbs and shaggy hair on his feet, was not very popular in England until after the Crimean War. In a period when horses furnished the only method of transportation, a farmer naturally preferred one that could be ridden, driven on the road, or worked in the fields, as necessity demanded.

In the fifteenth and sixteenth centuries, the English horse was rather small, as the result of large strains of native pony in his blood—*i.e.*, Welsh, Exmoor, New Forest, or Highland—and this was not agreeable to a king like Henry VIII, who was always on the verge of war with someone or other, and who needed horses for cavalry mounts. He and other kings promulgated various decrees designed to increase the size of horses bred in England, and it was declared unlawful to turn out onto the commons, moors, and heaths, where horses of every type and belonging to many different owners ran together, "any stoned horse above the age of two years, not being fifteen hands high . . ." The natural result of this was the practice of gelding most horses, a practice which is continued to this day. Gelding did not originate, as is apparently the general belief, only because stallions were high-spirited and difficult to manage, but because of the edicts mentioned above. A collateral light is thrown on this matter by the fact that gelding is much less universal in France than in England and America. A visit to any of the French government studs, such as the one at Pau, where one can see stallions of all types and degrees, proves that many stallions are perfectly tractable when treated like anything but savage beasts; and it is of incidental interest that the great majority of draught horses used in the streets of Paris are entire horses, and even the best fed and conditioned of them are absolutely quiet and peaceable.

To return to a discussion of the dams, they were probably the half-bred which was known as a "cocktail," and the cocktail was a general purpose horse of the best type. The royal edicts had accomplished their purpose, and when Eastern blood was imported so largely in the seventeenth century—infusions of Arab and Barb blood were on a rather small scale prior to that time—it found a good fifteen-hand horse to cross with in the native English horse, if he may be so named without raising a storm of protest from the purists among horse-breeders. Whatever the name, the cocktail was the result of this union, and he himself was Hackney, or "Chapman"—pack horse (later known as the Cleveland Bay)— or the Yorkshire Coach Horse, an offspring of the Cleveland Bay and the thoroughbred. These three types of light horses are now quite separate and distinct breeds, but any one of them might have been called a cocktail, and they all have a considerable amount of thoroughbred blood in them; any perusal of the ancestry of the Hackney or the Cleveland Bay shows that conclusively.

The Hackney had not at that time degenerated into a horse who could do little but lift his knees to his chin, and was a powerful, useful horse on the road or in the field. Cocktails were used for almost everything, including racing, and cocktail races were a regular feature of every small country meeting. A good cocktail stallion was a valuable possession, and when crossed with a thoroughbred mare produced a splendid kind of weight-carrying hunter. The invention of the steam engine, and later the motor car, did away with the necessity for the general purpose horse. TheCleveland Bay and the Hackney lost their great prominence in the field of their original use, and the half-bred hunter became the result of a cross between a thoroughbred sire and a draught mare. Aside from the obvious disparity in courage and spirit between the heavy draught horse and the old general purpose horse, one has only to look at the bone of the thoroughbred, the cocktail, and the draught animal through a microscope. The first is hard and close-knit and almost like ivory in consistency, the second is somewhat like it, but the draught horse has bone of a coarse porous type, clearly not adapted to carrying weight at hunting field speed.

The hunters who ran in the early Nationals—and they really were hunters, in the sense that they followed hounds with some regularity, for it was considered rather sharp practice to keep a horse purely for steeplechasing—could more truly be described as three-quarter-bred, for the sires, where known, were generally clean bred, and many of them have become famous as being among the early originators of the thoroughbred horse. Lottery, for example, was by a horse bearing the same name, and his sire, Tramp, was a grandson of Eclipse. Verulam, another son of Tramp, sired Wanderer, the National winner of 1855. The great Brutandorf put his stamp on the early days of the National—he was by Blacklock out of a Pot8os mare, and was therefore very inbred to Eclipse—for he himself got Gaylad, and his son Physician sired Cure-all, National winner of 1845, and The Cure, who got Jealousy, National winner of 1861, as well as The Doctor, who ran second to The Colonel in 1870.

The Cure had an extraordinary career. He won the Champagne Stakes in his youth but soon went down in the world, was turned out of Lord Airlie's stud as a worthless sire, and was trained for the hunting field. This project was nipped in the bud when he refused to rise at his fences and broke a groom's leg. A doctor then bought him for the ridiculous sum of seven shillings and sixpence and used him for a hack. Some of The Cure's get began to show ability about this time, however—one of them, Lambton, was a very successful steeplechaser—and the medical gentleman made a nice little profit by selling his hack for two hundred and fifty pounds. The Cure was eventually leased to the Royal Stud at Hampton Court, where several of his yearlings were sold for over a thousand guineas!

The breeding of thoroughbreds has always been a sort of lottery in which the most careful plans have a habit of working out into nothing at all, and in which, conversely, the casual or accidental union bears fruit of unexpected richness. Emblem and Emblematic were the daughters of a horse who was not expected to get jumpers, namely Teddington, winner of the 1851 Derby, and son of Orlando, by Touchstone. Orlando, incidentally, was the horse who reaped the rewards of the Running Rein scandal of 1844. Running Rein won the Derby that year, but was subsequently found to be a four-year-old, was disqualified, and Orlando was declared the winner. Commotion was not considered much of a horse, but he got Disturbance, a really good horse over Aintree; and Trumpeter, the sire of Casse Tête, was supposed to get horses who could not stay. Casse Tête may have won with luck in 1872, but win she did, and any horse that is first in the National must have some staying power. The classic example of chance breeding, however, was furnished by Shaun Goilin, who won the National of 1930. His dam, Golden Day, was at grass in a paddock in Ireland, and in the adjoining field were a number of two-year-olds. In the course of the night several of these colts jumped the intervening fence, and the result of this accidental union was Shaun Goilin. It is certain that he is a well-bred horse, for all the colts were of excellent stock, but just which one is his sire will never be known.

There are certain blood lines which seem to do badly in the production of steeplechasers, and others whose descendants inherit a natural ability for jumping. In America, the imported Atheling and his son, Bryn Mawr, have produced generations of good steeplechasers, and in England one of the greatest blood lines in both kinds of racing traces back to Pocahontas, by Glencoe-Marpessa, by Muley. Her best sons were Stockwell, Rataplan and King Tom, and their blood has been made famous on the flat by such horses as Doncaster, Bend Or, Ormonde, Kingcraft and many others. Stockwell and Rataplan were full brothers, by The Baron, son of Birdcatcher-Echidna, by Economist.

It is probably safe to say that 75 per cent of the horses running in the National at the present time can trace their pedigrees back to Pocahontas, and it is remarkable how her blood keeps cropping up all through the last two-thirds of the National's history. Mr. Hobson's Austerlitz was by Rataplan, Mr. Yates's Harvester was by Stockwell, Pathfinder was by Mogador, a son of King Tom, and Regal, Captain Machell's third winner, was by Saunterer out of Regalia, by Stockwell. Regal thus had a double cross of Birdcatcher blood, for Saunterer was by Birdcatcher. That very good double winner, The Colonel, was by Knight of Kars-Boa-

dicea, and Knight of Kars was by Nutwith-Pocahontas. In most
accounts of The Colonel's breeding it is averred that he was always spoken of as a half-bred but that he may not have been one.
It is difficult to see just why this mistake should have been made;
there is certainly a legend about his dam's ancestry which may
prove her to have been clean-bred, but there is no question whatsoever that Nutwith, and, through him, Knight of Kars, had a
bar sinister, and a very interesting one. Nutwith's pedigree can
be traced back to a mare by Blank out of an Exmoor pony mare,
and Blank was a son of the Godolphin Arabian from Captain
Hartley's Little Mare, by Bartlett's Childers. At one time the
Little Mare came in for a lot of attention, which was aroused by
the belief that her son Shakspere, and not Marske, was the sire
of Eclipse. This belief was pretty thoroughly destroyed, but it is
remarkable that in an old print showing Eclipse and Shakspere,
the two horses do seem to have much in common. Mr. William
Scarth Dixon discusses it in his book *The Influence of Racing and
The Thoroughbred Upon Light Horse Breeding;* he dismisses it, as we
must do here, as "not a little puzzling."

The legend about the pedigree of Boadicea has been told many
times. Some generations back in her ancestry appears a mare
called Modesty. To all intents and purposes she was a half-bred,
but her alleged adventures shortly after her entry into this world
remind one of the reply given by the small boy who was asked to
describe the habits of the irresponsible cuckoo: "Please, sir, he
don't lay his own eggs." The story goes that she was really a
thoroughbred substituted at birth for a half-bred filly so that she
could run in—and presumably win—half-bred races on the bor-
der. If this is true, she was clean-bred, and The Colonel half-

W. A. Rouch

The Colonel, who won in 1869 and 1870.

W. A. Rouch

Cloister, winner in 1893, after being second the previous year.
His time of 9 minutes 32·2/5th seconds is unequalled.

bred on only one side, but the Stud Book does not deal in legends, and for the purposes of that publication Boadicea must remain a half-bred.

Voluptuary, who won the National in '84 on his first appearance over fences, was by Cremorne, whose dam was by Rataplan, and it is possible that he started at 10—1 in spite of his inexperience partly because the experts in breeding had such great confidence in the jumping ability of the Pocahontas blood. These are only a few of the descendants of the great mare who have distinguished themselves in the National, and her name will appear again at the end of this chapter in the discussion of other pedigrees. It is interesting that Pocahontas was not a handsome mare; on the contrary, she was ugly and decidedly lacking in quality, but was remarkably hardy and strong, and lived to be more than thirty years old. Her sire, Glencoe, was sold into America in the later years of his life, and had a great influence on the thoroughbred horse there.

Teddington was the first sire to get two National winners, and no other stallion had that distinction until the heyday of Ascetic, perhaps the greatest sire of steeplechasers who has ever lived. Ascetic, by Hermit-Lady Alicia, was of no account as a race horse, and, except for his pronounced "jumping bone," did not look to be the sort of horse one would expect to sire good steeplechasers. He was very high in the withers, not very deep in the chest, and his head was set high and upright for a stayer. Yet he got Cloister, which was glory enough, and then went on to sire Drumcree and Ascetic's Silver, Grand National winners respectively in 1903 and 1906. Cloister was chance bred if ever a horse was; his dam, Grace II, was bought in Ireland by the late Lord

Fingal and trained as a hunter. She proved absolutely worthless for this job, however, and was put casually enough to Ascetic, the nearest available sire, who was used at that point as a hack and was ridden into town every day for the post—and the foal from this happy-go-lucky union was the great Cloister! The aftermath was equally casual, for Cloister was not impressive as a foal, and he and his dam were sold a short time later for the sum of 31 guineas. Grace II never did anything else worthy of note, for her subsequent foals were poor weaklings and all died, I believe, before they were broken to the saddle.

Hackler got two winners in Jenkinstown and Covertcoat, and is the third and last horse who got more than one National winner.

On several occasions, however, horses with the same sire have finished in the money in the same race. Seaman and Cyrus were sons of Xenophon, a descendant of Orlando, and Gregalach and Easter Hero, both sons of My Prince, finished first and second in 1929. Zoedone, incidentally, who was third in Seaman's race and first the year after, was by New Oswestry, another son of Knight of Kars, and thus she has in her veins the same Exmoor pony blood as The Colonel. This union of the thoroughbred and the Exmoor established a remarkably successful line of horses who carried the words half-bred after their names; from it sprang a very good mare called Mrs. Taft, who won the Cesarewitch of 1851, and through Knight of Kars, who joined with it the Pocahontas strain, it has influenced steeplechasing blood to the present day.

The Cure had an eventful life before he finally settled down at the stud, but the career of Old Buck, another good sire of steeplechasers, is perhaps even more tempestuous and extraordinary. After making a very moderate record on the race-course, Old Buck became a third-rate sire at Epsom with practically no patronage. A gentleman named Bletsoe, however, put some mares to him as an experiment, and the results were so satisfactory in the way of good hunters that he tried to buy the horse, but met with an unexpected obstacle. Old Buck had turned savage—it is curious that he was a demon in every stable but Mr. Bletsoe's, where he was considered quite gentle—and Colonel Hill, his owner, had tried to calm the ferocious spirit by putting him in a dog-cart. The horse promptly kicked it to pieces, and fought the plough when they tried to harness him to that. His ire was thoroughly aroused by this time; he wandered round the field until he found a farm horse, whom he took by the throat and deliberately murdered. Colonel Hill simply gave up after this performance, and, determining to get the horse out of the district, refused to sell him to Mr. Bletsoe and sent him to a Mr. Tyler in Devonshire. Old Buck maintained his wild reputation so completely with his new owner, however, that Mr. Tyler was only too glad to get rid of him, and Mr. Bletsoe brought him back triumphantly. Old Buck was soon established as a successful steeplechase sire, and the best of his get was Grudon, who won the famous snowstorm National of 1901.

Another well-known stallion whose success at the stud came as a surprise is Gallinule, the sire of Gauntlet, third in 1898. Gallinule was a very good horse, but his tendency to break blood vessels kept him from making much of a career in racing, and when he became a roarer, he was given up in despair. At the stud, however, he was unexpectedly brilliant, and sired a tremendous number of winners, among them that fine racing mare, Pretty Polly.

A good many great classic winners have sired horses who have distinguished themselves in the National. Elliman, third in '99, was by Melton, and the unbeaten Barcaldine was the sire of Barsac, who just managed to beat Manifesto for second place the year after. Roi Herode, the progenitor of that tribe of greys which has been made famous by the exploits of The Tetrarch, Stefan the Great, Tetratema, and many others, was the sire of Sir Lindsay, third in 1930, and of Double Chance, the 1925 winner—although there is some question about Double Chance's paternity, and he may have been a son of Day Comet. These are only a few of the horses who have shown ability to get steeple-chasers, and some of the others whose names appear again and again in the pedigrees of modern National horses are White Eagle, Zria (sire of Troytown), Wavelet's Pride, Captivation, Bridge of Earn, and The Raft.

Sprig, the 1927 winner, a sturdy dependable type of horse who finished fourth on two other occasions, is by Marco, who sired, among others, Omar Khayyam, a very successful American race-horse. The two American-bred horses who have finished in the money are Rubio and Billy Barton. The former, who won the National of 1908, was bred by Mr. J. B. Haggin at the Rancho del Paso Stud in California, and was out of La Toquera, while his sire was Star Ruby, a half-brother of the great mare, Sceptre. Star Ruby was a success at the stud in America, and one of his sons was Africander, who won the Belmont, the Realization, and the Saratoga Cup in 1903.

Billy Barton is by Huon, the only son of the great Ard Patrick to be imported into America, and his dam is Mary Le Bus, by St. Savin-My Fair Kentucky. St. Savin, incidentally, was also the sire of Mr. E. M. Weld's good steeplechaser, St. Charlcote, who beat such horses as Cherry Malotte, Skibbereen, and Martian, and who ended his days in the hunting field with Mr. A. H. Higginson. St. Savin's sire was the great St. Simon, by Galopin, and his dam, Aboyne, was a daughter of Hampton. Huon, Billy Barton's sire, was a marvellously bred horse. He was foaled in Germany, for Ard Patrick was bought by Count Lehndorff from Mr. John Gubbins for 20,000 guineas, and he stood in Germany for many years. Ard Patrick, winner of the Derby, and of the Eclipse Stakes, in which he beat Sceptre and Rock Sand, was by St. Florian, a son of St. Simon, and his dam was Morganette, by Springfield. Huon's dam was Hyeres, by Isonomy, by Sterling, and her dam was St. Marguerite, by Hermit.

Billy Barton was bred in Kentucky in 1918, and ran first as a two-year-old at Lexington. After that he was taken to Cuba, where he won several important races during the succeeding two years, including the Cuba-American Handicap, the Cuban Derby, the American Club Handicap, and the Cuban Grand National Handicap. He won altogether $43,040 before he turned cunning and refused to try, and though this is a very respectable sum, he was not a really outstanding horse on the flat, for Cuban racing is not of the highest standard. He was retired when five years old and was bought by Mr. Howard Bruce, the Master of the Elkridge Foxhounds in Maryland. Mr. Bruce hunted him for a while, and then trained him for some of the races over post-and-rails that are such a pleasant feature of the Spring in Maryland and Virginia. He did remarkably well in these and in other races, and won the Maryland Grand National (twice), the Virginia Gold Cup, the Pennsylvania Hunt Cup, the New Jersey Hunt Cup, the Meadowbrook Hunt Cup, and best of all, the Maryland Hunt Cup, which is really the blue riband of all these races. In the last named he set the record, a record which endured until Brose Hover won in 1930.

He was so impressive in these victories that Mr. Bruce shipped him to England to run in the Grand National. He started twice at Aintree, was second to Tipperary Tim in 1928, when not as fit as he might have been, and the next year had the misfortune to suffer interference when going well. He was in excellent condition for this second attempt, and if he had managed to stay up might have had something to do with the finish. Billy Barton is not a very large horse, but he moves splendidly, is a fine jumper, and is as game and courageous as a horse can be.

Obviously it is not possible to say which is the best horse that has ever run in the Grand National, but there are certain ones who have beaten their fields in a particularly convincing manner, and who have done so under big weights. The four horses who have won with twelve stone seven pounds in the saddle are Cloister, Manifesto, Jerry M., and Poethlyn, and it may be of interest to compare their pedigrees with that of Easter Hero, who may be considered one of the best horses of recent years, despite the fact that he never won a National. Additional interest is given to this comparison because he has the same sire as Gregalach, who has given definite proof of his quality by winning one National and being second in another. Easter Hero is not "in the book," for his dam, Easter Week, is by Outbreak out of a mare of Arab ancestry, who has produced a number of good steeplechasers, but who has a blot on her escutcheon. His sire, My Prince, was a useful sort of horse who ran about the beginning of the War, and his best victories were the Tudor Plate at Sandown, the Union Jack Stakes at Liverpool, and the Gordon Stakes at Goodwood. His sire was Marcovil (sire of Hurry On) son of Marco, and his dam, Salvaich, by St. Simon out of a mare of the Woodbine family. He can thus trace to Pocahontas on his maternal side—Woodbine was by Stockwell—and his pedigree shows such mighty names as Galopin, Barcaldine and Hermit. It is notable that he had a maternal ancestress named Dinah, who was by Hermit-Birdcatcher's daughter; Dinah was thus bred very much like Ascetic, who was by Hermit-Lady Alicia, and Ascetic was Cloister's sire.

Pocahontas blood ran in the veins of all these five horses; Cloister had it through his dam, Grace II, and Manifesto through his sire, Man of War, who was by Ben Battle-Wisdom, by Solon. (This Man of War must not be confused with the American Man o' War, by Fair Play-Mahubah, by Rocksand). Ben Battle —also the sire of Ambush II, National winner in 1900—was a son of Rataplan out of Young Alice, whose grandsire was Melbourne, and Melbourne was also grandsire of Ascetic. Man of War was one of those rather rare stallions who is not only dangerous, but dangerous all the time; he was a man-eating killer with no lucid intervals. Mr. Harry Dyas, who owned him and bred from him not only Manifesto but a good steeplechase mare called Gentle Ida, had a fairly large stable at one time, and Man of War was its terror and amusement. There are certainly some people who can handle with safety horses that no one else can go near, but men who felt they had that ability were unfailing game for

Mr. Dyas. In the course of a tour of the stables someone would remark that he had never seen a horse that would not eat out his hand, or words to that effect, whereupon his host would state that while this was undoubtedly true, he was going to see one now. A small bet usually resulted, and the meeting would adjourn to the other end of the stables, where the confident gentleman would take one look at Man of War parading up and down his box, breathing battle, murder and sudden death, and admit defeat without a trial.

Jerry M.'s dam was a mare by Luminary, and his sire was Walmsgate, who was very fashionably bred. Walmsgate was by Hampton, who was by Lord Clifden, by Newminster (also the sire of Hermit), and Hampton's dam, Lady Langden, was a grand-daughter of Rataplan. Walmsgate's dam was Flying Footstep, by Doncaster-Atalanta, by Galopin out of a mare cross of Woodbine family. and Walmsgate thus had a triple of the Pocahontas blood. Walmsgate never ran, but was a remarkably successful sire, both of flat racers and steeplechase horses.

The last of the four winners who carried 12—7 is Poethlyn, by Rydal Head-Fine Champagne. Rydal Head was by St. Frusquin (a son of St. Simon), out of Rydal, a daughter of Bend Or and Windermere by Macaroni. Thus the Pocahontas blood crops up once more and proves again what an influence the ugly daughter of Glencoe has had in the breeding of National horses. It is somewhat remarkable that not one of the sires of these five horses, who can truly be called great as far as the National is concerned, was in any way an extraordinary horse in racing. Ascetic and Rydal Head were very average, Walmsgate never ran, and My Prince, although useful, never approached classic form. Man of War might also have been termed useful, although he was probably not as good a horse as My Prince. He won several races as a three-year-old in Ireland, but failed on the flat the following year in England, and was made into a hurdler. He won nine races over hurdles during the next two years, and was then retired to the stud. Whatever the ability as race-horses of these five sires, it is clear that they had very much the same combination of blood in their veins; and an examination of the pedigrees of other good National horses shows these same lines appearing again and again.

CHAPTER SEVEN

1886 *to* 1906; *Cloister and Manifesto*

OLD JOE was the type of horse that makes people say that the National has been won by all sorts of queer ones. He had been a hunter, a harness nag, and a show jumper at very small shows before he became a steeplechaser, and—until he ran in the National of 1886—was distinguished only for a quiet mediocrity at all these trades. No one bothered very much about him at Aintree, except perhaps the bookmakers who seemed to know something or other, for they resolutely refused to lay odds longer than 25—1. Old Joe was not well backed at a "damned short price for a horse who had done everything but play the fiddle," and the fast brilliant jumper Coronet was favourite. Coronet went out at the start and looked very good for one round, but he was no stayer, and finally finished sixth. Old Joe was beautifully ridden by Skelton, and beat Too Good and Gamecock in the run in by sheer stamina. These were not the only good horses in the race, for Old Joe had plenty to beat, and his owner, Mr. Douglas, was so delighted that he gave a thousand pounds to his trainer and presented Skelton with the stakes of thirteen hundred pounds.

Visions of so much gold must have been in Skelton's mind again the following year when he had another chance of victory. He led on Savoyard coming into the straight, but good jockey as he was, he could not resist temptation with the goal in sight and made his run too soon. Daniells lay behind him until two hundred yards from home, and then got Gamecock up to win by a head in a driving finish.

That fine mare, Frigate, should have won in 1888. It was her third appearance in the thankless position of second, and nothing but sheer bad luck put her there. Frigate and the favourite, an Irish horse called Usna, went away with a big lead to the Canal Turn, where the latter dislocated his shoulder and carried the mare almost off the course; by the time Mr. Beasley got her going again most of the field had gone by and left them, but even so she was second to Playfair. If she and Usna had avoided misfortune they would probably have fought out the finish before the rest were over the last fence, for these two were very much the class of the race. The following year Mr. Tommy Beasley, the only one of the Beasley triumvirate who had not yet been in the money on Frigate, rode her in a National full of good horses such as Voluptuary, Roquefort, Gamecock, Why Not, and the great raking mare Bellona; but Frigate's bad luck had run out at last, and she won most convincingly. Frigate was curiously enough the daughter of a very old horse, Gunboat, who was in turn the son of Sir Hercules, who was way along in years when Gunboat was born—so we have the winner of the National of 1889 being the grand-daughter of the horse whose son, Arthur, ran second in the National forty-nine years before!

Arthur Nightingall's name will always be associated with that of Ilex, in spite of his later victories on Why Not and Grudon, and he has always said that Ilex was the best he ever rode. In 1888 Nightingall was engaged to ride at a small meeting at Leicester, and after weighing in for the Hunter's Steeplechase, he wandered out to the paddock to have a look at his horse. The look was not encouraging, for what he saw was a chestnut horse with no apparent neck or shoulders, and a remarkable amount of belly. A friend of his offered him five pounds not to ride, in the fear that the horse would kill him. Five pounds was the sum he was to receive for riding, but he had already weighed in, and the offer was regretfully declined. To his intense surprise Ilex gave him a beautiful ride, and they won in a common canter. He rode him again at Leopardstown shortly after, and was third behind Captain Owen on Kilworth. Nightingall had seen enough of Ilex by this time to know that he was something out of the ordinary, and when he came up for sale at Tattersall's he persuaded Mr. George Masterman to buy him and send him to the Nightingall stable to be trained. Arthur and his father did wonders with the horse, and in 1890 he started favourite for the National and won easily. He was third the next two years, but after that was not sound enough to stand a preparation for racing, and Arthur Nightingall made a hunter out of him.

Ilex was never very much to look at, even in his best days, and his common appearance brought about some amusing situations in the hunting field. One day a certain young buck from London looked Ilex over as hounds were drawing, remarked that he had never seen a steeplechase jockey on a good hunter yet, and laughed at the comparison between the jockey's ugly brute and his own handsome mount. As luck would have it, the hounds ran like blazes that day over a very stiff bit of country, and the Londoner was astonished and enraged to find the despised Ilex giving him a lead at one fence after another. He managed to stick along until the leader rose to a great hairy fence with a ditch beyond it, which the race-horse got over with ease, but the hunter fell, and his rider emerged from a sea of black mud to be greeted by his hilarious friends and the information that he had been trying to match strides with an erstwhile Grand National winner!

The horse who ran second to Ilex on his first appearance at Aintree was the rogue Pan, the horse that Captain Machell had tried so hard to buy. The Hon. George Lambton owned him for a while, then sold him to Mr. Hartopp, who in disgust passed him on to Mr. Woodland. Pan was good enough—there was never any question about that—but he simply would not try. If he had not been a quitter he might have given Ilex a race for it. As they came into the straight, with Pan well up, Mr. Hartopp, turning to Mr. Lambton in the stands, said: "My God, there is Pan going to win the National!" Then he dropped his glasses on some unsuspecting head below, and nearly fell out of the stands himself!

In 1891 the mighty Cloister ran in his first National. Cloister was the *beau ideal* of the steeplechaser of the big powerful type —a dark bay gelding, with beautifully laid shoulders, great depth through the chest, a clearly defined jumping bone, and muscular quarters with remarkable length from great square hips to big well-formed hocks. He was a big horse in every sense of the word, but had great freedom of action, and galloped and jumped with seeming absence of effort. He was a hard puller, but otherwise a thoroughly comfortable ride when one got used to his peculiar manner of jumping. He ran with his head very low, like most great stayers, and would keep it low until his jockey felt sure he could never get it up in time. Then, just at the last moment, when he apparently had not seen the fence at all, up would come his head, and a big fence would be thrown behind him as lightly as a little hurdle.

Cloister ran the first time in the colours of Lord Dudley, and was prepared for the race by Richard Marsh, who was later trainer to King Edward, and then to King George. Lord Dudley had another horse in Marsh's stable, a stallion called Royal Meath, who, like Cloister, was a son of Ascetic. Marsh says that Royal Meath was an even better Aintree proposition than Cloister, but this unfortunately was never proved, for Royal Meath never ran in the National. He won some very good races in France, but subsequently jarred a suspensory ligament when carrying a big weight at Sandown, and was retired to the stud, where he became a very successful sire of steeplechasers, among them being the brilliant jumper Rory o' Moore. When Royal Meath went wrong they had to "fall back" on Cloister, as Marsh puts it. No doubt many stables would have been more than pleased to have such a horse as a second string!

The race was full of good horses in '91. Roquefort, Voluptuary, and Gamecock were running, Nightingall rode Ilex, Mr. Harry Beasley had the mount on Come Away, the favourite, and Cloister had the services of the famous Captain Roddy Owen. The last two waged a grim battle up the straight, two splendid horses ridden by two great jockeys, and for once Captain Owen seems to have had the worst of it. Come Away was ahead half a mile from home, but Cloister was moving up, and after the last fence Captain Owen tried to pass on the inside. Beasley let him get up to his horse's shoulder, but then bored in toward the rail. Cloister was fairly boxed, and they finished in that position. Captain Owen promptly objected and was very much irritated with Beasley, against whom he vowed all sorts of vengeance. There was a great hullabaloo—the Irish furious at the objection to their idol, and Owen equally furious at Beasley. His friends managed to calm him down and to prevent him from resorting to fisticuffs—Richard Marsh remarked that he'd better be careful or he might be second again—but the Beasley supporters were still foaming at the mouth, and surrounded Captain Owen in the weighing room. He was much more interested in the decision which was then in the making than in their fulminations, and putting his back to the wall, remarked coolly: "All right, but wait till it's settled, then I'll fight everyone of you, single handed or the whole lot of you together!"

The stewards finally decided that Beasley had acted within his rights and that Owen should not have tried to pass on the inside. A similar decision occurred some years later, incidentally, in the race for the Goodwood Cup of 1913. Danny Maher, the American jockey who rode so well in England, was leading on Arda, with Frank Wootton on Jest in second place. Wootton tried to pass on the inside, as Captain Owen had done, and found himself boxed in exactly the same way. The Goodwood stewards came to the same decision as their Aintree colleagues before them, and Arda was not disqualified. Jest was probably the better of the two, and was a great success at the stud; her first foal was Humorist, who won the Derby of 1921, and died of tuberculosis shortly afterwards.

Captain Owen rode a beautiful race the following year (1892) and won on Father O'Flynn, a horse of considerable ability but very difficult to ride, for he would not try unless held together by really expert horsemanship. Even at his best he was not the equal of Cloister and Ilex, who carried big weights into second and third places; and it was only his light weight and Captain

Owen's skill that made Father O'Flynn beat the better horses. Cloister had passed into the hands of Mr. C. G. Duff shortly after his second to Come Away, and was trained this year and the next by Mr. Arthur Yates at Bishop's Sutton.

Cloister had now served a thorough apprenticeship, and in 1893 he won perhaps the most remarkable victory in the history of the National. Until this year it had been considered impossible for a horse to win the great race with twelve stone or more in the saddle, but so well had Cloister run through the winter, that he started favourite in spite of his twelve stone seven. The race was run on a course so dry that the horses raised dust as they galloped, and the heat was terrific for March. Dollery, who had the mount on Cloister, tried to place him at the first two fences, but the horse had his own ideas about jumping, and the jockey quickly decided to let him alone. They went into the lead after the second fence, and from there on it was a procession and merely a question of how much Cloister would win by. He entered the straight fresh and full of running, with the rest of a brilliant field far behind, and he was moving so well and easily that the cheering started when he was still two fences from home. He finally finished eased up, forty lengths ahead of Aesop and Why Not, in 9:32⅔, the best time since the course had been altered in 1863.

Though nobody even guessed it at the time, this was Cloister's last appearance in the National, for his subsequent career was a chapter of accidents, and provoked almost as much controversy as the famous alleged poisoning of the Duke of Westminster's Orme. A few weeks after this great victory, Cloister ran at Sandown and was astonishingly beaten by Horizon, a very average horse. At the time this could not be accounted for, and he was taken out of training for the rest of the year in the belief that possibly he had had too much racing—but it was really the beginning of much worse troubles.

Early in 1894 he was prepared for the National and did his work splendidly. The public was filled with confidence, and in the middle of March was still backing him enthusiastically at the incredible odds—for the National—of 6—4. Suddenly he went back in the betting, and was quoted at 6—1. On the same day that the odds changed he came back from a school over the Sandown fences with a slight lameness. A veterinary surgeon was called in and everything possible was done. Cloister recovered slightly, but the moment he was put over a fence the lameness and pain in the sciatic nerve returned, and he was struck out of the National a few days before it was run. In his absence, Why Not, who had run with varying degrees of success in several Nationals, was made favourite, and, well ridden by Arthur Nightingall, won after a gruelling race from Lady Ellen II. Three quarters of a mile from home Why Not was in third place and not going well, but he was a very game, honest horse, and just lasted to win by half a length. The finish was a terrific affair, and Nightingall always considered it the hardest race he ever rode in.

The next year the Cloister sensation was trotted out once more. The horse had been made favourite again, and there seemed no reason for alarm. But exactly a year—to the very day—after Cloister had first been scratched from the National, the news went forth that all was not well with him. Escott was training him in '95, and that morning sent him out for a gallop over fences. Cloister went perfectly for a mile, then collapsed without warning on the flat and lay on the ground with his tongue hanging out. He was finally got to his feet, but was obviously in pain, and was forthwith taken out of the National.

The uproar surpassed that of the year before and Mr. Duff was loud in his assertions that the horse had been "got at." Cloister's owner seems to have had a foul play complex, for he had the horse surrounded by plain-clothes detectives most of the time, even when at home in his trainer's stable, a performance which must have been mildly annoying to the trainer. After the '94 fiasco, Cloister was taken away from Mr. Yates and turned over to Escott, which would seem to indicate that Mr. Duff doubted the probity of someone in Mr. Yates' stable. He had no better luck in the stable of the new trainer, and the thing occurred over again in exactly the same way.

What was really the matter with Cloister can never be proved, of course; various veterinary surgeons had theories about it, but Mr. Yates disagreed with most of them. He always believed that Cloister had hurt himself during his National victory in '93, and cited as a proof of it his astounding defeat at Sandown shortly afterwards. Cloister was a horse who required very little schooling over fences—he did not have to be taught to jump!—and was not jumped to any great extent after the Sandown disappointment until a few weeks before the '94 race. His first serious schoolings over fences then and a year later were the forerunners of his going wrong, and Mr. Yates' theory is that the jumping brought out the weakness developed in 1893, and that Cloister was never a really sound horse after he won the National.

There are two objections to Mr. Yates' theory, and neither of

W. A. Rouch

Manifesto, who won in 1897 and 1899.   Out of eight starts he
won twice, was third three times, fourth once, and ninth at
the age of sixteen.

W. A. Rouch

Rubio, the only American-bred winner, first in 1908,
H. B. Bletse up.

them impinges in any way upon his reputation, for his name and that of his stable have always been synonyms for all that is honest and fine in the British Turf. First and unexplainable is the fact that Cloister, trained by Escott, ran in and won the Grand Sefton at Aintree in November of '94. He won it with no difficulty whatsoever, and did not break down during the race or after it. Second, the bookmakers in London knew all about Cloister's two accidents almost as soon as they had happened, which certainly looks as though someone had a direct interest in keeping them posted, and from that as a starting point one can possibly deduce that the accidents may have been expected. It seems unlikely, however, that two such reputable training stables should have contained a tout, or a boy who was acting for one—one stable might have, but two seems one too many. The only other alternative is that Mr. Duff inadvertently dug his own grave with his constant espionage system. A great many private detectives were employed at one time or another to watch Cloister, and it is just as logical to assume that they were the villains as to say that one or both stables harboured a traitor. It is certainly within the realm of possibility that one of them may have dropped a word, either by accident or malice aforethought, into the ear of one who wanted to know, and who thereupon set the wires humming for the benefit of the London bookmakers. Whatever the case, Cloister never ran again in the National, and was thereby deprived of two more probable victories, for he was infinitely the best in an era of very good horses.

Wild Man from Borneo won for Mr. Joe Widger the year of the second Cloister sensation and running fourth behind him was the seven-year-old Manifesto. Mr. Dyas, his breeder, had given

Manifesto plenty of time to mature, and this was his first appearance in the National. Cloister was gone, but another horse as great or greater had come upon the scene. Cloister and Manifesto were to the National what Bobby Jones is to any golf tournament he plays in—given an even break, they were sure to be there or thereabouts when the field straightened out for the run home. Manifesto was a bay, as was Cloister, but he was a lighter, more blood-like horse than the other, in spite of his ability to carry great weights. In 1896 he fell after being interfered with, and The Soarer won, beautifully handled by Mr. D. M. G. Campbell, who was at that time a young subaltern in the 9th Lancers. The victory must have been a mixed pleasure to Mr. Campbell, for he had trained The Soarer himself very well and successfully, and had sold him only a few days before the race. This same Mr. Campbell is now General Sir David Campbell.

The Aldershot steeplechase course certainly has nothing to do with the Grand National, but there is an amusing story connected with it. A certain very athletic officer in His Majesty's Royal Artillery, to wit, Mr. R. H. Allen—now Major Allen—once remarked in the presence of various of his colleagues that steeplechasers had nothing very much to do, that the jumps were not of prodigious height, and that even a man could negotiate the Aldershot course without great difficulty. Several brother officers promptly did what they considered calling his bluff and bet him that he couldn't jump the course himself. The bets were as promptly taken, and on a certain day Mr. Allen appeared all complete in running clothes to make his attempt. The scoffers were there in force to watch the grief, but shortly were filled with amazement as Mr. Allen pursued his way round the course, "lepping" the fences in fine style, and eventually made good his boast, to the detriment of many sceptical pockets. The Aldershot fences are certainly not as big as those at Aintree, and they may even be smaller than some of the largest on the Park Courses, but they are quite high enough from the point of view of a man on his own feet. One is inclined to question the ability of the average man to "get round," but Mr. Allen proved beyond any doubt that a man *could* jump the course—provided, at least, that that man was himself!

Manifesto never fell again at Aintree, and the following year he won absolutely as he pleased. He undoubtedly would have been made favourite in 1898, but in the early spring of that year he escaped from his box one day, hopped a five-foot gate, and rapped a fetlock so badly that he had to be laid off for several months. The stable boy who was responsible for the accident was so terrified at the result of his carelessness that he vanished as though the earth had swallowed him up, and was discovered only by chance many weeks later in another stable, where he was working under an assumed name! All of which gives a very unfair impression of Mr. Dyas, who though justifiably annoyed, had not the slightest intention of boiling the poor boy in oil!

The Manifesto-less race was won by Drogheda in a blinding snowstorm. The spectators, and indeed most of the jockeys, had a very vague idea of what was happening most of the time. The well-backed Barcalwhey fell, no one knows how, and his jockey Chalmers was knocked out. He came to after a while, and was eventually found sitting in the slush nursing a battered jaw. "That's won it," he said. "I don't know what happened—all I do know is that I've earned a fiver, and that it'll cost me twenty pounds for some new teeth!"

Manifesto came back to the race in 1899, this time under the ownership of Mr. Joseph Bulteel. In Mr. W. H. Moore's stable, where he was trained, was a mare called Gentle Ida, who was listed as a half-bred; her dam, Promptress, was not "in the book," but she and Manifesto had the same sire, as has been noted already. Somehow the rumour got round that the stable preferred her chances to those of Manifesto, and she started favourite at 4—1, while Manifesto was next in demand at 5—1. Good steeplechaser as Gentle Ida was, the rumour seems unlikely to have been founded on fact, but if it was so, the stable was sadly at fault, for Manifesto won very easily, and did it with twelve stone seven in the saddle, the same weight that Cloister had carried. The next year he carried six pounds more, and ran perhaps his greatest race to finish a close third to Barsac, who was in receipt of no less than forty-three pounds from the great horse.

The winner was the lightly weighted Ambush II, who belonged to King Edward, at that time Prince of Wales, and the National thus acted as a curtain raiser to the greatest year the Royal colours ever had, for that same summer Diamond Jubilee won the Two Thousand Guineas, the Derby, and the St. Leger for the Prince. His National victory was immensely popular, and crowds flocked round him as he led Ambush from the course. The enthusiasm was nearly as great as on another occasion when the Prince was having difficulties in reaching his victorious horse because of the crowd. A cordon of police was thrown about him to clear the way, and as he moved forward thus protected by the

Law, a voice shouted cheerily: "Never mind, Teddy, I'll come and bail you out!"

There have been several Nationals run in snowstorms, but in 1901 there was a regular blizzard. The whole course was white, the fences were mere mounds of snow and were getting higher every minute. After a lot of discussion it was determined to run the race anyway, in spite of a petition signed by many of the jockeys, including Arthur Nightingall, who had the mount on Grudon. Mr. Bletsoe, Grudon's owner, had an inspiration just before starting time. He rushed off to a grocer, and came back bearing several pounds of butter, which he hurriedly stuffed into Grudon's feet. As a result they did not "ball," and while the others were slipping and sliding about, Grudon pursued his way cheerfully over the course, and won in a canter. He came over the last fence way ahead, and was feeling so much within himself that he playfully hopped a footpath which crossed the course a short distance from the finish, and almost unshipped his jockey—who thought that jumping was over for the day—as well as half scaring to death those who had bet on him.

Manifesto was given a year off in 1901 but ran third to Shannon Lass a year later, and third again behind Drumcree in 1903. In both of these races he was carrying big weights and was beaten by horses at the very bottom of the handicap. He came out for the last time in 1904, at the age of sixteen, when he finished ninth, and thus completed a great and honourable career. Whether or not he was the best horse who ever won the National can be debated, but his record is unequalled, for out of eight attempts, he finished seven times, won twice, was third three times, fourth once, and ninth at an age when most horses have been retired.

The 1904 race was won by Moifaa, a great, ugly gelding from New Zealand. He was seventeen hands high, with withers like a camel's hump, but at his best was a really good steeplechaser. He was very difficult to ride, and no one could hold him; it was merely a question of guiding him into the right places. He would jump any fence he saw, and was, as Lord Marcus Beresford described him, "a great machine at high pressure over fences." His early career in England was not impressive, for he failed three times in succession, but in New Zealand he gave away three stone successfully on more than one occasion, and Aintree was ideal for such a mighty jumper. The fences were higher than usual this year, but Moifaa seemed to revel in them, and won easily.

There is a sort of Robinson Crusoe tale current in America with regard to Moifaa's victory which seems to be unknown in England, but it makes a splendid legend. According to this story Moifaa was shipwrecked off the Irish coast at the end of his voyage from New Zealand and was given up for lost. Some fishermen, however, while about their business on an early morning a few days later, discovered the horse parading back and forth on the strand of a small island on which he had taken refuge, and ferried him ashore. Refreshed by his icy swim in the waters of the North Atlantic, he is reputed to have entered into his training with a vim, and eventually strolled round the Aintree course to win the National. In view of this story there is humour in the fact that Moifaa's sire was a horse called Natator.

The next year Moifaa ran in the colours of the Prince of Wales, but he had gone bad in the wind and fell at Becher's the second time round, and Kirkland won. In 1906 the favourite was John M. P., a big powerful horse of great speed and stamina, who later ran brilliantly in America. He started at 7—2, but he was one of the impetuous sort that run their races from in front at a great pace, and are not seen at their best in the National. Coming into the Canal Turn his attention was attracted by the crowd; he put his mind too late to the business of jumping and went down. The race was won by Ascetic's Silver, and his rider was the late Hon. Aubrey Hastings. Ascetic's Silver was a good horse, but won few races, due to his unfortunate propensity for breaking blood vessels.

I had the great pleasure during the summer of 1930 of spending a day at the stable at Wroughton, on the Wiltshire Downs, where Mr. Hastings trained horses with such success for upwards of twenty years. Since Mr. Hastings' sad death in 1929, Mrs. Hastings has carried on the stable with the assistance of Ivor Anthony, a very fine steeplechase jockey who finished in the National "money" on three occasions. Mr. Hastings' record of training four Grand National winners is unequalled during the history of the race. Ascetic's Silver was the first, and after him came Ally Sloper, Ballymacad, and Master Robert. The last of these was not a thoroughly sound horse when he won. He had been troubled for some time with lameness, and in the hope of curing him was driven barefoot many miles on the hardest roads available. This eventually did him good, but he was always a bit tender on his feet, and that tenderness caused the amateur jockey, Mr. P. Roberts, to make a decision which seemed rather sensible at the time, but which he must have regretted many times since. He had ridden Master Robert in various races and was offered the mount in the Grand National. After some consideration he declined the offer, largely because of the horse's unsoundness and because he had the chance of riding Palm Oil, who was not so afflicted. Trudgill was then put up on Master Robert and proceeded to win by several lengths, while Palm Oil and the unfortunate Mr. Roberts came a cropper.

Among the many good horses that Mrs. Hastings had in her care when I saw the stable was Colonel Sir Harold Wernher's Brown Jack. He is not very inspiring to look at in his box. Like Jerry M., the great National horse of twenty years ago, he slouches and stands lazily over at the knee, but there is nothing lazy or over at the knee about him on the racecourse. He began his career as a hurdler and was the best in England at that sport. Then, at the suggestion of Steve Donoghue, he was trained for the flat, and with that great jockey in the saddle shortly proved himself one of the best long distance horses in the country. He is the real type of a long, lean stayer, and is one of the game, honest sort who give their best, and who like to win races. In spite of always carrying top weight, or nearly so, he has won most of the important races in England for stayers, and when he does not win he is generally placed behind some lightly weighted horse or horses. Among his victories are the Ascot Stakes, 1929, the Alexandra Plate (three times), the Goodwood Cup, and the Doncaster Cup, both in 1930. He was third in the Cesarewitch of 1929, in which he gave away a lot of weight to West Wicklow and Friendship, the two horses who beat him, and was third in the Ebor Handicap of 1930 behind a dead-heating first and second. His race for the Chester Cup in 1931, however, was perhaps the best he has ever run. As usual, he was at the top of the handicap, and it was generally assumed that he would not be able to give weight to Trimdon, a very good horse, and a first-rate stayer. Trimdon was made a good favourite, and for the first half of the race it looked as though the backers had been right for once, but when Brown Jack was called on he came away from the field in fine style, and galloped past the post with his ears pricked, looking as pleased as Punch.

Brown Jack is a horse of character and has his little habit which must not be interfered with. He dislikes standing in his box and much prefers to sit, which he does on the edge of his manger, and the manger is worn smooth from the contact. He scratches round in the bedding below it for several minutes, then hunches his quarters against the manger and sits down comfortably. Anthony told me that they tried to give him something softer to sit on and with great difficulty had the edge of the manger padded with felt; but Brown Jack would have none of it. He sniffed the felt a couple of times, then grabbed it in his teeth, ripped it off, and dropped it neatly outside the door of the box. They put it on again, and again it was torn off and dropped outside, so they decided that Brown Jack knew more about his own comfort than they did, and he now sits in lordly style on a cold, hard manger!

Mr. Howard Bruce's American-bred Billy Barton, whose career is taken up in another part of this book, was trained for his English engagements by Mr. Hastings, and I saw the fence over which he was schooled for the Grand National. When he first came to Wroughton he astonished everyone by his terrific leaping, for he jumped in post and rail style, and cleared each fence by a good few inches, which differed considerably from the broad jumping, scratching-through-the-top method employed by a horse who is used to negotiating brush fences with a ditch on one side or the other. It was Mr. Bruce's intention to start Billy Barton in the National of 1930, but unfortunately he hurt himself slightly, and it was thought he might not stand a preparation.

CHAPTER EIGHT

Some Great Jockeys Who Won the National

SO many great steeplechase jockeys have ridden in the Grand National during the nearly one hundred years of its existence that only a very bold man indeed would pronounce any particular one as the best. Mr. Arthur Yates used to say that pluck and determination made jockeys but that neither of these qualities was of much use without opportunity; and when one adds to this the element of luck which must always be present in steeple-chasing, from the very nature of the sport, it becomes clear why so many very perfect horsemen have failed to pilot a winner of the great race. From the point of view of statistics, however, George Stevens stands head and shoulders above all rivals as the only man to have ridden five horses into first place. If he was not the best of all, he certainly has never had a superior, and if a jockey may be said to have made his own luck, Stevens was that jockey, for his manner of riding was carefully calculated to eliminate the possibility of interference.

Perhaps the most noticeable thing about Stevens was his extreme caution. Not a very valuable quality in a jockey, one might think, for before a race he was inclined to be nervous, sometimes as much so as a novice wearing silk for the first time, but once in the saddle he was all cool confidence, and his caution was the result, not of nervousness, but of hard-headed thought. Other jockeys have preferred to take the chance of being slipped to that of being knocked over, but very few have had a knowledge of pace good enough to take that chance to the extent to which

Stevens took it. The moment the race started he would take his horse back into the ruck, and it was quite usual to see him trailing in last place all the first round of the Aintree course. He would wait until there seemed no possible chance of his getting up in time, and then come with a rush which carried him to the leaders just when the pace and the distance were telling on them. He certainly saved his horse in this way, leaving him just that extra fraction of stamina which means a length advantage at the finish, and he knew exactly when to move up and deliver his challenge. One can judge of the mental effect on a jockey whose horse was striding along in the lead when he knew that Stevens was waiting back there with his "sword of Damocles," all ready to challenge at the very moment when he was least ready to give battle.

Stevens' victories were scored on Freetrader in 1856, Emblem and Emblematic in 1863 and '64, and The Colonel in 1869 and '70. He was third on Emblematic in 1865 and rode The Colonel into fourth place in 1871, which was his last mount in the National. In June of that year he was jogging home on a cob when his hat blew off; a boy picked it up, and in the act of giving it back frightened the cob, who bolted down the hill, fell, and hurled Stevens against a rock at the side of the road. His skull was fractured, and he died the next day, killed by a cob after surviving nearly twenty years of steeplechasing without an injury of any importance, for his career had been singularly devoid of accident.

Six jockeys have won the National three times, three of them amateurs, and three professionals. Tom Olliver was the first in point of time, and was, indeed, the first to ride more than one

Sport & General

Becher's Brook in 1925.
Double Chance (right), the winner, and Silvo, who finished fifth.

winner. His mounts were Gaylad, 1842, Vanguard the year after, and Peter Simple in 1853. Olliver was a strong resolute rider over fences, but probably not the equal, in his own estimation or anyone else's, of Jem Mason, Lottery's rider. On one occasion, when a great deal depended on a horse of his own winning a race, he persuaded Mason to take the mount in his stead. When the horse arrived in the paddock, Mason took off the terribly severe bit in which Olliver rode him and made the horse go very well in an ordinary snaffle—which certainly shows the difference in ability between the two jockeys. Mason would probably have won the National more than once if Lottery had not been handicapped out of the race—apparently that was the opinion of those who thus handicapped him, at least. But it is a curious fact that Lottery did not like his jockey, however well they may have gone in the hunting field or on the race-course.

Mason was a quite extraordinary character and perhaps the most famous jockey of the early days of steeplechasing. He was very particular about his clothes, and dressed in such splendid fashion that he was frequently mistaken for a member of the nobility. It is said that Poole, the London tailor, made coats for him for nothing, and his boots were the real acme of dandyism. To make them, two separate boot-makers co-operated, one making the legs and the other the feet!

Whatever the quality of Olliver's horsemanship, he was a fine teacher, and gave many hints to the brilliant amateur Captain Little, who won on Chandler in 1848. Chandler was an ugly animal and was described by a certain gentleman as a "fiddle-headed brute," but there was nothing the matter with his ability to jump, and he has become famous for a leap he made at

H

Warwick, the year before his National victory. One of the obstacles to be surmounted was a brook, which had been so swollen by the rains that it spread out over the fields, and it was impossible to tell where the brook itself began. There seemed to be a good chance of some splendid falls, and spectators placed themselves in good position to see the "grief," but Chandler treated them to something even better. He came down at the brook like a whirlwind, took off well away, and landed safely on the other side. The distance was promptly measured, and proved to be, from hoofmark to hoofmark, just over thirty-nine feet!

The professionals remained in the background of the three-winner picture for some years after Olliver's time. Mr. T. F. Pickernell took up the running, and under the *nom de course* of "Mr. Thomas" he rode in nineteen Grand Nationals. His three victories were scored on Anatis, 1860, The Lamb in 1871, and Pathfinder four years later. He was erratic at times, but on his best days was a brilliant horseman, and had many successes on the continent as well as at home. He arrived at Nice one day to ride in a race and was straightway challenged to a duel by a Frenchman who believed himself insulted in some vague manner. Mr. Pickernell suggested settling the matter in the good old Anglo-Saxon way, but the Frenchman was horrified—particularly as he would not have had a chance—and swords were decided on, in the use of which weapon Mr. Pickernell was about as expert as his opponent was with his fists. The duel eventually took place, but little ferocity was displayed by either gentleman; they waved their swords at each other from a safe distance, shook hands, and left the arena arm in arm, and the necessity for bloodshed was averted forever.

A similar challenge was received at Baden-Baden by Captain George Warwick Hunt, who rejoiced in the nick-name of Jonas, and who was one of the few members of the famous Light Brigade that came "back from the mouth of Hell" at Balaclava. At the conclusion of a race in which Captain Hunt had ridden his hardest to finish fairly near the winner, a Frenchman named M. Thomas, much annoyed at the loss of the money which he had bet on the Captain's horse, shouted in no uncertain tones that Captain Hunt had deliberately pulled his horse. Tired and irritated, Hunt seized M. Thomas by a long and tempting nose, yanked him out of his carriage, and knocked him down. Of course nothing but blood could wipe out such an insult, and M. Thomas called for swords. Hunt put himself in the hands of the stewards of the race-course. They decided that the duel must take place, but that the Englishman's preference for pistols should be acceded to. The matter was arranged, and Hunt's seconds called on those of his opponents to agree on a place of meeting, only to be astonished by a complete and abject apology. It was later discovered that some unidentified person had filled M. Thomas with discretion by the statement that Captain Hunt put out his bedroom candle every evening with one shot from a Palais Royal pistol!

Mr. Tommy Beasley followed in the footsteps of Mr. Pickernell. The Beasley family supplied a constant stream of riders to Aintree; Mr. Harry Beasley won once, and was second several times, and William of the same family was second on Frigate in '88. They seemed to have passed Frigate from one to the other like a loving cup, for each of the three brothers was placed on her at some time during her long career in the National. Tommy was the one who brought her home in front, however, and his other wins were on Empress and Woodbrook in '80 and '81. Just which of the three was the best jockey is a question, but it is remarkable that from 1878 to 1891 there were only four Grand Nationals in which the name of Beasley did not appear as the rider of one of the placed horses!

In 1890 the professional, Arthur Nightingall, started his winning career with a victory on Ilex, after which he won with old Why Not in '94, and again with Grudon in the snowstorm of 1901. His record comprises three wins, one second, and four thirds out of fifteen rides, but leaves out the fact that he was amusingly and indirectly responsible for Playfair's victory in '88, for without Nightingall Playfair would not have finished at all. Nightingall rode The Badger, and Mawson had the mount on the winner. Playfair hit a fence very hard, and Mawson was thrown forward on to his horse's head, where he stuck tight in spite of frenzied scrabblings to get himself back where he belonged. The horse headed cheerfully for the next jump, paying no attention to his rider's undignified position; but just in time Nightingall ranged alongside on The Badger and pulled Mawson back into the saddle—whereupon Playfair went on, benefited by the accidents to Usna and Frigate, and won the race, while his saviour struggled home among the also-rans!

Nightingall's race on Grudon carries him over into the 1900's, but only two jockeys have ridden three winners since the turn of the century. The professional, Ernest Piggot, was the first to complete his triple; he was a very good horseman, and enjoyed the advantage of riding unusually good horses. He had the mount on Jerry M. in his come-back year of 1912, and rode Poethlyn in

1918 and 1919, which gives him the distinction of having brought home in front two horses carrying the biggest weight that the race has been won under.

Mr. J. R. Anthony is the other rider of three winners in the twentieth century, and thus makes the honours even between the professionals and the amateurs. His fame began with his victory in 1911, and no more brilliant feat of riding has been seen at Aintree than his artistry in nursing the unsound Glenside round the course and home in front in that race of rain and mud. His next success was with Ally Sloper in 1915, and he won again on Troytown five years later. Shortly after this he became a professional, as many of the amateurs did after the War, and was second twice on Old Tay Bridge, and then third on Bright's Boy in 1927. Thus he completed some sort of a record, for in each of these three successive years he was first over the last fence, only to be beaten in the run in by a faster horse—not because of any weakness of his, certainly, for he was a strong finisher. Anthony retired in 1928 to become a trainer, and has already done very well in that branch of the sport. Among the many good winners in his care is Easter Hero, who has blossomed forth into his full powers since Anthony has had him.

The first of the jockeys whose career includes two National victories is Mr. Alexander Goodman. He did little race riding after his win on Miss Mowbray in 1852, and when he came out again to ride Salamander sixteen years later few people recognized in the grey-whiskered veteran the mighty horseman of by-gone days. A great trainer once said that no professional could put a horse at a fence as well as Mr. Goodman, and he proceeded to demonstrate that this was still true by bringing the despised Salamander home a long way in front of his field. When he rode the horse to the unsaddling enclosure after the race, his expression is said to have been one of delight at winning the race mingled with obvious disgust at having so under-rated his mount that he had wagered only ten pounds to win!

Mr. Maunsell Richardson's two successes on Disturbance and Reugny, and his retirement from the saddle have already been discussed. In the case of Reugny, his victory might have been termed a double one, for he not only rode the horse, but trained him too, and did the one job as well as the other. The horse came to him the summer preceding the race in very bad condition and completely chest-foundered. A summer at grass with no grain worked wonders, however, and by autumn Reugny was getting one feed a day, though he stayed in the paddock until the end of November. He came in covered with long hair and looking like a farm horse, but he was absolutely sound. At Aintree he appeared so heavy that a certain expert refused to believe at first that Reugny was fit, and when convinced of his error, remarked that he never saw a horse who was ready to go look so big. Reugny was not a real stayer, but Mr. Richardson rode one of his most finished races, and won in the last hundred yards from Chimney Sweep, a very good black horse who ran in the colours of Lord Marcus Beresford, and who was at one time that gentleman's cavalry charger, when he was in the Seventh Hussars.

Mr. Richardson was very popular in the hunting society of Lincolnshire, and was naturally a brilliant rider to hounds. As already mentioned, his love of hunting was the primary cause of his retirement from the ranks of the gentlemen riders;

and he was in a position to rest upon his laurels if ever a man was, for he had won every important steeplechase in England at least twice. His amazing agility earned him the sobriquets of "Pussy" and "Cat," and he was one of those people who can leap on to mantelpieces with no apparent exertion. In all-round athletic ability he was a perfect example of that school of gentleman riders of the last century who excelled at all sports, for in addition to being a great horseman he was a remarkably fast runner, a good boxer, cricketer, fencer, racquet player, and an unusually fine shot.

Other jockeys with two National victories to their credit are Mr. E. P. Wilson, John Page, and Percy Woodland. Mr. Wilson was a really extraordinary horseman, for he won on horses that no one else could ride well and that had every reason in the world for failing to win the National. The first was Voluptuary, the flat racer with no steeplechase experience, and the year after that he brought Roquefort home in front. Page was one of the old school of professional jockeys and one of the best of that school; his first victory came in 1867, when he won on Cortolvin, who carried eleven stone thirteen, the highest weight carried by any winner from the time the race became a handicap in 1843 until Cloister broke all sorts of records fifty years later. His other win was decidedly lucky, for it was the remarkable year of 1872 in which three good horses had such bad luck in the straight that Casse Tête was enabled to struggle in first; but it was largely due to Page that the weedy mare got round the course at all. Percy Woodland was in his prime thirty years after Page, and rode in many Nationals; he won on Drumcree in 1903, and again on Covertcoat in 1910. He has since become a trainer, and has produced a lot of winners in both kinds of racing.

One of the greatest racing arguments of the nineteenth century was whether Mr. Richardson or Mr. George Ede was the best amateur who ever rode a National winner. Mr. Ede, who rode as "Mr. Edwards," won the race only once, on The Lamb in 1868, and the only other time he ever came near to winning, either before or after, was when he came in second on Weather-cock ten years previously. But there are many people who believe that he never had an equal. A close driving finish to a race may mean only that the winner was prevented by his rider from winning more easily, but Mr. Ede's wins meant riding, and his race on The Lamb was horsemanship at its best. All through the straight he battled with Tomlinson on Pearl Diver, a first-rate horse, and it was nothing but perfect riding that brought The Lamb home by a head. What further glories Mr. Ede might have acquired will never be known, for he met his death in 1870 at the age of thirty-six. He had ridden Guy of Warwick in the National of that year and was leaving the course to go home with Mr. Yates for a day's hunting from Bishop's Sutton, when Mr. Carew rushed up and begged him to ride Chippenham the next day. Mr. Yates tried to persuade him not to take the mount, and his last words were: "Don't ride the brute, George, he'll kill you." But Mr. Ede decided to stay on, for he liked riding horses from the stable of Ben Land, Chippenham's trainer, and Mr. Yates went home alone. Chippenham fell at the small fence before the Water Jump and rolled on his jockey, who died without regaining consciousness. Mr. Ede was not only a brilliant steeplechase jockey, but he was just as good on the flat, and many trainers of his day said they would rather have him in the saddle than any professional they could think of, whether the race was over fences or not—and in flat racing the professional is usually pre-eminent.

Captain E. R. Owen, generally known as "Roddy," was another gentleman rider whose career stopped short at its height, but his retirement was intentional, and not the result of any accident. He had always said that when he achieved the ambition of his life by riding the winner of the Grand National, he would give up racing and take himself to the army with all seriousness, a statement that was treated by his friends with no solemnity whatsoever. He was a very successful jockey and rode many times for Mr. Ernest Benzon, whose extraordinary gambling propensities gained him the title of the "Jubilee Plunger." At one meeting he won five races for Mr. Benzon, but his first appearance in the Aintree limelight was when he finished second on Cloister in the memorable race with Come Away. The next year he begged for the mount on Cloister again, but it could not be arranged, and he was obliged to be satisfied with Father O'Flynn, on whom he surprised everyone and possibly himself by beating the horse he had been so anxious to ride. He now proved the sincerity of his vow to give up racing after winning the National by immediately applying for active service; and that autumn he went off to Egypt, where he died of cholera during the Dongola Expedition of 1896.

The late Captain G. H. Bennet was one of the best jockeys of recent years, and he it was who steered Sergeant Murphy to victory in 1923. L. B. Rees had a well-earned success on Music Hall the year before that, and his brother Fred, won on Shaun Spadah in 1921. He is one of the finest jockeys of the present day, and is riding now perhaps better than he ever has. Ted Leader is

a strong dependable horseman who rode very well in 1927 to
keep the tired Sprig going long enough to withstand the challenge
of Bovril III and Bright's Boy. Tim Cullinan is the most recent
jockey to leap into the limelight, and in three years has established himself as one of the best. His first National ride was in
1928, when he remounted Billy Barton to finish second in a race
of forty-two horses of which only two completed the course. Billy
Barton came down with him the next year when he jumped on a
fallen horse, and in 1930 Cullinan was engaged to ride Easter
Hero, who seemed a very possible winner until lameness threw
him out of training. Frank Hartigan then secured his services for
Shaun Goilin, the Grand Sefton winner that he was training for
Mr. Midwood, and the Easter Hero disappointment was alleviated
from Cullinan's point of view, anyway, when he shoved his last
minute mount past the winning post a few inches ahead of Melleray's Belle.

CHAPTER NINE

Some Great Jockeys Who Did Not Win

A STORY of the life of Mr. Arthur Yates forms a practical history of English steeplechasing from 1855 until the beginning of the Great War, as well as a history of the Grand National for the same period, for though he trained and rode horses in both kinds of racing, steeplechasing was his first and greatest love, and his name will always be particularly identified with that sport. Mr. Yates was an excellent jockey, whether on the flat or over fences, and no gentleman rider before or since has won as many races in a year as he did in 1872, when he set up a record of piloting sixty-seven winners. He never had the good fortune to ride the winner of the Grand National, but this fact is best explained by his having only four mounts in that race. Three of them were not very good, and the fourth was Harvester, on whom he almost certainly would have won in Casse Tête's year but for incredibly bad luck at the last fence.

Arthur Yates was born in 1841 with what may be termed an inherited interest in racing, if an interest may be inherited, for his grandmother was a sister of Mr. Elmore, Lottery's owner, and both his father and his grandfather were great sportsmen. As a small boy he saw the famous Lottery and watched the old horse perform his parlour trick of leaping a luncheon table, which had been set up in the garden, all complete with food and cutlery. He rode his first race at the tender age of ten. It began with an informal contest in Hyde Park and ended in a mad dash past the Marble Arch and down Oxford Street—now a mass of London traffic—with irate mounted policemen in pursuit; but the pony was fast, and the jubilant youngster escaped. Six years later he had his first mount in a steeplechase, and from that time until 1885 he was one of the most successful of amateur jockeys and rode altogether four hundred and sixty winners. Increasing weight finally put an end to his career in the saddle. He became very portly indeed, and his friends spent weary hours trying to persuade him to give up riding, but he quite reasonably said that he could win races just the same, so why stop? At last, however, as he rode Lord Wolverton's good horse Settling Day into the enclosure after winning a race at Kempton in December of 1884, a lady of his acquaintance decided the matter by speaking in this wise: "Well ridden, Arthur, well ridden! But the joint is rather too big for the dish now, you know." This unflattering description of his appearance put even the winning of races in the background, and he rode for the last time at Plumpton, where he won again on Settling Day, and thus had the pleasure of winding up with a victory.

Mr. Yates' race for the Croydon Cup in 1866 filled a vast multitude of spectators with hysterical laughter, and perhaps shows what he meant by determination in a jockey. There were only three horses in the race—Flyfisher, Cortolvin, who later won the National, and Harold, owned and ridden by Mr. Yates. Cortolvin went off in the lead and looked the winner all over when the other two fell at the Water Jump, but Mr. Yates, like Captain Paul Jones, had "just begun to fight." As Harold struggled to his feet and trotted leisurely away, his jockey leapt from the mud, pursued him valiantly down the course, and caught him by the tail. Harold did everything but shriek with amaze-

Sport & General

The Water Jump in 1926. Bright's Boy, who finished third, in the lead.

ment, and the speed promptly increased. The faster Mr. Yates ran, just so much faster ran Harold. They covered a good deal of ground in this remarkable manner, with the man strung out like the tail of a comet, when suddenly he was seen to make a super-human effort. Inch by inch he pulled and scrabbled his way forward and got into the saddle in some unexplained and miraculous fashion. Cortolvin in the meantime had fallen, and Harold won the race amidst cheers which would have been louder if the cheerers had not been holding their sides with merriment.

Mr. Yates rode, owned, and trained horses who ran in the National, but his successes were confined to the last of those three fields. He came heart-breakingly close to riding a winner in 1872, however, on his own horse Harvester. Harvester was very well bred, being by Stockwell-Greta by Voltigeur, but had proved a failure on the flat, in spite of standing as early favourite for the Derby, a distinction to which he had no real claim—and as it turned out, he did not even start in the race. He was the best steeplechaser Mr. Yates ever owned, and was expected to do very well in the National. The going was hard and dry in '72, so that Mr. Yates shod Harvester with steel studs. The horse jumped brilliantly and was ahead at the last fence, but on landing, the stud in a hind shoe caught in the heel of a forefoot and tore the heel nearly off. Mr. Yates felt the horse falter under him, looked down and saw what had happened, and immediately pulled up, to watch Casse Tête, whom Harvester had beaten easily in the past, go on to win.

Mr. Yates was not alone in his hard luck, however, for riding Scarrington was Robert I'Anson, one of the best professionals who ever raced at Aintree. Scarrington was going very well along with Harvester, but he twisted a plate and just lasted to take second place from Despatch, with blood dripping down a fetlock cut by the loose shoe.

In I'Anson's first steeplechase he was coached and given advice throughout the race by Mr. Ede, who was then in his prime. The amateur told the young professional where and how to jump each fence, and to such good effect that the pupil beat his teacher by a head at the finish! I'Anson eventually became a brilliant horseman, but the Grand National persistently eluded him. The ride on Scarrington was the closest he ever came to winning the race, and his only other "place" was a third on the rather poor Shifnal in 1876. Shifnal won two years later, but was ridden by Jones instead of I'Anson.

Harvester came nearer to winning the National than any other horse owned by Mr. Yates, but during the next few years he trained a number of horses for various people, and some of them performed fairly well. In 1880 Jupiter Tonans started at 50—1 and proceeded to horrify the backers and send the bookmakers into paroxysms of delight by leading most of the way. But delight and horror were alike premature, for he was no stayer, and finished fourth. Mr. Yates discovered Roquefort about this time, and though the horse won races, his temper was so uncertain that his owner suffered no qualms when he sold him to Captain Fisher. Roquefort was still trained at Bishop's Sutton, and though he ran third in the National of 1884, he did it in such a haphazard fashion that no one had a good word to say for him, and a few weeks before the race in the following year he changed hands twice more and left Mr. Yates' stable. Mr. Wilson promptly instilled some sort of magic into him, and Roquefort won, to the chagrin of the various owners who had sold him so casually. If Mr. Wilson had continued to ride him he might have won again, but without that able jockey he relapsed into his old ways, and his best effort in later years was fourth in '91.

Cloister was bought by Mr. Duff after his battle with Come Away and sent to Mr. Yates to be trained. The varying fortunes of this great horse have been described. Mr. J. C. Dormer was second on him in '92, and Dollery rode him to victory the following year. After the first of these two races it is said that Mr. Duff saw fit to engage a famous portrait painter to do a picture of Cloister, with Mr. Dormer all complete in silk on his back. But when he won the next year with another jockey, the painter is alleged to have been requisitioned again, the unfortunate Mr. Dormer stricken out, and Dollery put in his place!

Cloister was the last great National horse trained by Mr. Yates; the nearest his stable came subsequently was when Van der Berg was third in 1895, and Cathal second three years later. It is remarkable how well his horses were going in Cloister's time, however, and his record at Aintree in '93 is a shining example of a "stable in form." Three horses went to Aintree from Bishop's Sutton for the Spring Meeting that year. Drumlina won the Altcar Steeplechase on the first day by ten lengths, Cloister led the Grand National field by forty lengths on the second, and on the third and last day of the meeting The Midshipmite cantered home six lengths ahead in the Champion!

For some time the stable at Bishop's Sutton raced in the name of the head stableman, John Swatton, for it was not considered quite respectable in those days for a gentleman to train horses, but in later years all that changed, and Mr. Yates became the acknowledged head. It was a fine organization of the old-fashioned sort in which the jockeys pitched in and worked like stable boys, and the *esprit de corps* was remarkable. The three best stable jockeys, Childs, Sensier, and Dollery, were developed by Mr. Yates himself, and the stable took its tone from its master and betted practically not at all. Mr. Yates often had a pound or two on his horses for reasons of sentiment, but rarely more, and was that *rara avis*, a dyed-in-the-wool racing man who did not bet. He went beyond his limit in 1893 and had fifty pounds on Cloister because he knew he was the best horse he had ever seen, and the same amount on The Midshipmite, because that horse always beat Cloister in his home gallops—Cloister needed a real race-course to show in his true colours. But his only other adventure into the high finance of betting was a failure. For twenty-five pounds on a horse was high finance to Mr. Yates' way of thinking, if not to other people's, and he put that sum on Settling Day in a race in which he was riding the mare himself, because she seemed incapable of losing. No one ever discovered why she ran so badly, and she not only lost, but finished a remarkably poor last behind a lot of very slow horses.

A story is told of Mr. Yates in the paddock at Sandown which delightfully illustrates his attitude about betting. He and a friend were looking over a Bishop's Sutton mare that was about to start in a race, and on whom Mr. Yates had already invested his limit of two pounds. The friend remarked that she looked very well. "My word, she does," said Mr. Yates. "Look here, I'll have *three* pounds!"

Swatton was thoroughly competent in his position of head stableman, but his knowledge of race riding was purely theoretical.

The day before Dollery's first National ride, Swatton took him round Aintree and showed him just where to jump each fence. Like another cheery sportsman years before, he stuck a little piece of paper in the weakest place of one jump after another, and told the jockey to follow them carefully. Dollery listened gravely and never remarked on a fact that his kindly mentor had not noticed—that the indicated spots were sometimes on the right of the fence and sometimes on the extreme left. A horse following Swatton's little signposts would have zig-zagged back and forth like a humming bird, and would have added a mile or two to the regular distance of the race, as well as leaving an air-minded observer with the impression that he was watching a dodging race. Dollery took great pains to neglect the pieces of paper when the race was run next day, and rode very respectably to finish fairly close to the placed horses.

Mr. Yates gave up training in 1913, and his last winner was St. James's Park, who carried off the Royal Artillery Gold Cup at Aldershot in March of that year. He lived until a few years after the War, and went to his grave loved and respected by all who knew him, and with the imposing record of having trained two thousand nine hundred and fifty winners on the flat and in steeplechasing.

Mr. George Ede was one of Mr. Yates' greatest friends, and another was Mr. Fred Hobson, who won on Austerlitz in 1877. Many aspersions were cast upon Mr. Hobson's riding because he habitually took hold of the cantle of his saddle when jumping, but it was nothing but habit, and he won many races in spite of it. In his time the race-courses were still infested with gangs of rowdies looking for trouble, and one day when Mr. Hobson was crossing the Croydon course on his way home in the evening, a huge ruffian, who had backed one of his losing mounts, sprang out at him from behind a fence. "Ha!" shouted the giant, "now I've got you, you———! Put 'em up, can you fight?" "No," said Hobson, "at least not a great big fellow like you, but I tell you what I can do—I can run like the devil!" Which he promptly did, and fled away over the grass like a rabbit!

Many of the professional jockeys before the Eighties were hard-bitten, uneducated men, whose lives were bounded by horses to an extent that is almost unknown now, and such a one was James Adams. He rode for upwards of thirty years, and was a fine horseman despite his inability to read and write, which would seem, after all, to have little to do with riding. Like many illiterate people, he had an amazing memory, and would go to great lengths to prevent others from realizing his deficiency. One day he was fairly caught, however; he was discovered reading with great concentration a newspaper which he was holding upside-down. Some one drew his attention to this fact, but Adams merely remarked: "Any bloody fool can read it the other way," and went on "reading" without reversing the paper! James Snowden was another of the same type, and history fails to reveal whether or not he could distinguish the three R's, but he was a mighty man with a bottle of beer. On one occasion, when he had imbibed very freely, he walked up to his horse in the paddock, inspected the blinkers the horse was wearing and told the groom to take them off. The groom remonstrated that the horse would not go without them—whereupon Snowden grunted that it was bad enough having a blind jockey without a blind horse as well, took the blinkers off, and went out and won the race.

One of the best amateurs of his day was the Hon. George Lambton, but he never won the National, nor even finished in the money. To ride a National winner was his greatest ambition, and he tried many times, but he must have been unlucky as far as that race was concerned. In 1888 he rode Savoyard, and coming to the last fence they were in the lead. Mr. Lambton heaved a sigh of relief—at last he was going to win!—but Savoyard was lazy at fences unless driven, he took off carelessly at the little hurdle, crashed into it and came down. A year later Savoyard was well fancied by his connections, and Mr. Lambton went out on him to do or die. He tried to keep to the right—as horses rarely refuse in that direction, and thus to avoid interference— but at the second fence Merry Maiden ran up the right side of the fence just as Savoyard was taking off; they collided in mid-air, and Savoyard was out of it again!

A great friend of Mr. Lambton's was Mr. Charles Cunningham. He was a big man for race riding, for he stood over six feet and weighed more than twelve stone in normal condition, but by pro-digious wasting got down to ride Why Not at eleven stone five in 1889, and was rewarded by coming in second. For a man of his size his record as a jockey was remarkable, for in his three best years he won one hundred and forty-four out of two hundred and seventy-six races. He died at a comparatively early age, largely as the result of a bad fall on Why Not in 1890, from which he never really recovered, though it is probable that the real reason was the privations to which he subjected himself in the effort to make riding weight, and which must have lowered his resistance to a great extent.

Mr. Lambton tells an amusing story of a race in which he and

Mr. Cunningham were the central figures. It was at a meeting at Ludlow, and the last race of the day. The going had been bad to begin with, and by the end of the afternoon the course was a morass. Messrs. Lambton and Cunningham were way ahead of the field a long way from home, and were struggling for the possession of a narrow path which was the only piece of good going in the whole course. The former finally got it, but both horses were exhausted, and Mr. Lambton's fell at the next fence, in spite of attacking it at a place where a huge gap had been made earlier in the day. The rider was not hurt but was pinned to the ground, and as he wriggled in an effort to get free, he suddenly saw his opponent creeping slowly through another gap on the wrong side of the flag. Lambton's horse shortly struggled to his feet and followed slowly in the wake of the other, while the two riders carried on a violent argument. "You'll not object to me," shouted Mr. Cunningham—the incident occurred out of sight of the stewards—"I only missed the fence to avoid jumping on you." "That won't do," came the reply, "there was plenty of room to my left!" "Damned if there was," bellowed Mr. Cunningham, "you were in the only gap, and look at my bloody horse!"

The last speaker eventually finished in front, but Mr. Lambton promptly filed an objection and said that Mr. Cunningham had admitted going the wrong side. "I admit nothing," said that gentleman, "but if I hadn't done it I'd have jumped on you, and next time I'll do it and kill you!" The race was awarded to Mr. Lambton, who says that Cunningham ever after insisted that he, Lambton, had behaved like a cad—and that he isn't sure that Cunningham wasn't right!

Captain Arthur Smith was a contemporary of Mr. Lambton,

and like him failed to gain a "place" in the National, in spite of
being a fine horseman. He was a great man to hounds, and survived many extraordinary accidents such as the following, out
of which only an omnipotent Providence brought him alive:
Hounds were running at a great pace over a country which Captain Smith did not know at all, but he stuck with them through
thick and thin, and when he saw them disappear beyond a beck-
oning hilltop, he charged the solid thorn fence on the brow of that
hill with all the confidence in the world. In the next field, however, was a farmer who did know the country, and who knew that
on the other side of that fence was a great gravel pit, twenty-five
feet deep. He was horror-stricken to see the captain and his
mount silhouetted against the sky above that fence, and galloped
up in breathless haste to peer over the edge. What he saw made
him sway in his saddle with amazement, for the supposed man-
gled corpse was unconcernedly guiding his horse up the side of
the quarry, and a cheerful grin greeted the horrified face above.
The farmer shut his sagging lower jaw, turned his horse, and
went on his way with the muttered comment: "Well, sir, you
were not born to be killed out hunting!"

There have been a lot of jockeys in the past twenty years who
have had all the ability but none of the luck required to win the
National; but very few have been as downright unfortunate as
Mr. Harry Brown, who is a really brilliant horseman. He not
only rode good horses, but rode them so well that it seemed impossible that he should not win eventually. He has had four
mounts in the National, one of which, Southampton, in 1922,
was "unsighted" and fell at the first fence, but with each of the
three others victory stared him in the face until the very last

moment. In 1920 he finished third on The Bore, a very game little horse of his own. The following year he rode The Bore again, and came in second after falling at the last fence when level with the winner, Shaun Spadah. But in 1924 his cup of ill luck was filled to overflowing. He had the mount on Conjuror II, a very good horse who had been third the year before after suffering bad interference, and who started favourite at 5—2. Halfway through the second round they were sailing along many lengths ahead of the nearest rival, and it looked as if the jinx was beaten at last—but a loose horse barged into them, and Mr. Brown was done out of it again. In 1927 he was slated to ride Mr. Schwartz's Jack Horner, who won so cleverly the previous year, but the fates were still against him. Jack Horner went wrong and was scratched, and Mr. Brown has not been seen in the National since Conjuror was so sadly knocked over.

CHAPTER TEN

1907 *to* 1928

IN 1907 Arthur Newey survived great difficulties to win on Eremon. He lost a stirrup at the beginning of the second round, and as he reached feverishly to regain it, the riderless Rathvale ranged alongside and almost barged into him. He did everything he could to get rid of this unwelcome visitor, but Rathvale was a permanent fixture and evinced a great affection for Eremon. With this new problem to tackle Newey gave up all hope of his dangling stirrup, rode as best he could, and eventually won the race with only one iron, and with the loose horse "in his pocket" every inch of the way.

The American-bred Rubio won the next year, and provided a complete upset by so doing, for his past was anything but brilliant. He was brought to England as a two-year-old and sold to Mr. Septimus Clarke at Newmarket for fifteen guineas. Mr. Clarke passed him on to Major Douglas-Pennant for ninety-five guineas, and he was certainly worth that, for he followed hounds for a season without a fall. He was then put into training, but broke down after winning three rather unimportant steeplechases. In order to callous his legs, Major Douglas-Pennant sent him to a hotel keeper at Towcester, where Rubio drew a humble hotel bus to and from the station for several months. This seems to have had the desired effect, though he was never really sound, and was supposed to be done at the end of a couple of miles of racing. Nobody thought he had a chance at Aintree. He started at 66—1 and was merely one of the outsiders whose names many people do not even know until they look at their race cards. But he won with no difficulty, and apparently was all ready to run some more. Another American touch was given to this race by the presence of Prophet III and Chorus, both of whom belonged to Mr. Foxhall Keene. The first named fell early in the race, but Chorus stood up, and eventually came in eighth.

The Grand National has been won five times by horses only five years old, and Lutteur III was the last one. He ran several times at Aintree, but was never as good as in his victorious year of 1909. That year he was thoroughly the equal of Austerlitz, whom Mr. Hobson rode to victory in 1877, and who was probably the best of the other horses of that age. Lutteur was bred and trained in France, and was ridden by the French jockey, Georges Parfrement, who gave him an excellent ride to win from a field of thirty-two horses, of which, surprisingly, nineteen completed the course.

The following year Jenkinstown was first, ahead of the great Jerry M., who belonged to Mr. Assheton-Smith. This gentleman is none other than Mr. Duff, the owner of Cloister, but he had inherited a new name shortly after the turn of the century. In 1911 he was made a baronet, and we shall meet him again in these pages under the title of Sir Charles Assheton-Smith. Jerry M. ran very well under top weight, and afterwards won the Grand Steeplechase de Paris at Auteuil; but he hurt himself in that race, and went into retirement for two years, thus avoiding the famous muddy race of 1911.

The favourite that year was Rathnally, a very good horse who was a continuous source of disappointment to his owner, Mr. O. H. Jones, his trainer, Coulthwaite, and to the public in general.

In home gallops he was superb and did all and more than was asked of him, but race-courses and crowds seemed to upset him, and he never showed at his best in public, unless indeed in this race, when he had bad luck. The course was a perfect morass, and one horse after another slid, slipped, and was counted out. Caubeen and Rathnally were going well side by side until the former was taken into the lead, when he promptly fell and knocked the other over. Rathnally ran about a bit before being remounted, and even so finished second some sixty yards behind Glenside, the only horse of the thirty-three who did not fall. Glenside had only one eye, he was not really sound, and he was ill when the race began. But in some miraculous manner Mr. Jack Anthony got him round the course. Shady Girl was third, and the only other horse to finish was Foolhardy, a fifty guinea hunter, whose rider, Mr. MacNeill, had taken the short end of a bet of twelve hundred to three that he would get round and past the winning post. It is very probable that both Rathnally and Shady Girl were better horses than the winner, but that only enhances the performance of Mr. Anthony, who practically carried Glenside over the last few fences, and the horse was so exhausted that he slowed almost to a walk in the run in.

There was a great deal of speculation about Jerry M.'s comeback in 1912. He had never been a really handsome horse, for he had a long back and a ewe neck, but he was immensely powerful, a brilliant fencer, and a thorough stayer. He was a particularly massive horse, with tremendous bone, and many believed that when such a one had broken down seriously he could never be brought back to condition. He had appeared only once on a race-course since his victory in France in 1910—at Hurst Park, a

few weeks before this National—and though he had run well
enough there, people shook their heads, stated ominously that
Hurst Park was not Aintree, and reminded each other that he was
carrying Cloister's and Manifesto's weight of twelve stone seven.
The most pessimistic were silenced, however, when Jerry M. was
led into the paddock at Aintree. Gore had him ready to the
minute, and he was bursting with vitality. The public took one
look at him, and hurried off to see their bookmakers, with the
result that he started equal favourite at 4—1 with Rathnally.

The minimum weight had been raised this year to ten stone,
and Jerry M.'s twelve-seven was the top of the handicap. Fifteen
pounds below him was Bloodstone, a very fast horse and a good
one; he led for most of the race, and came over the last fence still
ahead, but his superior speed and light weight were no match for
Jerry M.'s staying power, and the latter won easily in the run in.
Rathnally let everyone down by falling at the third fence, and as
Glenside had collapsed the jump before, the first and second of
the previous year were out of it before the race was fairly started.
Rathnally disappointed again in the Champion the next day; he
had gone such a short distance in the National that it could not
have affected him at all, and he was universally expected to win.
The Champion is just half the distance of the National, and should
therefore be just half as trying, but Rathnally was a poor second
to Lord Rivers, who was a very average horse.

Three foreigners created an international atmosphere in the
paddock before the race in 1913. Highbridge, an American
horse, had impressed the public by his second to Strangeways in
the National Hunt Steeplechase at Cheltenham, Trianon III was
the French hope, and Jamagata had come all the way from Aus-

tria to try his luck. The international atmosphere lasted only about five minutes after the race got under way, however, for Highbridge fell at the first fence, Trianon came down at Valentine's, and the Austrian found the course too much for him. Covertcoat, owned by Sir Charles Assheton-Smith, gave that gentleman his third winner by coming in a quarter of a mile ahead of Irish Mail, and Carsey was third. The last named was the unlucky horse of the race, for he had the race very much in hand at the last fence but went into that obstacle in a very slovenly manner and fell in a heap. When remounted he went very big over the same fence, and finished quite undistressed.

The French were at it again in 1914 with Trianon III and Lutteur III, the latter being the horse which had won so handsomely five years before. Nobody knew just which to bet on, for Covertcoat was beaten by the French pair at Hurst Park early in March, and it was a question which of them was the best. Lutteur III had been suffering from a strained tendon, and had been stopped in his training, but was supposed to be thoroughly fit again. Another public fancy was Rory O'Moore, a son of Royal Meath, who jumped brilliantly, but whose stamina was doubtful.

The going was good, and the fences had been trimmed to such an extent that the whole field survived the first five. Sunloch, lightly fancied at 100—6, went out into the lead almost from the start, and was never headed. Rory O' Moore stuck to him until near the end, but could not stay, and the Frenchmen caught him in the straight and gradually forged ahead. Lutteur III was probably the better of the two—he carried eleven pounds more than Trianon—but the interruption to his training was fatal, and he had to be satisfied with third place just behind his compatriot. Sunloch began his career in farmers' hurdle races, and never did any good in subsequent Nationals, but he won this race like a good horse.

1915 saw the stands half empty, and those who were there, clad in khaki. This was the last National run at Aintree for three years, and the victor was Ally Sloper, with Mr. Jack Anthony in the saddle. Jacobus and Father Confessor were second and third, and fourth place was occupied by Mr. Barnard's American horse Alfred Noble. The Aintree course was then closed for the duration of the War, and the scene of the great race shifted to the South.

The "War Nationals" were run at Gatwick, and in the first year the race was known as "The Race Course Association Steeplechase," but after that was called simply "The War National." The fences were raised, and everything possible done to make it like a real Grand National, but the difference was naturally manifest. The race in 1916 was run very slowly, two selling platers kept up with the leaders during the first round, and one of them managed to finish third behind Vermouth and Irish Mail in a National with only one fall. The jumps were still higher the next year, and the pace was faster. Templedowney went out like a sprinter and maintained a lead through most of the race; but Limerock caught him at the last fence and was winning easily when he astonishingly crossed his legs on the flat, fell, and left Ballymacad a very lucky winner. Chang was second, and close behind him came Ally Sloper, who had won at Aintree in 1915.

Poethlyn was the best horse that appeared during the war

years, and romped home ahead of his field in 1918.   He was
favourite the following year, when the race was moved back to
Aintree, in spite of the people who insisted that Aintree and Gatwick were so different that victory in a War National meant
nothing now that the race had come back to its own place.   There
were not many sceptics, however, and Poethlyn started at 4—1
and looked the winner all the way.   He carried twelve seven, and
thus increased the number of winners with that weight to four.   It
is not likely that he was the perfect steeplechaser that Cloister,
Manifesto and Jerry M. were, and it may be said that he had
nothing very much to beat, but he looked a good horse and won
as a good horse should.   Whatever his exact position in the ranks
of the great, he was certainly good enough to win the National
twice, and he must have made his breeder wonder why he had
sold him as a young horse for the sum of seventeen pounds!

Mr. Jack Anthony was the hero of another rain storm in 1920.
The going was awful, and the weather so thick that no one could
see very much, but Mr. Anthony had a very different type of
horse this time; there was considerable doubt in some minds as
to Troytown's ability to stay the course, but apparently there was
none in the mind of his jockey, for he took Troytown out to gallop
the field off its feet, rain or no rain.   All went well with them until
two fences from home, when Troytown made a bad mistake, and
almost came down.   Mr. Harry Brown on The Bore passed them
as Troytown struggled to keep his feet, but Mr. Anthony steadied
his mount, got him going again, and caught The Bore at the last
fence.   After that it was all Troytown, and The Bore, game as he
was, could not save second place from The Turk II.

This race was the first of several which were marred by the

favourite falling at the first fence. Poethlyn was the public choice at 3—1, but went down in the rush for the initial jump and blasted the hopes of many backers. Even if he had not done so, he would have been hard put to it to defeat the winner, for Troytown was probably one of the best horses that ever won the National. He never had another chance to prove it, however, for unfortunately he fell and broke his back in a steeplechase in France a few months later. He had been sent to France for the Grand Steeplechase de Paris in which he finished third with Jack Anthony in the saddle, and the race following that one was his last.

The first fence problem had another airing in 1921, when several well-backed horses went down at that point. The reason for it all, of course, was the large size of the fields. With so many horses rushing into the jump together, it was only too possible for one or more of them not to see the fence at all until it rose up and hit them in the nose. It is of interest, however, that the problem does not seem to have come up to a very large extent during the last century, when the fields were often as big as they were in Troytown's time and when the first fence was nearer to the start than it is now. The explanation may lie in the fact that the first fence in those days was merely a hurdle which could be knocked over without great difficulty. By the time the horses reached the big solid jumps they were more strung out, and each one had an open chance at each fence.

However, to return to the race of 1921, the first fence was not the only one to bring them down. The going was slippery, and they fell in droves, until only Fred Rees on Shaun Spadah and Mr. Brown on The Bore were left. Neither jockey had ever won the National, and each realized just before the last fence that he had only the other to beat. Together they raced for the jump. Shaun Spadah cleared it safely, but Mr. Brown was unlucky, and The Bore fell. Horse and rider were up again in a moment, the latter with a broken collar bone, but he got back into the saddle and finished second, with his right arm swinging loosely at his side. Way behind in third place came All White; like The Bore, he had been remounted, and the winner was the only horse in the race who did not fall.

Shaun Spadah was not very fast, but he could stay and was a clever jumper, and his victory brought him many followers in 1922, when he emulated Poethlyn by falling at the first fence in company with the unfortunate Mr. Brown on Southampton. Music Hall won from Drifter and Eavesdropper, and fourth in the race was Sergeant Murphy. This old Aintree campaigner was then bought by Mr. Stephen Sanford, and the following year, at the age of thirteen, he won and made his new owner the first American to win the Grand National. Captain Bennet gave the horse an excellent ride, and did well to hold him up after his slovenly jump at the fence beyond Valentine's.

Mr. Harry Brown's sad mishap on Conjuror II has been described in Chapter Nine. If Conjuror had not been knocked over, he almost certainly would have won; as it was, however, the 1924 honours went to Master Robert, who had pulled a cart at one time in his career. Fly Mask was second, and third place was taken by Mr. Midwood's Silvo, the great jumper who won the Grand Steeplechase de Paris in 1925. Mr. Sanford had two horses running—Drifter and old Sergeant Murphy—and though they did not win, they ran very creditably and finished fourth and fifth.

The National of 1925 saw Old Tay Bridge in the money for the first time. He had run in the race several times without success and had developed into a splendid jumper, but he was a big bodied horse without very much speed. He came over the last fence slightly in front of Fly Mask, and the two of them were struggling on the flat when the speedy Double Chance came from behind to beat them both. Old Tay Bridge won the battle for second place, Sprig was fourth, and Silvo fifth.

The next year the horses were an impressive looking lot as they appeared in the paddock. The dark bay, Silvo, was in perfect condition, and looked well worth the ten thousand pounds Mr. Midwood had paid for him; his brilliant victory in France the spring before had brought him many supporters, and he was now considered the best jumper in Great Britain. Old Tay Bridge looked better than ever, and Sprig was favourite at 5—1, although the other two were close behind at sevens and eights. Another horse who attracted a lot of attention at the last minute, although it seemed not to affect his starting price of 25—1, was Jack Horner, who had run seventh the year before. His owner, Mr. A. C. Schwartz, was an American, and a newcomer to the National who had bought Jack Horner only a few weeks before the race. Jack Horner was never a thoroughly sound horse, but Leader had him trained to the minute, and never before or after was he in such splendid shape. He looked marvellously well in the paddock, much better than the betting indicated, and his running that afternoon was quite up to his good looks. It is to be regretted that increasing unsoundness led to his retirement two years later. I saw him run at Gatwick in the National Trial of '28, which was one of his last appearances in public, if not indeed the last, and so changed was he from that day at Aintree that for a moment I hardly recognized him.

The start this year was a good one, and the horses went away in a solid phalanx. Silvo had no chance to justify his fine appearance, for he was "unsighted" at the first fence, fell, and shortly galloped riderless past the stands. The good mare, Grecian Wave, was another first fence casualty, but the rest got over, and little Darracq took the lead, which he maintained most of the way. Entering the straight, however, he tired, and Old Tay Bridge took up the running. He was first over the last fence, with Bright's Boy close up, but Watkinson brought Jack Horner with a rush and galloped away from the other two in the run in. Old Tay Bridge was second, Bright's Boy third, and Sprig finished fourth, with Darracq tailed off behind him.

A curious thing happened in this race. After it was all over I went down on to the course to have a look at the Water Jump. In front of the water is a thorn fence two and a half feet high and the same in width. It is a very strong, solid fence and remarkably unyielding. Somehow or other, in the act of taking off, a horse had thrust his foot into the base of this fence for a distance of about eighteen inches—yet no horse fell at the Water Jump that year! Anything that was pushed into that fence was very hard indeed to get out again, as I proved by experiment. I communed with various policemen and others who had been standing by the jump during the race, but none of them had noticed any horse having particular difficulty there. How a horse managed to spread himself over a total distance of fifteen feet, with one foot stuck fast in the grave, so to speak, it is impossible to say, but the mark was there, for all who wished to see—a long sliding print

K

of a shod hoof, carried well in under the spruce fence.

Sprig was favourite again in 1927. He was a big muscular chestnut, with a rather common but wise looking head, and was just the clever, balanced type of jumper that is dependable at Aintree. He had proved his ability to "get the course" by finishing fourth two years in a row, and his jockey, Ted Leader, understood him thoroughly. Bright's Boy had the top weight, three pounds more than Sprig, and it was destined to prove too much for him at the most critical moment in the race. This good little horse was, paradoxically, too good to be successful at Aintree, for his known excellence caused an allotment of just a little more weight than he could win under. Lord Stallbridge's good hunter Thrown In—who was sold at one time for seventy-five pounds—ridden by his owner's son, the Honourable Hugh Grosvenor, was the Prince of Wales' tip, and as such had a big following at 18—1. Of the others, the most popular were Master Billie, ridden by Fred Rees, the little mare Silver Somme, the five-year-old Grakle, and White Park, a good winner during the winter and a horse who always looked thin and tucked up, in spite of the most superhuman efforts to put flesh on him. This lightness of condition never seemed to bother him, for he was very successful on the Park Courses, and was so well thought of by the handicapper that he carried a pound more than Sprig.

Again a popular fancy was unsighted at the first fence, and this time it was Thrown In. Silver Somme refused early in the race, and going away from Valentine's the speedy Grecian Wave dashed into a terrific lead, only to run out unaccountably as she neared the stands. Test Match fell at the Water Jump, and Sprig led the field away for the second round. Coming into Becher's a

loose horse crossed in front of him, but Leader showed what a
jockey he was by letting Sprig solve the problem for himself.
Sprig checked for a moment and then bucked over the fence as
best he could. He pecked a bit on landing, and by the time
Leader got him going again he was lying fifth, and took off for the
Canal Turn in that position. Such a terrific leap did he put in
there, however, that he landed in first place and started for home
in the lead again. Along the straight Jack Anthony crept up with
Bright's Boy and was even with Sprig as they approached the last
fence. Bright's Boy jumped a little faster than the other, and for
the third time in as many years Jack Anthony was ahead at the
beginning of the run in. The stands were cheering the battle between Leader and Anthony, when suddenly a bay horse appeared
on the scene and challenged them both. The finish was fast and
furious, with Sprig eventually winning from the bay outsider by
a length, and Bright's Boy the same distance away in third. The
surprise horse placed second was Bovril III, a one-eyed hunter
owned and ridden by Mr. Gerald Pennington, an amateur only
less experienced than his horse. No one paid them any attention
at the start, and they were quoted among "the others" at 100—1,
but Bovril jumped brilliantly and came very close to winning,
for Sprig was a thoroughly tired horse when he passed the post.
Behind Bright's Boy came Mr. J. B. Balding on Drinmond. This
was Mr. Balding's first National ride, and he gave a very excellent
performance by finishing where he did, for Drinmond, though a
great jumper and stayer, was definitely lacking in speed.

This was a very popular victory, and even more so than Sprig's
position of favourite warranted. His original owner was Richard
Partridge, a lieutenant in the Shropshire Yeomanry, who was

killed shortly before the Armistice. Sprig had been kept in training at his request, and the young officer's mother was the recipient of many sincere and heartfelt congratulations when the horse won in such honest fashion.

Mr. Grosvenor never rode again at Aintree. Some months after this race he went out to Australia to act as Aide to the Governor of New South Wales, and it is sad to have to record that he was killed there in an aeroplane crash in 1929. He was very popular and a fine sportsman, and his death, while still a young man in his twenties, was mourned by his many friends in England.

In 1928 there were so many horses who had run well during the winter, or had thoroughly satisfied their trainers in home gallops, that opinion was divided as to whether they were all very good, or all equally bad. A few weeks before the race Mr. Frank Barbour sold Koko to Captain the Hon. "Freddie" Guest. Koko, a wonderfully good-looking horse, was considered the best in training over the Park Courses, but he was inclined to "chance" his jumps, and was very erratic. Amberwave had won the National Trial at Gatwick in splendid fashion from a number of good Aintree horses, Grakle was good, but like Koko, erratic; and little Carfax and the powerful Trump Card carried the hopes of Yorkshire. Mr. Barbour sold Easter Hero, his other National entry, a few days after he parted with Koko, and the buyer this time was the late Mr. Alfred Lowenstein. Easter Hero had not then developed into the great steeplechaser he was to become; he was known to be very fast and a brilliant jumper, but he was headstrong to an unusual degree and this was to be his first attempt in the National.

The dark horse of the race was the American-bred Billy Barton, owned by Mr. Howard Bruce, Master of the Elkridge Foxhounds in Maryland. His past career has been dealt with, and he arrived in England with a fine reputation, which was greatly strengthened when he won at Newbury, in his first race after landing, with consummate ease. He immediately became a National tip, but his subsequent running was disappointing. Just before the National, the Hon. Aubrey Hastings, his trainer, secured the services of the Irish jockey, Tim Cullinan, a recent recruit from the amateur ranks, and this was supposed to be all in Billy Barton's favour, but the public remained wary. His official starting price was 33—1, although 25—1 was quoted by some bookmakers. The dependable Sprig and Bright's Boy were popular as usual, Drinmond had run fourth the year before, and Fred Rees was riding Master Billie, who had finished sixth behind Jack Horner. Bovril III had been well supported in the future books, but he unfortunately went lame in the middle of March, and though hopes were held out for his recovery, he was scratched at the last minute when it became evident that he could not possibly run.

Billy Barton was not the only American-bred horse in the race, for he had a compatriot in Burgoright, who belonged to Mr. B. L. Behr, M.F.H. of "Mr. Behr's Hounds" in Illinois. Burgoright had won many races in America, but had gone wrong in the wind and was not at all impressive in England. He was ridden in the National by the American amateur, Mr. F. A. Bonsal. There were several French-bred horses in the race. Mr. Victor Emmanuel, an American, had entered The Coyote; Maguelonne, owned by the Comte de Jumilhac, had lived up to her good French reputation by performing well at Hurst Park, and The

Ace II was running in the colours of Mr. R. B. Strassburger of Philadelphia. The Ace won some good races in France, but he had an unfortunate habit of shedding his jockey at critical moments without falling himself, and had distinguished himself on many occasions by winning without a jockey in the saddle.

The result was a race that seemed peculiarly open and which might have been won by anybody, but this seems to have given the public betting fever, or the bookmakers cold feet, for an extraordinary number of horses started at short odds. In years when the field was of normal size, 5—1 was considered a fair price against any horse even to finish; yet in this race with forty-two starters, the greatest number in the history of the National up to that time, the odds shortened rapidly as starting time drew near, and Master Billie was the final favourite at 5—1, with several others at only slightly longer prices. The betting this year seems amazing in view of the frequent disappearance of favourites at the first fence; in the light of subsequent events, it was not only amazing, but thoroughly ill-advised!

The public was prepared for the big field to produce something unusual, in spite of its wild betting, but what did happen was beyond anyone's maddest imaginings. Amberwave was held up at the start, in the hope of thus avoiding the crush at the first fence—where nobody fell, incidentally—and he got over that obstacle successfully; but there were enough horses down between there and Becher's to discourage him completely. He refused half-heartedly several times and finally fell before the race had proceeded very far. Bright's Boy and Sprig both came down early, and the two old dependables were thus out of it before the real tragedy occurred, as was Koko, who landed upside-down in

Central News

The Last Fence in 1928. Tipperary Tim, the winner, on the left; the riderless Great Span, and Billy Barton, who is about to fall.

the ditch at Becher's, and was pulled out only just in time for the field to come by in the second round.

Easter Hero sailed away into a big lead right from the start and sprinted along several lengths ahead of the rest. At the Canal Turn he took off too soon, landed on top of the fence, and stuck there. Some of the horses nearest to him, amounting to nine in number, managed to get by—Billy Barton put in an incredible leap, clearing the fence and part of Easter Hero as well—but the others were not so fortunate. By the time they arrived on the scene Easter Hero had fallen back into the ditch, and was parading up and down it—and they would have none of it. One after another, singly and in pairs, their jockeys put them at it, but they refused. Mr. Balding tried eight times with Drinmond before giving up, but to no avail, and after a time the ground inside the course was dotted with horses and jockeys returning sadly homewards. Twenty odd horses were thus put out of it at one blow, and among them was the favourite, Master Billie.

In the meantime the lucky first squadron was going on with the race. The visibility was so bad that those in the stands could not see what had happened at the Canal Turn and were amazed when so few horses came out of the mist, but an American cheer went up as Billy Barton came on in front, dropped a foot in the Water, but got over safely and led the field away into the country again. At the Canal Turn this time the number was even smaller. Billy Barton was still ahead, though he seemed tired, and Maguelonne seemed least distressed. Her French jockey, Bedeloup, was equal to the occasion, but she slipped up and fell three fences further on, leaving Billy Barton, Tipperary Tim, and Great Span to fight it out. Great Span was unlucky, for he was staying well and probably would have won if his saddle had not slipped two fences from home. It turned just as he took off, and Payne, his jockey, was dropped neatly into the ditch. Now there were only two—with the riderless Great Span between them, they rose for the last fence approximately together, but the American horse was done and he hit the top. Cullinan was down, up, and on again like a flash, but it was too late, and Tipperary Tim went on to win, the only horse not to fall, and Billy Barton the only other to finish. At the Canal Turn Stand no one knew who had won for some time; curiously enough the numbers of the two finishers were 52 and 25, and these were juggled round for what seemed like ages before they were finally settled in place.

CHAPTER ELEVEN

The Nationals of 1929 *and* 1930

THE uproar was terrific. The greatest steeplechase in the world had been won by a tubed horse, a 100—1 outsider, who had never been in the money in a first-class race! The Grand National was pure luck and nothing else! Back and forth across the land went the argument as to whether this victory proved that the winner was a good horse hitherto unrecognized, or that he was merely the luckiest horse in the world. His subsequent career rather inclines to the latter conclusion, for he has not done anything very good since, and fell in the National of 1929.

The uproar continued, in the newspapers and out of them. There was a great deal of talk about the Aintree fences being too big, and about the whole race being a brutal thing to subject a horse to; there were even rumours of introducing a Bill into Parliament to try to "do something" about it, but fortunately that thought died of inertia. Then someone suggested that the ditch in front of the Canal Turn fence be filled in, and the obstacle which had so offended be thus made easier. This was at length done—in the face of much opposition from those who contended rather reasonably that the Canal ditch was really no worse than any other, and that if they were going to fill in one they might as well fill in all the others—and the obstacle at the Canal Turn is now merely a thorn fence five feet high and three feet three inches wide.

Another change was made, this in the conditions, and one which was intended to cut down the size of the fields. Hitherto there had been only one forfeit stage: for example, this part of the conditions for 1928 read " . . . a handicap of 100 sovs. each, 50 sovs. forfeit, or 5 sovs. only if declared by Tuesday, January 24th . . ." But the huge field in that year had brought to a head the criticism stirred up by the number of horses who had been "unsighted" at the first fence, as well as by the number of horses in the race, and it was determined to give owners plenty of opportunity to scratch horses who could have no possible chance. The result of this determination was the following phrase in the conditions for the Grand National of 1929: " . . . handicap of 5 sovs. each, 50 sovs. extra if left in after January 22nd, an additional 25 sovs. if left in after March 12th, and 20 sovs, extra for starters . . ."

The framers of these new conditions had a very difficult fact to contend with, however: the race the year before had been won by a 100—1 shot of no great merit, and a horse at similar odds had been second to Sprig the year before that. Under these circumstances the words "no possible chance" just didn't mean anything, and it is not surprising that anyone with a steeplechaser of any merit whatsoever should have wanted to try him at Aintree. The incredible had happened once, almost twice, so why not again? On January 22nd, the first forfeit stage, there were one hundred and twenty-one horses down for the race, and sixty-six of them were still in when the flag fell at Aintree a month later.

During the winter Easter Hero and Maguelonne had been bought by Mr. J. H. Whitney, an American, and were being trained by Jack Anthony. The French mare unfortunately went wrong, and so much so that the great Aintree hopes entertained for her by her connections had to be discarded once and for all.

She had won the Grand Steeplechase de Paris in 1928 by a
brilliant run in the last quarter mile, and there were many
people who believed she was very likely to win the National
before she was through. Her racing days are now definitely over,
and she had been retired to the stud, where, I am told, she has
been put to My Prince, the sire of Easter Hero and Gregalach.
If Mr. Whitney was disappointed in Maguelonne, however, the
reverse was true of Easter Hero. He developed amazingly under
his new trainer, put on weight and muscle, and became a little
less impetuous and headstrong. He proved himself about the
best hurdler in England during the early part of the season of
1928-29, and when put back to fences won the Cheltenham Gold
Cup in convincing style. This could not be overlooked, in spite of
his fiasco of the previous year and his top weight of twelve stone
seven, and he started favourite at 9—2. Billy Barton was in
again, fitter than in 1928, and ready to do himself full justice.
Old Sprig and Bright's Boy were running as usual, the former
looking as well as in the days of old, but sixty-six horses were a
great many, and the thought of the possible scrimmage at the
first fence was a fearful one.

This race has already been described in the first chapter.
Sprig and Bright's Boy did little better than the year before, and
the ditch in front of the third fence settled the ambitions of many.
Easter Hero led through the first round, and Billy Barton was
well up, but the latter fell at the Canal Turn—where he had
jumped so well twelve months previously—and though remounted, was shortly knocked over at the Open Ditch. Easter
Hero held his lead until Valentine's in the second round; just
beyond that fence he spread a plate, and Gregalach came like the

wind to win from the favourite with Richmond II a poor third.

Just before Easter Hero spread his plate he was one of three horses who staged a most extraordinary show. Going away from the fence after Becher's, Richmond II and Sandy Hook went out to challenge the leader. They drew almost level with him, and the three galloped into the Canal practically abreast—Easter Hero on the inside, then Sandy Hook, then Richmond II. They rose at the fence as one horse, and as one horse they made the turn left-handed toward Valentine's, with not a foot separating the jockeys' knees at any point during the jump or the turn. For a distance of perhaps a hundred and fifty yards they ran "locked," and as is usually the case, it left them pretty exhausted. It finished Sandy Hook completely—he fell at the fence after Valentine's—Richmond II had no gallop left in him, and Easter Hero was tired, though still galloping on. It is possible that he might have withstood Gregalach's challenge with some success if he had not had to fight out that "locked" battle with the other two.

Gregalach at this time was a real puzzle. He had won at Tipperary Tim's odds of 100—1, but one only had to look at him to realize that here was no doubtful horse. Somehow or other, it just didn't occur to anyone that he might figure prominently in that great field of sixty-six, and it was a problem to know just how good he was. He is a grand horse to look at, big-boned and powerful, with great range and scope, and his career since the National of 1929 has proved abundantly that he was not merely lucky in that race. He was trained then by Tom Leader and was considered the least of the three Leader horses in the race, the others being Sprig and Mount Etna. He had an advantage of

Sport & General

Becher's Brook in 1930. Glangesia leading, Toy Bell in centre, and Shaun Goilin, the winner, at top of fence.

seventeen pounds in the weights over the favourite, and had not been subjected to such a battle at the Canal Turn, but even so he overhauled and beat Easter Hero like a good horse.

There was a great deal of discussion as to just how much Easter Hero was affected by his spread plate. It is logical to assume that he would have done better without such an accident, and a number of shrewd judges of racing who examined him afterwards say that it must have decreased his efficiency by twenty-five per cent. On the other hand, I am told that both Mr. Frank Barbour, his former owner, and Moloney, who rode him, believe that he was tiring under his top weight, and that Gregalach would have beaten him in any event. Whatever the rights and wrongs of the argument, Gregalach's fine race in the National of 1931 proved conclusively that Easter Hero was up against a first-class steeplechaser, and one that no horse in the world could give seventeen pounds to with impunity over four and a half miles of Aintree.

It was perfectly logical that these two should have been the early favourites in the betting for 1930, and in the absence of Billy Barton, who had been retired from racing, they seemed likely to dominate the race between them. Before the month of March had advanced very far, however, trouble attacked them both. Gregalach's stock was raised by his second in February to the brilliant young Gib, who had won eight races in succession, but was decidedly lowered by an amazing last at Hurst Park, and after this race there were rumours of all sorts. There was a mix-up of some kind, and the upshot of it was that Gregalach left Ted Leader's stable, and H. Waldron completed his training. On top of this came news of a bad splint; he was obviously a doubtful starter, and went out in the betting.

Easter Hero had done well through the winter, and his race for the Gold Cup at Cheltenham was awaited with interest, not only because it came so shortly before the National, but because in it his major opponent would be Gib, the seven-year-old gelding who had been carrying all before him, and who was acclaimed as a great one in the making. He had been bought as a foal by Lord Fingal, who had hunted him during the season of 1927-28, and his career as a race-horse had been one long success. He was criticized as being too tall and leggy for a National prospect, but no one denied his abilities over the Park Courses, and as he had not been entered at Aintree, Cheltenham would be his only chance to match strides with the mighty Easter Hero.

The presence of the two cracks discouraged the other trainers, Grakle and Donzelon were the only others to come out for the Gold Cup. Easter Hero dashed into the lead in his customary manner, and the other three fell in behind him. Donzelon came down before the first round was completed, and Grakle jumped very big and much too slowly, but Gib stayed nicely within striking distance. Three fences from home Fred Rees brought Gip up, and drew level with the leader; the two horses rose at the fence together, but Gib fell, and Easter Hero went on to win a very hollow victory from Grakle by twenty lengths. How much of a race Gib would have made of it if he had not fallen is a question, but fall he did, and Easter Hero looked better than ever as a National proposition.

The victory, however, was a costly one, for a few days later came the report that Easter Hero had hurt himself at Cheltenham and was lame. The betting situation rolled over and stood up again in a completely different shape. Grakle, who had been

Sport & General

The same fence a second later.

beaten so badly in the Cheltenham race, was about equal favourite with Sir Lindsay, a gelding by Roi Herode that Anthony had bought out of a hunting stable for Mr. Whitney. Neither of them had great Aintree reputations to boast of. Grakle had precipitated a scrimmage at the Canal Turn in Sprig's year, had been one of the refusing mob at the same place a year later, and his greatest ray of light was supplied by his completing the course in 1929. He was a fine horse to look at, and had won a number of races, but was inclined to "chance" his fences. Sir Lindsay had run only one race in his life—exclusive of point-to-points—and that one was the National Hunt Steeplechase at Cheltenham. He had the benefit of a beautiful ride from Lord Fingal on that occasion, and certainly won with astonishing ease, for after coming over the last fence side by side with Possible, Sir Lindsay had galloped away on the flat like an absolutely fresh horse; but this still seemed hardly a sufficient career for a National favourite. Next in order were Shaun Goilin, winner of the Grand Sefton, and the property of Mr. Midwood, who had owned Silvo; Melleray's Belle, fourth the year before; and Merrivale II, a lightly weighted horse of whom much was expected.

And suddenly violet-ray treatment worked wonders with Easter Hero and he went absolutely sound! The odds described another evolution, and were just settling down in their new guise, when Easter Hero had a relapse and was definitely out of it.

On the day of the race Grakle was favourite, Shaun Goilin, Sir Lindsay and Gregalach were at slightly longer odds than he was, and Melleray's Belle was well backed. Gregalach had improved somewhat and moved very well in a gallop on the morning of the race, but he had a large splint for all beholders to see. There was little confidence in him, and not very much money placed at his odds of 100—6. Among the outsiders was a horse called Peggie's Pride, who received a prodigious amount of support from the theatrical profession. The operatta, "Bitter Sweet," was in the midst of a long run at His Majesty's Theatre in London, and its leading lady was the charming American actress Miss Peggy Wood. The cast of "Bitter Sweet" considered this a direct invitation to bet on Peggie's Pride—and it was probably as good a reason for betting on an outsider as any other! But the horse, unfortunately, was less pre-eminent in his field than Miss Wood is in hers, and he failed to complete the course. Another outsider, and one who was destined to give an excellent account of himself, was Glangesia, a grey Irish horse, who belonged to Mr. Richard Mellon, an American. Mr. Mellon is the Master of the Rolling Rock Foxhounds, who hunt over a stiff post-and-rail country in Pennsylvania, and he had hunted hounds on Glangesia for two seasons before bringing him to England as a race-horse. There were forty horses in the race, nothing like the great cavalcade of the previous year, but still quite enough for trouble. The going, however, was very good, and the sun was out most of the race.

The field got off to a good start, and at Becher's showed the unusual spectacle of two grey horses out in front. Gate Book was ahead, with Glangesia going easily at his shoulder. Tootenhill moved up at the Canal, and the three led off to Valentine's. Gregalach was close to the leaders as they passed the Canal Stand, but he was interfered with at Number Eleven, fell, and was pulled up. Tootenhill came down in the ditch at this same fence, and Gate Book put in a terrific leap to clear him, but lost his balance on landing, and fell. This left Glangesia in the lead, and he showed the way past the stands, and out into the country again. Just before Becher's he slowed a little, but jumped so big and so quickly at that fence that he pulled himself back into first place, and stayed there until Melleray's Belle forged ahead at Valentine's. Shaun Goilin and Sir Lindsay also moved up, and these three entered the straight on fairly even terms. They took off for the last fence almost together, and there was much losing of stirrups. Williams on Sir Lindsay lost both irons, and Cullinan and Mason on the other two lost one apiece. The stands stood up and shouted as the three horses came down to the finish in a race as close as a five-furlong sprint, and Cullinan finally got Shaun Goilin up to win by a head from Melleray's Belle, with Sir Lindsay close up in third—a position which might have been bettered if his jockey had not been completely stirrupless, though it is true that he hit the last fence so hard that he was partially winded.

The gallant but tired Glangesia came in fourth, and Ballyhanwood and Royal Arch II, fifth and sixth, were the only other horses to finish.

L

CHAPTER TWELVE

The Altered Conditions, and the National of 1931

THE Grand National of 1930 did not produce the usual aftermath of criticism and obloquy, probably because the field of forty starters seemed small compared to the sixty-six of the preceding year, and because there was no spectacular collapse of a well-backed horse to supply dinner-table conversation for a week or two afterwards. The critics of the National in recent years may be divided into two classes: the few, who from real knowledge and careful consideration of the matter believe that some change is necessary; and that much larger group, who read an article in one of the more sensational newspapers, rely entirely on that for their information, and epitomize the whole race as disgraceful. The latter group want to know why the powers-that-be don't "do something about it," and seem not to realize that the said powers-that-be are infinitely more troubled by the problem of interference at the first and other fences than most of their critics, and are making strenuous efforts to find a solution. The first fence as it happens, has not lived up to its reputation to any extent during the last four years, but that is probably more good luck than anything else, and does not prove that it will not do so in the future, or that the problem no longer exists as completely as it ever did.

The proof that the Aintree authorities were taking a definite interest in this problem appeared when the conditions for 1931 were published. For the first time in the history of the race, the Grand National ceased to be an "open" race, in which any horse

Associated Newspapers

Becher's Brook in 1930.   May King falls.

in the world could compete, regardless of what he had done or failed to do in the past. In these new conditions, it was stated that the race was now for six-year-olds and upwards, that the bottom weight was raised to ten stone seven, and, most important, that the race was open only to horses, "which, by March 17th, 1931, have been placed first, second, or third (by the Judge), in a steeplechase of three miles or upwards, or the equivalent in foreign distances, or in a steeplechase of any distance at Aintree, Liverpool, or have won any steeplechase value 500 sov. to the winner (selling races in every case excepted) . . ."

The first of these changes, that which raised the minimum age from five years to six, was merely an acknowledgement of existing conditions, for only two five-year-olds have started in the National since the War, and neither had anything to do with the finish. In addition, it is now generally admitted that the race is too hard for such a young horse. In similar manner, the raising of the minimum weight by seven pounds found few opponents, for if a horse is not good enough to carry ten stone seven, he has no business in the race at all. The third change, however, caused a tremendous amount of discussion, as was to be expected.

If some change of the sort was necessary, and apparently it was, this was probably the best that could have been devised, but unfortunately it accomplished nothing whatsoever. The original entry for 1930, when there was no such qualifying clause, was eighty-four, and there were forty starters; in 1931, with horses obliged to qualify as explained above, eighty-five were entered, and forty-three started. It is said that without this change in the conditions, the field would have numbered seventy or more; but aside from that unproven supposition, the problem seems to be exactly where it was five years ago—unless, indeed, it is a step forward to have proved that this method will not have the desired effect.

The usual amount of guessing as to who would win the Grand National went on during the winter preceding the 1931 race, and the resultant opinions were rather curious. Easter Hero's recovery from lameness, and the supposed return to form of Gregalach and Richmond II, caused a lot of speculation, most of which, in the light of subsequent events, was largely unprofitable. Easter Hero was of course given top weight, and immediately people all over the country announced that he would not be able to shoulder it successfully. This opinion seemed to be almost unanimous—yet he was promptly installed as favourite, and with the exception of a few days after he was beaten at Lingfield, he remained in that position right along, and on the day of the race was so popular with the betting public that he started at 5—1.

Gregalach was the subject of great interest. He was rumoured to be back in his best form, and that seemed quite possible until he ran miserably in three races, one after the other. It was assumed that he must have some obscure internal trouble, and the interest in him died out until starting time, when it revived and brought his odds to 25—1. Richmond II came out looking very well indeed, and ran nicely in a couple of races, but he had always "had a leg," and eventually it asserted itself, and he was scratched.

Aside from these three, there were so many horses who were apparently going to win, or who seemed to have about equal chances, that it was a problem to know what to think of any of

Associated Newspapers

A second later.

them. It was not reasonable to assume that a great number of angels were being entertained unawares; it seemed more logical to say that they were all very moderate, yet for once logic was wrong, and it is probable that more good horses ran in the National of 1931 than in any race since the War.

All the horses who had completed the course the previous year were in again, but Melleray's Belle was the only one who approached favouritism at starting time. Sir Lindsay shared that honour with Easter Hero in the early betting on the strength of his third in 1930, but he ran so badly on various occasions that his price soon lengthened. Shaun Goilin had a big knee, but even so carried more of the confidence of Hartigan's stable than Kakushin, a brilliant jumper, but one whose stamina was doubtful. Gib was somewhat of a mystery, for he had jumped badly when running second to Kakushin in the Becher 'Chase at Aintree in November, but it was said that he was not right at the time, and Mr. Topham had given him twelve stone five to carry.

Much of the interest was centred on a number of horses who had never run in the National. There were the three sons of Drinmore: Drin, winner of the Grand Sefton, Ballasport, who had run excellently through the winter, and Drintyre, who distinguished himself on several occasions. Two young horses, Solanum and Oxclose, were tipped as likely winners, and there were others with equal right to consideration. At the Aintree gallops on the morning of the National, Drintyre was in every mouth; no less than nineteen people assured me that morning that Drintyre was sure to win if he stood up, and that Ballasport was the only possible danger. Everyone seemed as certain that Drintyre was going to win as they were that Easter Hero was not going to—yet Drintyre started at 20—1, and Easter Hero at fives!

The international atmosphere was furnished by Gyi Lovam! who had been brought all the way from Czechoslovakia by his owner-rider, Captain Popler. It was a very sporting effort, and Captain Popler had the sympathy of everyone when bad weather and ill luck prevented the horse from having more than one race in England before the National. Gyi Lovam! had won the Great Pardubice Steeplechase, which is the chief race over fences of Central Europe, twice in succession, but either the Aintree fences were too much for him, or his preparation suffered too much interference, for he was not one of the finishers.

Very little rain fell at Aintree during the weeks preceding the National, and the going was remarkably good. The weather was hot and sunny, so much so that the spectators enjoyed the unusual experience of taking off their coats and still being too hot at a Grand National. It was probably the nearest approximation to the conditions of 1893, when Cloister set the record of 9 minutes $32\frac{2}{5}$ seconds, and there seemed an excellent possibility of that record being broken.

Forty-three horses went to the post, and after one breakaway, the flag fell, and they were off over the Melling Road in a cloud of dust. Gib led them over the first fence, where Apostasy acquired the distinction of being the first horse to fall at that point since 1927. Gregalach moved up as they dashed into Becher's, and was jumping like a stag as he came over the Canal Turn with Gib and Big Black Boy. Ballasport, Easter Hero and Drintyre were next in order. At Valentine's Big Black Boy fell, Gib jumped on him, and both were out of it. Remarkably few horses had come down,

Central Press

He drops into the ditch.

however, and for the first time in history the stands saw thirty horses clear the Water Jump and go away for the second round. Gregalach was leading at the Water, with Great Span, Easter Hero and Solanum close up. Next came Theras, and Grakle, going well within himself, then Shaun Goilin, Drintyre, and Ballasport.

Solanum rushed into the lead as they galloped at Becher's for the second time, and took off close behind the riderless Tamasha, who went deep into the fence, but got over all right. Possibly this was too much for Solanum; something was, anyway, for he pitched forward on landing, and rolled over right in the path of Easter Hero, who was just in front of Ballasport. Easter Hero dodged to the left, then quickly back to the right, jumped right out from under Fred Rees, and deposited that jockey at Solanum's heels. Easter Hero stumbled, recovered, and went on riderless. Ballasport, coming up fast, barged into Easter Hero, whose loosely swinging reins whipped round the left leg of Williams, Ballasport's jockey, and tangled in the stirrup. Williams managed to get his leg free, but the stirrup, leather and all, was torn from the saddle, leaving him only one iron and eight fences still to go.

Sir Lindsay, who landed over Becher's just as this scrimmage was breaking up, was so unsettled by it that he almost fell, and promptly refused at the next fence. In the meantime, Gregalach and Great Span had jumped Becher's close to the rail, had suffered no interference, and gone on to the Canal with Tamasha running on their right in an aimless manner, and Grakle leading Drintyre close behind them. Was Tamasha going to swerve to the rail and cause more grief? For a moment it looked so; then he blundered into the jump on the far outside, and that danger was eliminated.

Gregalach was going very fast when he took off for the fence at the Canal. He jumped perfectly, but his momentum carried him wide, and by the time he had turned left-handed for Valentine's, Great Span, Ballasport, and Drintyre had swung inside, and were a good three lengths ahead of him, while Grakle was right at his side. Those three lengths were important later on. Next in order, piloted by the riderless Easter Hero, came Shaun Goilin, Melleray's Belle, and Glangesia, with Ballyhanwood and Drin at their heels. They jumped and turned, all but Drin, who swung too sharply, fell, got up without Speck, cantered a few yards, and went down again with a broken hip.

And long after the rest had gone by came Captain Popler on Gyi Lovam! He had come a terrible cropper at Becher's, but had remounted, and drove into the Canal with all the determination in the world. The Canal Stand cheered him loudly as he cleared that and Valentine's, then groaned as he came down at the next fence—and this time there was no remounting, for Gyi Lovam! went on alone.

Down the course Great Span had fallen, Drintyre, dead beat, had refused two fences from home, and Grakle had crept up to lead Gregalach by half a length at the last fence, where Ballasport, lying third, humped himself a little roughly to get over. Williams had given him a splendid ride all the way, in spite of his lost iron, but now he was exhausted by his one-sided effort, and toppled off. For a moment he clung to the reins, and almost got to his feet, but Ballasport kicked him in the stomach, and he was done.

And is pulled out.

The two leaders now had the finish to themselves. Moloney took up his whip, and Gregalach responded nobly. He ranged up beside Grakle, and for an instant the two horses were level, but Grakle on the inside had the shorter way to go, and his superb condition began to tell. Inch by inch he went ahead until he had a length and a half advantage, Gregalach was too tired to come again, and they finished with that distance between them, in 9 minutes 32⅘ seconds, only two-fifths of a second slower than the record.

The 100—1 shot Annandale was a bad third, behind him was the French horse Rhyticere, ridden by a French jockey, and then Ballyhanwood, who thus beat all the horses who had beaten him the previous year. Shaun Goilin was sixth, Glangesia seventh, Melleray's Belle eighth, the remounted Great Span ninth, Starbox tenth, Harewood eleventh, and Royal Arch II, with another French jockey in the saddle, twelfth and last. Of the six horses who had finished the year before, only Sir Lindsay failed to do so this year.

The race was marred by two fatal accidents to horses. Drin's fall has already been alluded to, and the other victim was Swift Rowland, who fell at Becher's the first time round, was jumped on and killed instantly by the horse behind him. It is very sad and rather ironic that such accidents should have happened in a year when the going was perfect, when more than the usual number of horses completed the course, and when such an unusual number survived the first round. Of incidental interest is the fact that there have been only thirty-five fatal accidents to horses in the whole ninety-three years of the Grand National's history, and that considerably more than half of these took place before 1890.

In addition to that, if one compares the list of horses killed and injured at Aintree, in proportion to the number of starters, with a similar list of Park Course statistics, one finds that Aintree has had fewer accidents, not only to horses, but to men. In all the years of the National, only one man has been killed, and that was seventy years ago.

Grakle and Gregalach were originally in the same stable before they were bought by Mr. Taylor and Mrs. Gemmell, their respective owners. Mr. Taylor had his choice of the two, and on the advice of Tom Coulthwaite picked Grakle. At first it seemed an unfortunate choice, for Gregalach won the National of 1929 on his first attempt, whereas Grakle finished behind him in that race, and failed to "get round" in three other Nationals. Coulthwaite never lost faith in Grakle, however, and in 1931 produced him at Aintree as fit as a horse can be. He had at last learned to jump like a gentleman, and this was all that was necessary to make him a really fine steeplechaser, for physically he has always been very good indeed. He and Gregalach are both roughly the same type of big-boned weight carrier which shows to its best advantage at Aintree; Gregalach, certainly, is twice the horse at Aintree that he is over the Park Courses.

The 1931 Spring Meeting at Aintree saw the passing of Easter Hero. It is a matter for regret that he could not run in the National of 1930, for he was probably at his best that year, and it is sad to see such a brilliant horse go out of racing without a Grand National to his credit. Shortly before the '31 race he was beaten at Lingfield, which was decidedly out of character for a horse who had been invincible for three years over the Park Courses. In the National he did not look himself, and showed none of the impetuous vitality which had run all opposition into the ground in other years. He had begun to drop back before the scrimmage at Becher's, simply because he could not go the pace—and the old Easter Hero was accustomed to make the pace too hot for the others. He came out again next day in the Champion, but jumped badly at the last two fences, and finished in a dead heat with Coup de Chapeau, an unknown French horse. The real significance of this appears when one realizes that he was at equal weights with Coup de Chapeau, which was the first time in years that any horse had finished near him without a real pull in the weights. After this race Mr. Whitney announced that Easter Hero would be retired and would run no more.

PART TWO

$\mathcal{N} O T E$

IN the data given in the following pages the reader will please note that:

1. The conditions of a particular race have not been substantially changed unless otherwise indicated.

2. In starting prices all odds are listed against.

Key to abbreviations is to be found at the end of this part.

THE GRAND Liverpool Steeplechase.—A sweepstakes of 20 sovs. each, 5 forfeit, with 100 added; 12 stone each, gentlemen riders; four miles across country; the second to save his stake, and the winner to pay 10 sovs. toward expenses; no rider to open a gate or ride through a gateway, or more than 100 yards along any road, footpath, or driftway.

Going: DEEP

Weather: CLEAR

Starters: 17

Date: FEBRUARY 26

Time: 14 MIN. 53 SEC.

Horse	Jockey	Owner	Position at Finish
LOTTERY *by Lottery—Parthenia*	Jem Mason	Mr. J. Elmore	1
SEVENTY FOUR *by Memnon*	T. Olliver	Sir George Mostyn	2
PAULINA	Mr. Martin	Mr. Theobald	3
TRUE BLUE	Mr. Barker	Mr. Stephenson	4
THE NUN	Mr. A. McDonough	Lord McDonald	5
RAILROAD	Mr. Powell	Capt. Marshall	6
PIONEER	Mr. T. Walker	Sir D. Baird	7
DICTATOR	Carlin	Mr. J. S. Oswell	F.
CONRAD	Capt. Becher	Capt. Childe	F.
CRAMP	Wilmot	Mr. Robertson	F.
RAMBLER	Morgan	Mr. H. S. Bowen	F.
DAXON	Owner	Mr. Ferguson	F.
BARKSTON	Byrne	Mr. Ferguson	F.
RUST *by Master Bagot*	Mr. W. McDonough	Mr. Ferguson	P. U.
CANNON BALL	Owner	Mr. Newcombe	F.
JACK *by Marmaduke*	Wadlow	Capt. Lamb	F.
CHARITY *by Woodman*	Hardy	Mr. Vevers	F

CONDITIONS the same, except: 150 sovs. added; 30 sovs. to second horse, third to save his stake.

| *Going:* GOOD | *Starters:* 12 | *Time:* 12 MIN. 30 SEC. |
| *Weather:* CLEAR | *Date:* MARCH 5 | |

Horse	Jockey	Owner	Position at Finish
JERRY *by Catterick*	Mr. Bretherton	Mr. Villebois	1
ARTHUR *by Sir Hercules—Angelica*	Mr. A. McDonough	Mr. Barry	2
VALENTINE *by Fentiman*	Owner	Mr. Power	3
THE SEA *by Whalebone*	Owner	Marquis of Waterford	
LOTTERY *by Lottery—Parthenia*	J. Mason	Mr. Elmore	F.
SPOLASCO *by Master Richard*	Rose	Owner unknown	
THE NUN *by Calton*	Mr. Powell	Lord McDonald	F.
COLUMBINE	Mr. Won	Marquis of Waterford	F.
HASTY *by Sir Harry*	Rigg	Owner unknown	
SEVENTY FOUR *by Memnon*	T. Olliver	Sir George Mostyn	F
WEATHERCOCK *by Strephon*	Barker	Owner unknown	F.
THE AUGEAN *by Sir Hercules*	Christian	Owner unknown	

The records are very vague about this race. The placing of the first three horses is definite, as is the fact that certain horses fell; but it is uncertain how many finished, and the accounts of the race discuss a horse called Cruickshank, who does not appear in the entry. The cases of "owner unknown" may be explained by the likelihood of the horses belonging to the owner of the horse immediately above in the entry list, but in the absence of ditto marks this cannot be assumed definitely.

STARTING PRICES

3–1 The Nun	7–1 Seventy Four	10–1 Cruickshank (?)
4–1 Lottery	8–1 Arthur	12–1 Jerry

LOTTERY, JEM MASON UP.
Winner of the first Grand National.

CONDITIONS for this year the same as in 1840 with one addition, that the winner of the Cheltenham Steeplechase in 1840 should carry 18 pounds extra. The Cheltenham Steeplechase had already taken place and had been won by Lottery when these conditions were framed.

Going: GOOD *Starters:* 11 *Time:* 13 MIN. 25 SEC.
Weather: GREY *Date:* MARCH 3

Horse	Jockey	Owner	Position at Finish
CHARITY *by Woodman*	Mr. Powell	Lord Craven	1
CIGAR *by Petworth*	Mr. A. McDonough	Mr. Anderson	2
PETER SIMPLE *by Arbutus*	Walker	Hon. F. Craven	3
REVEALER *by Reveller*	Mr. Barker	Mr. Villebois	4
THE HAWK *by Prendergast*	Saunders	Capt. Nugent	5
SEVENTY FOUR *by Memnon*	Mr. Whitworth	Sir G. Mostyn	6
GOBLIN *by Phantom*	Bretherton	Lord Villiers	7 (R)
LEGACY *by Petworth*	Mr. W. McDonough	Mr. Robertson	F.
LOTTERY *by Lottery*	J. Mason	Mr. Elmore	P. U.
SELIM	Owner	Capt. Price	F.
OLIVER TWIST *by Flexible*	Mr. Oliver	Mr. Smith	F.

The wall was removed this year in deference to the scrimmage at that jump in 1840, and in its place was erected an artificial brook, ten feet wide and three feet deep, with a thick thorn fence on the take-off side.

STARTING PRICES

5–2 Lottery
4–1 Cigar

6–1 Peter Simple
12–1 Legacy
14–1 Seventy Four

14–1 Charity
100–6 The Hawk

T H E conditions for this year were changed as follows: the entrance fee was increased to 23 sovs. each, but there was no added money. The owner of the second horse received no prize from the stakes, he merely saved his stake. Lottery again carried 18 pounds extra for having won the Cheltenham Steeplechase two years before.

Going: MODERATE   Starters: 15   Time: 13 MIN. 30 SEC.
Weather: CLEAR   Date: MARCH 2

Horse	Jockey	Owner	Position at Finish
GAYLAD *by Brutandorf*	T. Olliver	Mr. Elmore	1
SEVENTY FOUR *by Memnon*	Powell	Lord Mostyn	2
PETER SIMPLE *by Arbutus*	Owner	Mr. Hunter	3
THE RETURNED *by Monreith*	Owner	Mr. W. Hope-Johnstone	4
SAM WELLER *by Strephon*	Barker	Mr. James Mason	F.
LOTTERY *by Lottery*	J. Mason	Mr. Elmore	P. U.
COLUMBINE	L. Byrne	Lord Waterford	
BANATHLATH *by Cameleopard*	Colgan	Mr. Ferguson	F.
LADY LANGFORD *by Sir Hercules*	Abbot	Hon. C. Forester	F.
BANGALORE *by Swap*	Capt. Peel	Mr. Ramsay	
ANONYMOUS *by Prince*	Owner	Mr. Moore	
SATIRIST *by Sir Gilbert*	Bretherton	Lord Maidstone	
LUCKS-ALL	Goddard	Mr. R. Ekin	
CONSUL *by Irish Napoleon*	Oldaker	Baron Rothschild	F.
HONESTY *by Sir Hercules*	Mr. W. McDonough	Lord Clanricarde	

The records give no definite account of how the horses, not marked under "position," finished, and do not even say whether or not they completed the course.

STARTING PRICES

5-1 Lottery
6-1 Seventy Four
6-1 Peter Simple
7-1 Gaylad

8-1 Sam Weller
10-1 Lucks-All
10-1 Consul

100-7 Satirist
15-1 The Returned
20-1 Banathlath
20-1 Bangalore

1843

T H I S year the race was called The Liverpool and National Steeplechase, and became a handicap for the first time. Top weight 12 stone 8 pounds, and winners from date of declaration to carry 5 pounds extra.

The Stone Wall was revived for this race, but was only four feet high. It was put together with masonry and had a layer of turf on top.

Going: HARD BUT GOOD   *Starters:* 16   *Time:* NOT TAKEN
Weather: COLD AND CLEAR   *Date:* MARCH 1

Horse	Weight	Jockey	Owner	Position at Finish
VANGUARD *by Belzoni*	11–10	T. Olliver	Lord Chesterfield	1
NIMROD	11	Scott	Mr. Mare	2
DRAGSMAN	11–3	Crickmere	Mr. Holman	3
CLAUDE DUVAL	11–7	Tomblin	Col. Anson	4
GOBLIN	11–6	Bretherton	Mr. Errington	5
BUCEPHALUS	11–5	Whitworth	Mr. R. Hunter	6
LOTTERY	12–6	J. Mason	Mr. Elmore	7
PETER SIMPLE	13–1 (5 lbs. extra)	Frisby	Mr. W. Ekin	8
THE RETURNED	12	Maj. Campbell	Mr. W. Sterling Crawford	9
CONSUL	11–12	Oldaker	Baron Rothschild	REF.
REDWING	11–10	Doolan	Lord Waterford	F.
VICTORIA	11–10	Owner	Mr. T. Taylor	F.
TINDERBOX	11–7	G. Moore	Mr. Hunt	F.
TEETOTUM	11–7	Owner	Mr. Kennedy	F.
CROXBY	11–6	Mr. W. McDonough	Hon. F. Craven	P. U.
THE ROMP	11	Holingshed	Mr. Lamplugh	REF.

STARTING PRICES

3–1 Peter Simple   4–1 The Returned   10–1 Nimrod
4–1 Lottery   8–1 Redwing   12–1 Vanguard
    10–1 Dragsman

1844

CONDITIONS same as previous year. The Stone Wall was banned forever, and a post and rail was put in its place.

Going: VERY DEEP AND BAD   *Starters:* 15   *Time:* A LITTLE LESS THAN 14 MIN.
Weather: HEAVY RAIN   *Date:* FEBRUARY 28

Horse	Weight	Jockey	Owner	Position at Finish
DISCOUNT	10–12	Crickmere	Mr. Quartermaine	1
THE RETURNED	12	Scott	Mr. W. S. Crawford	2
TOM TUG	10–7	Rackley	Mr. Tilbury	3
CAESAR	11–10	Barker	Lord Maidstone	4
LATHER	11–2	Ball	Lord E. Russell	5
THE ROMP	10–7	Byrne	Lord S. Bentinck	6
MARENGO	10–10	Sharkey	Mr. Bretherton	7
LITTLE PETER	10–12	Owner	Mr. Hollinshead	8
LOUIS PHILIPPE	11	Cowell	Sir J. Gerrard	9
PETER SIMPLE	12–12	Frisby	Mr. Ekin	F.
ROBINSON	12–7	Parker	Mr. Milbank	REF.
WIVERTON	12–4	T. Olliver	Lord Maidstone	F.
HESLINGTON	12	Mr. W. McDonough	Mr. W. Scott	REF.
NIMROD	10–10	Mr. A. McDonough	Mr. Mare	F.
CHARITY	10–7	Powell	Mr. Vever	F.

STARTING PRICES

5–1 Discount   8–1 Wiverton   15–1 The Returned
5–1 Marengo   13–1 Charity   20–1 Louis Philippe
8–1 Heslington   14–1 Nimrod   25–1 The Romp

1845

Going: HEAVY   *Starters:* 15   *Time:* 10 MIN. 47 SEC.

Weather: CLEAR BUT VERY COLD   *Date:* MARCH 5

Horse	Colour and Sex	Age	Weight	Jockey	Owner	Position at Finish
CURE-ALL	br. g.	a.	11–5	Loft	Mr. W. S. Crawford	1
PETER SIMPLE	gr. h.	a.	11–12	Frisby	Mr. Thornton	2
THE EXQUISITE	b. g.	a.	11–12	Byrne	Capt. Boyd	3
TOM TUG	blk.g.	a.	10–2	Crickmere	Mr. J. T. Blackburn	4
THE PAGE	ch. g.		11–10	Owner	Mr. Holman	REF.
CLANSMAN			11–6	Owner	Mr. J. Kelly	F. & D.
BRENDA	b.m.		11–7	J. Abbot	Mr. Perkins and Capt. France	R. O.
VANGUARD	b. g.		12–10	Owner	Mr. T. Olliver	P. U.
BOXKEEPER			11–4	Bradley	Mr. Barnett	
CEREMONY	ch. h.		11	T. Abbot	Mr. Atkinson	
PETER SWIFT	gr. g.		10–12	Mr. Powel	Mr. Milbank	
THE STRANGER			10–10	Hill	Lord Alford	
NIMROD	b. g.		10–8	French	Mr. Mare	
THE ROMP	ch. m.		10–4	Thompson	Mr. R. H. Jones	
BRILLIANT	blk. g.		10–4	Noble	Mr. Wesley	

Just before the race the favourite at 5—1, The Knight Templar, met with an accident and was scratched. This changed all the betting, and the horses started at the following prices. Cure-All was not quoted at all.

STARTING PRICES

4–1 Vanguard	6–1 Brenda	9–1 Peter Simple
5–1 Tom Tug	7–1 The Page	10–1 Brilliant.

1846

CONDITIONS unchanged, but distance increased to nearly five miles by accident.

	Colour and					Position at
Horse	Sex	Age	Weight	Jockey	Owner	Finish
PIONEER by Advance	b. g.	6	11–12	Taylor	Mr. Adams	1
CULVERTHORPE (H. B.)		a.	11–4	Rackley	Mr. Payne	2
SWITCHER		5	12–4	Wynne	Lord Howth	3
FIREFLY		a.	12–4	L. Byrne	Lord Waterford	4
EAGLE		a.	11–12	Capt. W. Peel	Mr. C. E. Brooke	5
CURE-ALL	br. g.	a.	12–4	Owner	Mr. W. J. Loft	
REGALIA	b. m.	a.	11–12	Doolan	Lord Waterford	
GOLDEN PIPPIN		a.	11–12	Nainby	Mr. Atkinson	R. O.
MAJOR A.		6	11–6	Blake	Mr. Windham	
TROUBADOUR (H. B.)		a.	11–6	G. B. Rammell	Mr. Austin	
CARLOW			11–4	T. Olliver	Mr. G. Lambden	
BRENDA (H .B.)	b. m.	a.	11–4	Mr. Powell	Mr. Hammond	
TINDERBOX		a.	11–4	P. Daley	Mr. Robertson	
PETER SIMPLE	gr. h.	a.	11–2	Frisby	Mr. Ekin	
HORNIHIHARRIHO (H.B.)		a.	11	Parker	Mr. H. L. Carter	F.
LANCET (H. B.)		a.	11	Mr. W. McDonough	Mr. Hey	Knocked over by mounted spectator
MAMELUKE			10–12	Mr. A. McDonough	Capt. Barnett	F.
PICKWICK			10–10	Dally	Mr. G. Lambden	
PERAMBULATOR (H.B.)		6	10–8	N. Stagg	Hon. F. Craven	
VELUTI (H. B.)		6	10–8	Mason	Mr. W. S. Crawford	B. D.
THE SCAVENGER		6	10–2	Bradley	Mr. Pearce	REF.
LADY GRAY			10	Thomas	Sir R. Brownrigg	F.

Going: GOOD   Starters: 22   Time: 10 MIN. 46 SEC.
Weather: CLEAR   Date: MARCH 4

The fact that some horses are marked h.b. (*i.e.*, half-bred) means that they are known to be half-breds. It does not mean that all the others were thoroughbred, but merely that their breeding is not known definitely.

STARTING PRICES

11–2 Veluti	10–1 Lancet, Mameluke	16–1 Perambulator, Cure-All
6–1 Eagle	12–1 Culverthorpe, Golden	100–6 Brenda, Peter Simple
7–1 Firefly	Pippin	25–1 Major A

1849

Going: HEAVY *Starters:* 24 *Time:* 10 MIN. 56 SEC.
Weather: COLD, WITH A DULL SKY *Date:* FEBRUARY 28

Horse	Colour and Sex	Age	Weight	Jockey	Owner	Position at Finish
PETER SIMPLE (H.B.) by Patron	b. g.	a.	11	Cunningham	Mr. Mason, Jr.	1
THE KNIGHT OF GWYNNE	ch. g.	a.	10–7	Owner	Capt. D'Arcy	2
PRINCE GEORGE	b. g.	a.	10–10	T. Olliver	Mr. T. Mason	3
ALFRED		5	10–6	Wynne	Mr. Buchanan	4
CHANDLER by Dr. Faustus	br. g.	a.	12–2	Owner	Capt. Little	5
THE BRITISH YEOMAN		a.	11–4	Mr. Bevill	Mr. Elmore	6
TIPPERARY BOY		5	10–9	Barley	Mr. Terry	
MULLIGAN		5	11–2	Ford	Mr. Westrop	
KILFANE		a.	11	Neale	Mr. J. H. Holmes	F., DES.
CORIANDER		a.	10–6	Bally	Mr. E. W. Rudyard	F.
BALLYBAR		a.	9–12	H. Bradley	Mr. Wesley	F.
KHONDOOZ		a.	9–10	Rackley	Mr. Tillbury	P.U.
THE CURATE		a.	11–11	Powell	Mr. Brettle	F. & D.
PROCEED		a.	11–11	Owner	Capt. Peel	REF.
WOLVERHAMPTON		a.	11–5	Owner	Mr. B. Bretherton	F.
ARAB ROBBER		6	11–2	Phillips	Mr. Russell	
THE IRON DUKE		5	11	Abbott	Mr. C. Price	
THE VICTIM		a.	10–11	Taylor	Lord Chesterfield	
SIR JOHN (H. B.)			10–10	Owner	Mr. Sharkie	
NAPOLEON		6	10–8	Archer	Mr. J. Bateman	P.U.
CHATHAM		a.	10–6	Frisby	Lord Strathmore	F.
EQUINOX		a.	9–12	Moloney	Capt. Peyton	F. & D.
JERRY		a.	10–4	J. S. Walker	Mr. J. S. Moseley	F.
SPARTA		a.	8–12	Wakefield	Mr. Bathurst	F.

STARTING PRICES

5–1 Prince George	9–1 Proceed	12–1 Alfred
6–1 The Curate	12–1 Wolverhampton	20–1 Chatham, Peter Simple
8–1 The Knight of Gwynne	12–1 to 15–1 The British Yeoman	50–1 Napoleon

Going: GOOD *Starters:* 32 *Time:* 9 MIN. 57½ SEC.
Weather: CLEAR *Date:*

Horse	Colour and Sex	Age	Weight	Jockey	Owner	Position at Finish
ABD EL KADER (H.B.) by Ishmael—English Lass	b. g.	a.	9–12	Green	Mr. Osborne	1
THE KNIGHT OF GWYNNE	ch. g.	a.	11–8	Wynne	Mr. J. Fort	2
SIR JOHN	b. g.	a.	11–8	J. Ryan	Lord Waterford	3
TIPPERARY BOY		a.	10	S. Darling	Mr. Hughes	4
FARNHAM		6	11–3	Abbott	Mr. Maugan	5
MARIA DAY		a.	10–5	Rackley	Mr. Treadgold	6
VENGEANCE		a.	9–10	Archer	Mr. Vever	7
PETER SIMPLE (H. B.)		a.	12–2	Cunningham	Mr. Cunningham	
THE BRITISH YEOMAN		a.	11–10	Philpot	Mr. J. Elmore	
RAT-TRAP		a.	11–7	Frisby	Lord Strathmore	
THE CHANDLER		a.	11–3	Owner	Capt. Little	
THE VICTIM		a.	11–2	Taylor	Mr. Hassall	
SPRING BUCK		a.	10–12	Smith	Lord G. Kennedy	P.U.
THE IRON DUKE		5	10–12	Hanlon	Mr. J. Bell	
MEATH		a.	10–10	Neale	Mr. Harrison	
MULLIGAN		6	10–10	Owner	Mr. Westropp	
ROY-DE-AISEY (H. B.)		5	10–10	Magee	Lord Lurgan	
QUADRUPED		a.	10–8	G. Arran	Mr. Cunningham	
LAUREL (H. B.)	b. g.	a.	10–8	Owner	Mr. Butler	
RAINBOW (H. B.)		a.	10–8	Dalby	Mr. J. C. Ranton	F.
EVERTON (N. S.)		a.	10–8	A. Salt	Mr. D. Lewis	
SHINSORE (H. B.)		6	10–5	Bradley	Mr. Williamson	
THE OAKS		5	10–5	Canavan	Mr. J. G. Murphy	K.O.
COLUMBINE		a.	10–4	T. Olliver	Mr. Pocket	
SOBRIETY		a.	10–4	J. Thompson	Mr. Sandford	
FISTICUFF		a.	10	Parr	Mr. J. Nicoll	
HOPE		a.	9–12 (carried 10–1)	Owner	Mr. Hunter	F.
KILKENNY		a.	9–10	Holman	Capt. Fraser	
LITTLE FANNY (N. S.)		a.	9	Fowler	Lord Sefton	
JOHNNIE BARRIE		a.	9 (carried 9–11)	Maitland	Mr. Laing	
PEGASUS (N. S.)		a.	8–10	Tasker	Lord Seaham	
THE PONY (N. S.)		a.	8–7	Maney	Mr. R. Brooke	

Abd el Kader was not quoted by the bookmakers at the start.

STARTING PRICES

5–1 Peter Simple
7–1 Sir John
9–1 Rat-trap

12–1 The Knight of Gwynne, Victim
15–1 Farnham, Vengeance
16–1 Chandler

20–1 Columbine
25–1 Maria Day, Little Fanny
30–1 The Oaks

ABD-EL-KADER.

Winner of the Grand Nationals of 1850 and 1851.

1851

Going: AVERAGE   *Starters:* 21   *Time:* 9 MIN. 59 SEC.

Weather: CLEAR   *Date:*

Horse	Colour and Sex	Age	Weight	Jockey	Owner	Position at Finish
ABD EL KADER by Ishmael—English Lass	b. g.	a.	10–4	T. Abbot	Mr. Joseph Osborne	1
MARIA DAY by Mundig	br. m.	a.	10–5	J. Frisby	Mr. C. Higgins	2
SIR JOHN by Windfall, dam by Middlethorpe	b. g.	a.	11–12	J. Ryan	Lord Waterford	3
HALF-AND-HALF (late SMALL-BEER)			10–8	R. Sly, Jr.	Mr. Oakes	4
VAIN HOPE			11–8	S. Darling, Jr.	Mr. Vevers	5
RAT-TRAP			10–10	J. Mason	Mr. T. F. Mason	6
MULLIGAN			10–2	W. Draper	Mr. J. Elmore	7
SHINSORE			10–7	Mr. Gaman	Mr. King	8
REINDEER (late FRANK)			9–8	C. Planner	Mr. May	9
TIPPERARY BOY			10–3	T. Olliver	Mr. Tollitt	10
SIR PETER LAURIE			11–7	W. Scott	Mr. W. Barrett	
PETER SIMPLE			11–7	D. Tubb	Mr. Cunningham	
THE VICTIM			10–13	W. Taylor	Mr. Palmer	
FUGITIVE			10–12	H. Bradley	Lord Lurgan	F.
CURRIG			9–12	J. Debean	Mr. Barry	
FUGLEMAN			10	D. Wynne	Col. Shirley	
HOPE			9–12	Mr. Green	Mr. S. H. Kemp	P.U.
VOLATILE			9–10	W. Fowler	Mr. W. Vevers	F.
MARE BY GREYSTEEL			9–10	Thrift	Mr. Onslow	
MAURICE DALEY (late FLYCATCHER)			9–6	C. Boyce	Mr. Cartwright	
PENRITH (late CHARLES XII)			9–4	McClory	Mr. Johnstone	

STARTING PRICES

6–1 Red-trap	8–1 Vain Hope	20–1 Half-and-Half
7–1 Sir John	10–1 Tipperary Boy	25–1 Sir Peter Laurie,
7–1 Abd el Kader	15–1 Fugitive	Mulligan, Currig
	100–6 Maria Day	

1852

Going: GOOD AS POSSIBLE Starters: 24 Time: 9 MIN. 58½ SEC.
Weather: CLEAR Date: MARCH 3

Horse	Colour and Sex	Age	Weight	Jockey	Owner	Position at Finish
MISS MOWBRAY	b. m.	a.	10–4	Mr. A. Goodman	Mr. T. F. Mason	1
by Lancastrian—Norma						
MAURICE DALEY	b. g.	a.	9–4	C. Boyce	Mr. Cartwright	2
(late FLYCATCHER)			(carried 9–6)			
SIR PETER LAURIE		a.	11–2	W. Holman	Capt. Barnett	3
CHIEFTAIN			10–12	Harrison	Mr. Atkinson	4
LA GAZZA LADRA		6	9–12	J. Neale	Mr. Goodwin	5
WARNER			10–8	W. Archer	Lord Waterford	6
SIR JOHN			11–10	J. Ryan	Lord Waterford	7
ABD EL KADER			11–4	D. Wynne	Mr. Osborne	P.U.
BEDFORD			9–12	A. Taylor	Mr. Chance	F.
MCIAN			9–10	J. Sadler	Mr. R. Jones	
PETER SIMPLE (N. S.)			11–2	Owner	Mr. G. S. Davenport	F.
BOURTON			10–10	S. Darling, Jr.	Mr. Martin	F.
(late UPTON)						
DOLLY'S BRUE			10	McGee	Mr. Maugan	
SILENT FRIEND			9–12	Parry	Mr. Courtenay	
LAMIENNE			9–7	Meaney	Mr. J. G. Murphy	
VICTIM			9–7	H. Bradley	Mr. Gooch	F.
ROYAL BLUE			9	G. Stevens	Mr. Harding	F.
BEDFORD			10–10	Ablett	Mr. Barling	F.
AGIS			10–10	T. Olliver	Capt. Little	REF.
MARIA DAY			10–6	J. Frisby	Mr. Higgins	F.
CARRIG			10–4	Debean	Mr. J. Bourke	P.U.
			(incl. 10 lbs. extra)			
EVERTON			9–6	Hewitt	Mr. Elmore	F.
			(carried 9–10)			
COGIA			9–6	J. Tasker	Mr. J. Bird	F.
			(carried 9–9)			
MALEY			9–6	Connor	Mr. Henderson	F.

NOTE: Lord Waterford declared to win with Warner.

STARTING PRICES

6–1 La Gazza Ladra	12–1 Bedford	50–1 McIan
9–1 Abd el Kader	12–1 Sir John	100–1 Royal Blue
10–1 Chieftain	30–1 Sir Peter Laurie	

1847

T H E name was changed this year to The Grand National Handicap Steeplechase, but the conditions remained the same. The post and rail, which had been substituted for the old Stone Wall in 1844, was now replaced by an artificial Water Jump, which has been at the same spot in front of the stands ever since.

Going: GOOD   *Starters:* 26   *Time:* 10 MIN. 39 SEC.
Weather: CLEAR   *Date:* MARCH 3

Horse	Colour and Sex	Age	Weight	Jockey	Owner	Position at Finish
MATTHEW		a.	10–6	D. Wynne	Mr. Courtenay	1
by Vestris						
ST. LEGER		a.	12–3	T. Olliver	Mr. Watt	2
JERRY		a.	11–6	Bradley	Mr. Moseley	3
PIONEER		a.	11–12	Capt. Peel	Mr. O'Higgins	4
CULVERTHORPE		a.	11–6	H. N. Powell	Mr. D'Arcey	5
BRUNETTE	ch.m. 13		12–6	Mr. A. McDonough	Mr. Preston	6
SAUCEPAN			12–6	Mr. W. McDonough	Mr. Power	
BALLYBAR		a.	11–12	Turner	Mr. Robertson	
THE FALSE HEIR		a.	11–4	Wilson	Mr. Hall	
THE PLURALIST	br. g.	a.	11–4	Denby	Mr. Hall	
FREDERICK			11–2	Abbot	Mr. Preston	
by Turcoman						
LATTITAT		a.	11	Owner	Mr. Bevill	
MARENGO		a.	11	Barker	Capt. Barnett	F.
CAVENDISH	b. g.		10–10	Scott	Mr. Walter	
AVOCA			10–10	Capt. Broadley	Capt. Gambier	
ST. RUTH	b. g.	a.	11–1	Canavan	Mr. R. J. Moore	
RED LANCER			10–8	Owner	Lord Strathmore	P. U.
BARMAID	b. m.		10–8	Owner	Mr. Lockwood	
GRENADE	ch. g.		10–8	Rackley	Mr. Anderson	
CLINKER	ch. g.	a.	10–7	Mason	Mr. Kirkpatrick	
GAYHURST			10–7	Owner	Mr. Wesley	
TRAMP			10–6	Archer	Mr. W. Hall	
QUICKSILVER			10–4	Rawson	Col. Taylor	
CUMBERLAND LASSIE	b. m.		10–4	Meddock	Mr. Smith	F.
VALERIA	b. m.	5	10–3	Dally	Mr. Oakley	
MIDNIGHT	br. m.	5	10–10	Gardner	Mr. H. B. Browne	

STARTING PRICES

10–1 Matthew—4–1 until   10–1 Culverthorpe   15–1 St. Leger, Pioneer, Avoca
   just before the start   100–8 Jerry   20–1 Red Lancer

1848

Going: VERY BAD | *Starters:* 29 | *Time:* 11 MIN. 21 SEC.
Weather: RAIN | *Date:*

Horse	Colour and Sex	Age	Weight	Jockey	Owner	Position at Finish
CHANDLER *by Dr. Faustus*	br. g.	a.	11–12	Owner	Capt. Little	1
THE CURATE	ch. g.		11–12	T. Olliver	Mr. Brettle	2
BRITISH YEOMAN			11–4	Mr. Bevill	Mr. Elmore	3
STANDARD GUARD			10–12	Taylor	Mr. Storey	4
WOLVERHAMPTON		a.	11–12	Bretherton	Mr. R. H. Jones	
SAUCEPAN	b. g.	a.	11–11	Abbott	Mr. W. Strickland	REF.
MATTHEW (H. B.)	br. g.	a.	11–6	Wynn	Mr. Courtenay	K. O.
JERRY	br. g.	a.	11–7	Sanders	Mr. Moseley	P. U.
FATHER MATTHEW (H. B.)			11–6	Lanplugh	Mr. W. S. Crawford	
PIONEER *by Advance*	b. g.	a.	11–6	Capt. Peel	Mr. Ouseley Higgin	B. D.
THE SWITCHER	ch. h.	a.	11–5	Owner	Lord Strathmore	
ASHBERRY LASS	ch. m.	6	11–3	Collis	Mr. J. W. Haworth	
CHEROOT	ch. g.	a.	11–2	McGee	Mr. Davies	
ARISTIDES	b. g.		11–1	Rowlands	Mr. G. Brettle	
SIR ARTHUR	br. h.	6	11–1	Murphy	Mr. Barry	
KHONDOOZ	h.		11	Rackley	Mr. J. Wilson	P. U.
SPHIA	b. m.	a.	11	Ford	Sir R. de Burgh	
THE IRISH BARD	b. h.	a.	11	Freeze	Mr. Arthur	
EAGLE	ch. g.	a.	11–4	J. Broome	Mr. C. C. Brooke	F.
PIONEER *by Pioneer (h.b.)*		a.	10–13	Neale	Mr. T. Harrison	B. D.
PICTON (H. B.)	b. g.	a.	10–13	Burke	Mr. J. N. Burke	
COUNSELLOR	ch. h.	a.	10–12	Frisby	Mr. W. Coutts	F., DES.
FORTUNE-TELLER	ch. g.		10–10	Stagg	Mr. Kennedy	
THE SAILOR	ch. g.	6	10–8	Holman	Mr. Mason	F., DES.
THE GIPSY QUEEN	roan m.		10–6	Whitfield	Lord Anson	
VARIETY	b. m.	a.	10–8	Powell	Mr. C. Towneley	
BLUE PILL *by Physician*	br. h.	a.	10–3	Allensby	Mr. E. Cary	F., DES.
SPARTA	b. m.	a.	10	Turner	Mr. R. Brooke	
NAWORTH	b. g.	a.	9–8	Archer	Lord Strathmore	

Apparently there were two horses named Pioneer in this race. The one by Advance was the 1846 winner. Another is mentioned as breaking down near the end of the first round, but it is impossible to tell which of them that was or which was the one quoted at 25—1 by the bookmakers.

STARTING PRICES

6–1 The Curate
8–1 Matthew
12–1 Chandler

15–1 Sir Arthur
100–6 Standard Guard

25–1 Pioneer, Counsellor, Khondooz
30–1 Fortune-Teller

1853

Going: VERY DEEP   Starters: 21   Time: 10 MIN. 37½ SEC.

Weather: CLEAR   Date:

Horse	Colour and Sex	Age	Weight	Jockey	Owner	Position at Finish
PETER SIMPLE by Patron	b. g.	a.	10–10	T. Olliver	Capt. Little	1
MISS MOWBRAY	b. m.		10–12	Mr. Gordon	Mr. Mason	2
OSCAR	b. g.		10–2	Mr. A. Goodman	Mr. Mason	3
SIR PETER LAURIE			11–8	W. Holman	Mr. W. Barnett	4
ABD EL KADER			10–10	Mr. T. Abbott	Mr. Osborne	5
THE GENERAL			10–4	T. Ablett	Mr. Land	6
CARRIG			10–5	D. Wynne	Mr. J. Bourke	7
KNIGHT OF GWYNNE			11–2	Donaldson	Mr. Drake	P.U.
BOURTON			11–2	S. Darling	Mr. Higginson	
TIPPERARY BOY			10–10	Butler	Mr. S. Lucy	
DUC AU BHURRAS			10–10	J. Ryan	Lord Waterford	
VICTIM			10–6	Tasker	Capt. Scott	P.U.
FIELD MARSHAL			10–4	Nelson	Mr. J. Roberts	
MAURICE DALEY			10–2	C. Boyce	Mr. Cartwright	
BETSY PRIG			10	Meaney	Capt. D. Lane	F.
POLL			9–10	Debean	Mr. Hudson	F.
VIEW HALLOO			9–10	W. Archer	Mr. Megson	
MALEY				E. Harrison	Mr. J. R. Henderson	
CHATTERBOX			9–8	Mr. McGaman	Mr. Bretherton	P.U.
CRABBS			9–2	W. Fowler	Mr. J. Henderson	P.U.
THE DWARF			9	H. Lamplugh	Mr. Morris	F.

NOTE: Mr. Mason declared to win with Oscar.

STARTING PRICES

5–1 Miss Mowbray   9–1 Peter Simple   100–6 View Halloo

6–1 Oscar, Duc au Bhurras   12–1 Sir Peter Laurie   20–1 Abd el Kader

7–1 Bourton   12–1 Victim   25–1 Others

     15–1 Carrig

1854

Going: GOOD   *Starters:* 20   *Time:* 9 MIN. 59 SEC.

Weather: DULL BUT CLEAR   *Date:*

Horse	Colour and Sex	Age	Weight	Jockey	Owner	Position at Finish
BOURTON *by Brayton* (*h.b.*)	b. g.	a.	11–12	Tasker	Mr. Moseley	1
SPRING	ch. g.	6	9–10	W. Archer	Mr. Barber	2
CRABBS	br. g.	a.	9–2	D. Wynne	Mr. J. Henderson	3
MALEY		a.	9–10	Thrift	Mr. Henderson	4
LADY ARTHUR		a.	9–10	T. Donaldson	Mr. Delamarre	5
HALF-AND-HALF		a.	10–8	Green	Mr. Bignell	6
BURNT SIENNA		a.	8–12	Burrows	Mr. Slater	7
PETER SIMPLE		a.	12	C. Boyce	Mr. Bignell	
OSCAR		a.	11–12	S. Darling	Mr. T. Mason	K.O.
PETER		a.	10–12	R. Sly, Jr.	Mr. Linnell	
BEDFORD (H. B.)		a.	10–4	Eatwell	Mr. Barling	B. L., DES.
LA GAZZA LADRA		a.	10	T. Abbott	Mr. J. Williams	REF.
MAURICE DALEY		a.	9–10	T. Olliver	Mr. Cartwright	
STAR OF ENGLAND		a.	9–10	W. White	Mr. Blood	
GERALDUS		a.	9–8	Debean	Mr. Barry	REF.
PRIDE OF THE NORTH		a.	9–8	R. James	Mr. Olliver	REF.
COCKCROW		6	9–8	Maher	Lord Waterford	
TIMOTHY		a.	9–6	H. Lamplugh	Mr. A. Sait	REF.
ROYALTY		5	9–4	Ennis	Capt. Rhys	
SHILLIBEER *by Faugh a Ballagh* (*h.b.*) (carried 9–4)		6	9	E. Southwell	Lord Sefton	

STARTING PRICES

4–1 Bourton
5–1 Maurice Daley
8–1 Half-and-Half

10–1 Crabbs
12–1 Peter Simple
15–1 Oscar
20–1 Spring, Peter

25–1 Cockcrow, Burnt Sienna
40–1 Timothy
50–1 Others

1855

Going: HEAVY *Starters:* 20 *Time:* 10 MIN. 25 SEC.
Weather: RAIN *Date:*

Horse	Colour and Sex	Age	Weight	Jockey	Owner	Position at Finish
WANDERER (H. B.) by *Verulam*	b. h.	a.	9–8	J. Hanlon	Mr. Dennis	1
FREETRADER	b. h.	6	9–4	Meaney	Mr. W. Barnett	2
MAURICE DALEY (H. B.)	b. g.	a.	9–6	R. James	Mr. Cartwright	3
JANUS		a.	9–10	Lamplugh	Mr. Elmore	4
DANGEROUS (H. B.)		a.	9	Fowler	Mr. Henderson	5
THE NUGGET		a.	10–4	W. White	Mr. C. Symonds	6
GARLAND		a.	10–2	Sly, Jr.	Mr. Minton	7
MISS MOWBRAY		a.	11–6	S. Darling	Mr. T. F. Mason	F., DES.
PETER		a.	11–4	Ablett	Mr. S. Mansell	
NEEDWOOD		a.	11–2	Fech	Mr. B. Land	
TROUT		a.	10–12	Tasker	Mr. Moseley	F.
HALF-AND-HALF		a.	10–4	Darby	Mr. Hutchinson	
BASTION		a.	10–4	T. Olliver	Mr. Roberts	
ESCAPE		a.	10–4	Knott	Mr. Buchanan	K.O.
BOUNDAWAY		6	10	J. Byrne	Mr. Magee	
CUTAWAY		a.	9–10	C. Boyce	Mr. A. Sait	
MALEY		a.	9–6	Fulman	Mr. Henderson	
PIMPERN		a.	9–6 (carried 9–8)	Weaver	Mr. H. Lewis	
LITTLE CHARLEY		a.	9–4	D. Wynne	Mr. C. Capel	K.O.
BURNT SIENNA		a.	9	T. Burrows	Mr. Jenkins	

STARTING PRICES

3–1 Trout
4–1 Miss Mowbray
6–1 Dangerous

12–1 Needwood
15–1 Bastion
20–1 Maurice Daley, Peter, Little Charley

25–1 Wanderer
33–1 Janus, Garland
50–1 Others

1856

Going: AVERAGE   *Starters:* 21   *Time:* 10 MIN. 9½ SEC.

Weather: CLEAR   *Date:*

Horse	Colour and Sex	Age	Weight	Jockey	Owner	Position at Finish
FREETRADER *by The Sea*	br. h.	a.	9–6	G. Stevens	Mr. W. Barnett	1
MINERVA (H. B.)	ch. m.	6	9–10	Sly, Jr.	Mr. Davenport	2
MINOS	ch. g.	a.	9–4	R. James	Mr. G. Hobson	3
HOPELESS STAR		a.	10–2 (incl. 6 lbs. extra)	W. White	Mr. Tyler	4
LITTLE CHARLEY		a.	9–4	T. Burrowes	Mr. C. Capel	5
EMIGRANT		a.	10–2	C. Boyce	Mr. G. Hodgman	6
SIR PETER LAURIE		a.	10–12	S. Darling	Mr. W. Barnett	B. & R. O.
JEAN DU QUESNE		a.	10–6	Lamplugh	Baron C. Lamotte	
FRANC PICARD		a.	10–12	Wakefield	Baron C. Lamotte	
THE PASHA		a.	10–4	D. Meaney	Mr. Hurley	
SEAMAN		a.	10–2 (carried 10–4)	F. Martin	Mr. A. McDonogh	
THE FOREST QUEEN		a.	10–2	J. Thrift	Mr. Harper	
JUMPAWAY (H. B.)		a.	9–10	J. Hanlon	Mr. Denison	
POTTER		a.	9–8	Kendall	Mr. Barber	
BRITISH YEOMAN		a.	9–4 (carried 9–7)	Mr. Goodman	Mr. T. F. Mason	B.D.
DAN O'CONNELL		a.	9–4	R. Archer	Mr. J. Tayleure	
BANSTEAD		6	9–4	Mr. W. Bevill	Mr. Dixon	F., DES.
VICTOR EMMANUEL		6	9–4	Seffert	Mr. Pickering	F.
STAMFORD		a.	(carried 9–2)	C. Green	Mr. Hodgman	
LIVERPOOL BOY		6	9	McLean	Mr. H. King	
HARRY LORREQUER		5	8–10	Fowler	Mr. J. Henderson	R.O.

STARTING PRICES

9–2 Jean du Quesne	15–1 Forest Queen	40–1 British Yeoman,
5–1 Harry Lorrequer	15–1 Stamford	Little Charley,
7–1 Seaman	100–6 Emigrant	The Pasha
10–1 The Potter	25–1 Freetrader, Minerva,	50–1 Banstead
12–1 Sir Peter Laurie	Hopeless Star,	Others not quoted
	Jumpaway	

1857

Going: VERY DEEP   Starters: 28   Time: 10 MIN. 6 SEC
Weather: RAIN   Date:

Horse	Colour and Sex	Age	Weight	Jockey	Owner	Position at Finish
EMIGRANT	b. g.	a.	9–10	C. Boyce	Mr. Hodgman	1
by Drayton						
WEATHERCOCK	b. g.	6	8–12	Green	Mr. B. Land	2
TREACHERY	b. m.	5	9	Poole	Mr. T. Hughes	3
WESTMINSTER			9–2	Palmer	Mr. T. Hughes	4
			(incl. 6 lbs. extra)			
DANGEROUS			9–8	F. Page	Mr. A. Rice	5
JEAN DU QUESNE			10	H. Lamplugh	Count de Cunchy	6
LADY ARTHUR			9–4	Weaver	Viscomte Lauriston	7
FOREST QUEEN			9–8	T. Donaldson	Mr. Harper	8
ESCAPE			11–2	Thrift	Mr. J. Merry	
MINOS			10–4	Mr. Goodman	Mr. Mellish	
CASSE CON			10–2	Johnson	Baron Monuecove	
STAR OF THE WEST			10	E. Jones	Mr. J. Colpitt	
HOPELESS STAR			10	D. Wynne	Mr. E. Parr	P.U.
FREETRADER			10	G. Stevens	Mr. Barnett	
LITTLE CHARLEY			10	T. Burrowes	Mr. Capel	
GARRY OWEN			9–12	J. Ryan	Col. Dickson	
SQUIRE OF BENSHAM			9–8	Mr. Coxon	Mr. W. P. Wrixon	
RED ROSE			9–8	J. Hughes	Mr. T. Hughes	
KING DAN			9–6	Escott	Mr. Jennings	
MIDGE			9–6	Mr. Black	Mr. J. Garnett	
ROMEO			9–6	D. White	Mr. T. Hughes	F.
ALBATROSS			9–6	Meaney	Mr. J. Dennis	D.
STING			9–6	Hanlon	Mr. J. Cassidy	
MAURICE DALEY			9–2	James	Mr. Laurence	
OMAR PASHA			9–2	J. Kendall	Mr. W. Williams	
TEDDESLEY			9	R. Ascher	Mr. Hylton	
FIRST OF MAY			9	R. Sly	Mr. Raxworthy	
HORNIBLOW			9–10	Dart	Mr. T. Day	

STARTING PRICES

100–15 Minos	100–7 Jean du Quesne	25–1 Weathercock
7–1 Escape	100–6 Omar Pasha, Romeo	30–1 Garry Owen
9–1 Hopeless Star	100–7 Little Charley	40–1 Maurice Daley
10–1 Emigrant	20–1 Forest Queen	50–1 Dangerous, Sting
12–1 Teddesley	25–1 Freetrader	Others not quoted

1858

Going: VERY DEEP AND BAD   *Starters:* 16   *Time:* 11 MIN. 5 SEC.
Weather: SNOW AND HIGH WIND   *Date:* MARCH 6

Horse	Colour and Sex	Age	Weight	Jockey	Owner	Position at Finish
LITTLE CHARLEY *by Charles XII*	b. g.	a.	10–7	W. Archer	Mr. Capel	1
WEATHERCOCK	b. g.	a.	11–7	Mr. Edwards	Viscount Talon	2
XANTHUS	g.	a.	11	Balchin	Mr. Craven	3
MORGAN RATTLER			10–4	T. Burrowes	Sir E. Hutchinson	4
CONRAD			8–4	E. Jones	Mr. Tempest	5 (R.)
ESCAPE			10–10 (carried 11)	T. Olliver	Mr. J. Merry	K.O.
CLAUDIUS			10–7	Poole	Mr. J. C. Manby	F.
ABD EL KADER			10–5	C. Green	Mr. Briscoe	F.
JOE GRAHAM			9–12 (carried 10–4)	Rutherford	Mr. Heron Maxwell	F.
TREACHERY			9–8	W. White	Mr. T. Hughes	P.U.
LOUGH BAWN			9–8	G. Stevens	Mr. Buchanan	REF.
BLACK BESS			9–6	D. Wynne	Mr. T. Bay	F.
LITTLE TOM			9–6	B. Land, Jr.	Capt. Connell	F.
HARRY LORREQUER			9	W. Fowler	Mr. J. Henderson	K.O.
GLENAMOUR (H. B.)			9	Knott	Mr. Heron Maxwell	F.
MOIRE ANTIQUE			9	F. Page	Mr. J. Henderson	F.

STARTING PRICES

4–1 Treachery
9–2 Lough Bawn
5–1 Little Tom
12–1 Harry Lorrequer

25–1 Weathercock, Abd el
    Kader, Moire Antique
14–1 Conrad

100–6 Little Charley,
    Morgan Rattler
20–1 Escape, Black Bess
33–1 Joe Graham, Xan-
    thus

1859

Going: GOOD   Starters: 20   Time: 10 MIN. 2 SEC.

Weather: CLEAR   Date:

Horse	Colour and Sex	Age	Weight	Jockey	Owner	Position at Finish
HALF CASTE *by Morgan Rattler*	br. h.	6	9–7	C. Green	Mr. Willoughby	1
JEAN DU QUESNE	b. h.	a.	9–9	H. Lamplugh	Viscount F. de Cunchy	2
THE HUNTSMAN	b. h.	6	11–2	B. Land, Jr.	Mr. Land	3
MIDGE			9–4	D. Meaney	Mr. Garnett	4
ANATIS			9–4	Mr. Thomas	Mr. Capel	5
ORKONSTA			9	G. Stevens	Viscount A. Talon	6
GHIKA			9–10 (carried 9–2)	C. Boyce	Mr. Moreton	7
ESCAPE			10–5	T. Donaldson	Mr. Merry	8
WEATHERCOCK			10–13	Enoch	Viscount A. Talon	B.D.
LITTLE CHARLEY			10–11	T. Burrowes	Mr. W. Barnett	
XANTHUS			10–7	F. Balchin	Mr. Craven	F.
CLAUDIUS			10	T. Olliver	Mr. J. L. Manby	
ACE OF HEARTS			9–12	J. Ryan	Lord Waterford	F.
THE BREWER			9–10	W. White	Mr. T. Hughes	F.
BORDER CHIEF			9–10	Watling	Mr. H. E. Johnstone	
JEALOUSY			9–8	Kendall	Mr. Bayley	
GIPSY KING (H. B.)			9	Edmunds	Mr. Slaney	P.U.
GIBRALTAR			9	Armstrong	Mr. Hope	
FLATCATCHER (H. B.)			8–12 (carried 9)	T. Holmes	Mr. Barling	K.O.
SPRING			8–7	Nightingall	Mr. Barber	F.

STARTING PRICES

100–30 The Brewer	100–8 The Huntsman	33–1 Weathercock, Midge
7–1 Half Caste	14–1 Little Charley	Orkonsta
10–1 Jean du Quesne	20–1 Escape, Ghika	40–1 Spring
10–1 Jealousy	25–1 Ace of Hearts, Anatis	

1860

Going: AVERAGE				*Starters:* 19	*Time:* NOT TAKEN	
Weather: VERY COLD AND WINDY				*Date:*		

Horse	Colour and Sex	Age	Weight	Jockey	Owner	Position at Finish
ANATIS	b. m.	a.	9–10	Mr. Thomas	Mr. C. Capel	1
by King Dan—						
The Switcher's dam						
THE HUNTSMAN	b. h.	a.	11–8	Capt. Townley	Capt. Hunt	2
XANTHUS	ch. g.	a.	10	F. Balchin	Mr. W. G. Craven	3
MARIA AGNES		6	9–8	G. Stevens	Mr. Golby	4
IRISH BOY		a.	8–12	Owner	Mr. W. Bevill	5
BRIDEGROOM (H. B.)		a.	10–6	Mr. Ekard	Sir George Wombwell	6
BRUNETTE		a.	12	Kendall	Mr. Barrett	7
REDWING		a.	10–8	Rourke	Mr. Aylmer	
HORNIBLOW		a.	10–10	Enoch	Mr. H. Blundell	
GOLDSMITH		a.	10–10	Ben Land, Jr.	Capt. Hunt	
TEASE		a.	10–2	W. White	Mr. Francis	B.D.
SIR ROBERT		a.	10–2	C. Boyce	Mr. J. Courtenay	P.U.
KILCOCK		6	10	D. Meaney	Mr. Aylmer	
TELEGRAM		a.	9–9	Palmer	Mr. Worthington	
MISS HARKAWAY		a.	9–8	Mr. F. Lotan	Mr. Barber	REF.
THE CURATE (H. B.)		a.	9–4	G. Eatwell	Mr. Burling	F.
SHYLOCK		a.	9–2 (carried 9–5)	T. Clay	Maj. Owen	
LEFROY		a.	9	C. Green	Capt. White	
CONGREVE		a.	9	Gammeridge	Capt. Clifton	REF.

STARTING PRICES

7–2 Anatis	12–1 Irish Boy	25–1 Shylock
7–1 Tease	100–7 Telegram	33–1 The Huntsman, Sir Robert
10–1 Maria Agnes, Xanthus	100–6 Brunette, Goldsmith	

1861

	Colour and					Position at
Horse	Sex	Age	Weight	Jockey	Owner	Finish
JEALOUSY	br. m.	a.	9–12	Kendall	Mr. J. Bennett	1
by The Cure						
THE DANE	b. h.	5	10	W. White	Capt. Christie	2
OLD BEN ROE	b. g.	a.	10–7	G. Waddington	Mr. W. Briscoe	3
BRIDEGROOM	b. g.	a.	10–7	Mr. FitzAdam	Mr. B. J. Angell	4
XANTHUS			9–8	C. Boyce	Mr. W. G. Craven	5
BRUNETTE			11	Owner	Mr. F. Rowland	
KIBWORTH LASS			11–3	Oliver, Jr.	Mr. Manby	REF.
			(incl. 6 lbs. extra)			
ANATIS			10–4	Mr. Thomas	Mr. Capel	F.
DIAMANT			10–4	Enoch	Mr. Manby	REF.
BROTHER TO						
LADY'S MAID			10–3	Harris	Mr. J. Stokes	
THE EMPEROR			10–2	Mr. Goodman	Mr. D. Briggs	
FRANC PICARD			10	Mr. Lamplugh	Baron de la Motte	
MASTER BAGOT			10	Mr. Edwards	Capt. Little	F.
WEE NELL (H.B.,N.S.)	b. m.		9–11	Knott	Mr. Mackey	
LONGRANGE			9–10	R. Sherrard	Mr. C. Watts	
KILCOCK			9–10	D. Meaney	Mr. Bowbiggins	
REDWING			9–7	Murphy	Mr. E. J. Gannon	F.
THE FRESHMAN			9–7	Mr. Blake	Mr. C. Symonds	F.
THE IRISH EMIGRANT			9	R. Sly	Mr. W. Owens	F.
THE UNKNOWN			8–12	G. Eatwell	Mr. Spencer Lucy	
			(carried 9)			
THE CONDUCTOR			8–12	Nightingall	Mr. G. Hodgman	R.,F.,DES.
DR. LEETE			8–8	W. Mason	Marquess of Hartington	
COCKATOO			8–8	C. Green	Mr. S. Gooderham	F.
THE ROVER			8–8	F. Page	Mr. J. S. Wilson	

Going: AVERAGE *Starters:* 24 *Time:* 10 MIN. 14 SEC·
Weather: CLOUDY *Date:*

STARTING PRICES

4–1 Anatis
5–1 Jealousy
7–1 Cockatoo
8–1 Master Bagot

10–1 Old Ben Roe
100–8 The Emperor
14–1 Franc Picard
100–7 The Freshman

25–1 Redwing, The Bridegroom
33–1 Brunette, The Dane
40–1 Kilcock, The Conductor
50–1 Xanthus

1862

Going: AVERAGE Starters: 13 Time: 9 MIN. 30 SEC.
Weather: CLEAR Date:

Horse	Colour and Sex	Age	Weight	Jockey	Owner	Position at Finish
HUNTSMAN by Tupsley	b. h.	a.	11	H. Lamplugh	Viscount de Namur	1
BRIDEGROOM	b. h.	a.	10–13	B. Land, Jr.	Mr. Angell	2
ROMEO	b. g.	a.	8–12	Owner	Mr. C. Bennett	3
XANTHUS (N. S.)	ch. g.	a.	9–6	R. Sherrard	Lord Sefton	4
BUCEPHALUS	b. h.		10–9	McGrillon	Mr. R. Rowan	5
ANATIS	b. m.	a.	10–12	Mr. Thomas	Sir E. Hutchinson	P.U.
PLAYMAN			10–8 (incl. 10 lbs. extra)	Nightingall	Mr. A. Yates	F.
THOMASTOWN	b. h.		10–4	J. Murphy	Mr. T. Naghten	REF.
WILLOUGHBY (H. B.)			10	Owner	Mr. H. Lington	P.U.
O'CONNELL			9–8	J. Wynne	Lord de Freyne	F.
THE TATTLER			9–7 (carried 9–8)	C. Boyce	Mr. W. G. Craven	P.U.
HARRY			9–5	G. Stevens	Mr. W. W. Baker	F.
THE POET			8–12	Gatt	Mr. J. Henry	F.

STARTING PRICES

3–1 The Huntsman	10–1 Bridegroom	20–1 Willoughby
6–1 Thomastown	10–1 Harry	25–1 Xanthus, Playman
9–1 Anatis	100–8 Romeo, The Tattler	33–1 O'Connell
	100–7 Bucephalus	

1863

T H E conditions were unchanged, but the course was lengthened by about a quarter of a mile. The fences were very low for the most part. Becher's and Valentine's were stiffened by the addition of a post-and-rail, which was put up in front of each of them; only two other fences, The Open Ditch, and the Water Jump, were at all difficult.

Going: VERY GOOD *Starters:* 16 *Time:* 11 MIN. 20 SEC.

Weather: CLEAR *Date:*

Horse	Colour and Sex	Age	Weight	Jockey	Owner	Position at Finish
EMBLEM *by Teddington*	ch. m. a.		10–10 (incl. 10 lbs. extra)	G. Stevens	Lord Coventry	1
ARBURY	a.		11–2	Mr. Goodman	Mr. J. Astley	2
YALLER GAL	ch. m. a.		10–13	Mr. Dixon	Mr. Briscoe	3
FOSCO (N. S.)	gr. g. a.		9–11	Owner	Mr. G. Holman	4
AVALANCHE	b. m.	6	10–9	Palmer	Baron de Mesnil	5
JEALOUSY	b. m. a.		11–10	Kendall	Mr. Priestley	6
MEDORA		12		Owner	Mr. F. Rowland	P.U.
FRESHMAN			11–13	Mr. Edwards	Mr. W. Maney	F.
THE DANE			11–6	W. White	Capt. Christie	P.U.
MASTER BAGOT			10–4	Knott	Mr. W. G. Craven	
LIGHT OF OTHER DAYS			10–4	Nightingall	Mr. W. W. Baker	
INKERMAN			9–11	Mr. Smith	Mr. W. E. Dakin	F.
THE ORPHAN			9–11	Mr. W. Bevill	Mr. J. C. Tilbury	F.
TELEGRAPH (N. S.)			9–11	G. Waddington	Mr. Campbell	F., DES.
BIRDBOLT			9–11	Owner	Mr. Spence	P.U.
REAL JAM			9–11	D. Hughes	Mr. T. Hughes	

STARTING PRICES

3–1 Jealousy 100–8 Master Bagot 25–1 Arbury
4–1 Emblem 20–1 The Light of Other 33–1 Avalanche
100–12 Medora Days, Real Jam, 40–1 Fosco
10–1 The Dane Yaller Gal

1864

Going: VERY GOOD   *Starters:* 25   *Time:* 11 MIN. 50 SEC.

Weather: BRIGHT AND CLEAR   *Date:*

Horse	Colour and Sex	Age	Weight	Jockey	Owner	Position at Finish
EMBLEMATIC	ch. m.	6	10–6	G. Stevens	Lord Coventry	1
ARBURY		a.	11–12	B. Land	Mr. J. Astley	2
CHESTER	b. g.	a.	10	W. White	Mr. Dalton	3
THOMASTOWN (H. B.)	b. h.	a.	12	J. Murphy	Mr. T. M. Naghten	4
OCEAN WITCH		5	10–2	W. Reeves	Capt. Lamb	5
REPORTER	b. h.		12–2	Mr. Dixon	Mr. Fiddaman	F.
SIR WILLIAM (H. B.)			11–10	Mr. Davison	Mr. T. Iven	
JERUSALEM			11–10	Mr. Edwards	Mr. W. Murray	P.U.
HARRY			11–10	Cassidy	Count Cossett	F.
BANTAM			11–8	G. Holman	Mr. Aspinall	P.U.
WEE NELL			11–6	Knott	Mr. T. Hunt	P.U.
LEONIDAS			11–4	C. Boyce	Capt. Machell	P.U.
			(incl. 6 lbs. extra)			
SERIOUS CASE			11–3	G. Waddington	Mr. T. S. Dawson	F.
ROMEO			11	F. Martin	Mr. De Gray	F.
LITTLE BAB			11	Pat Igon	Mr. W. Murray	
PORTLAND			10–12	Mr. Goodman	Mr. H. Matthews	F.
SATANELLA			10–12	D. Meaney	Marquess of Drogheda	F.
BELL'S LIFE			10–12	Griffiths	Maj. Wombwell	F.
			(incl. 6 lbs. extra)			
IRELEY			10–10	Mr. Blake	Mr. B. J. Angell	K.O.
NATIONAL PETITION			10–8	J. Monaghan	Mr. J. Lanigan	
REAL JAM			10–8	D. Hughes	Mr. T. Hughes	
BRIAN BORHOIME			10–4	Poinons	Mr. Lawrence	P.U.
MARTHA			10	J. Land	Mr. T. Wade	F.
MISS MARIA			10	J. Holman	Mr. H. Melville	
SILK AND SATIN			10	Jarvis	Mr. Spark	
			(carried 10–2)			

STARTING PRICES

9–2 Jerusalem	12–1 Portland, Wee Nell
5–1 Bantam	20–1 Ocean Witch
10–1 Emblematic	30–1 Bell's Life
11–1 Real Jam, Serious Case	33–1 Thomastown, Martha, Romeo

40–1 Arbury, Ireley, Chester, Reporter

50–1 Harry

1865

Going: SNOW ON COURSE   *Starters:* 23   *Time:* 11 MIN. 16 SEC.

Weather: CLEAR   *Date:*

Horse	Colour and Sex	Age	Weight	Jockey	Owner	Position at Finish
ALCIBIADE by The Cossack		5	11–4	Capt. Coventry	Mr. B. J. Angell	1
HALL COURT		6	11	Capt. Tempest	Capt. Brown	2
EMBLEMATIC		a.	11–10	G. Stevens	Lord Coventry	3
MISTAKE		5	10–8	Jarvis	Mr. F. Jacobs	4
MERRIMAC		a.	11–4	B. Land	Capt. Tempest	5
FLYFISHER		6	11–12	Mr. J. R. Riddell	Mr. Powell	6
EMBLEM		a.	12–4	W. Walters	Lord Coventry	P.U.
JOE MALEY		a.	11–10	D. Page	Mr. Hidson	P.U.
ACROBAT		a.	11–9	W. Mumford	Capt. Machell	REF.
MEANWOOD		6	11–9	Knott	Mr. Harvey	P.U.
ARBURY		a.	11–8	C. Boyce	Count A. de Dampoerre	F.
EXPRESS		a.	11–6	Owner	Mr. D. Collins	P.U.
LIGHTHEART		a.	10–12	J. Monaghan	Mr. A. W. Clayton	P.U.
PRINCESS DAGMAR		a.	10–12	G. Holman	Mr. H. Melville	P.U.
PHILOSOPHER		6	10–8	E. Jones	Mr. Turner	P.U.
STANTON		a.	10–8	G. Waddington	Mr. Harvey	P.U.
TUMBLER		a.	10–6	Mr. Drake	Capt. J. White	REF.
TONY LUMPKIN		a.	10–4	Mr. Thomas	Col. Forster	P.U.
BALLYCASEY		a.	11	T. Barton	Mr. J. A. Read	F.
FRESHMAN		a.	10–10	D. Meaney	Mr. W. H. Whyte	P.U.
THE CZAR		a.	10	Mr. Goodman	Mr. Goodliffe	F.
MARKET GARDENER		a.	10	Mr. T. Spence	Lord Sefton	REF.
THE DWARF		a.	10	Igoe	Mr. Studd	P.U.

NOTE: Lord Coventry declared to win with Emblematic.

STARTING PRICES

5–1 Emblematic
100–12 Joe Maley
9–1 Stanton
100–8 Princess Dagmar, Emblem, Arbury

100–7 Tony Lumpkin, Alcibiade
20–1 Lightheart, The Czar
25–1 The Dwarf

33–1 Merrimac
40–1 Freshman
50–1 Hall Court, Meanwood, Acrobat

1866

Going: VERY DEEP   Starters: 30   Time: 11 MIN. 5 SEC.
Weather: SNOW   Date:

Horse	Age	Weight	Jockey	Owner	Position at Finish
SALAMANDER by Fire-eater	a.	10–7	Mr. A. Goodman	Mr. Studd	1
CORTOLVIN	a.	11–6	J. Page	Lord Poulett	2
CREOLE	a.	10–10	G. Waddington	Mr. Welfitt	3
LIGHTHEART	a.	11–5	E. Jones	Mr. A. W. Clayton	4
MERRIMAC	a.	10–7	Capt. Tempest	Capt. Shaw	5
THE DOCTOR	5	10	G. Stevens	Mr. Mytton	
FRANK (N. S.)	a.	11–8	Mr. Lawrence	Mr. Cockburn	
L'AFRICAINE	a.	13–2	G. Holman	Mr. W. R. H. Powell	P.U.
EFFENBURG	a.	12–8	R. Twiddy	Count Furstenberg	
ALCIBIADE	6	12–2	B. Land, Jr.	Mr. B. J. Angell	F.
HALL COURT	a.	11–12	W. Reeves	Capt. Browne	F.
REPORTER	a.	11–4	R. French	Lord Poulett	
GLENCAVIN	a.	11–4	J. Jewitt	Mr. J. Stevenson	
THOMASTOWN	a.	11–4	Murphy	Mr. T. N. Naghten	F.
LAURA	5	11	H. Lamplugh	M. E. Bourgnet	F.
IBEX	6	10–12	C. Boyce	Mr. Brayley	F.
STANTON	a.	10–12	Welsh	Mr. J. Coupland	F.
G. by Turner	6	10–10	Reeves	Mr. T. Parr	
MISTAKE	6	10–9	Knott	Baron von Grootven	
SIR WILLIAM	a.	10–7	Ellison	Mr. T. Jones	REF., P.U.
STELLA	a.	10–7	Jarvis	Mr. Spark	F.
PHILOSOPHER	6	10–7	Wheeler	Mr. W. Murray	F.
GAROTTER	5	10–7	G. Ryan	Mr. Oliver	F.
ACE OF HEARTS	6	10–2	Mr. Edwards	Lord Poulett	F.
KING OF HEARTS	a.	10–2	A. Sadler	Mr. W. Robinson	F.
MILLTOWN	5	10–2 (carried 10–4)	Mr. Thomas	Mr. W. McGrane	
REAL JAM	a.	10	D. Hughes	Mr. F. Hughes	
CUTLER	a.	10	Thorpe	Mr. Barber	
WEST END	a.	10–5	W. White	Col. Forester	
COLUMBIA		10–10	W. Reeves	Mr. Reginald Herbert	

STARTING PRICES

7–1 Laura	100–7 L'Africaine	30–1 Hall Court, King of Hearts
8–1 Cortolvin	15–1 Creole	
9–1 Alcibiade	20–1 The Doctor	40–1 Salamander
12–1 Real Jam	25–1 Ibex, Mistake, Merrimac	1000–15 Columbia
		50–1 Others

1867

Going: GOOD   *Starters:* 23   *Time:* 10 MIN. 42 SEC.

Weather: CLEAR   *Date:* MARCH

Horse	Colour and Sex	Age	Weight	Jockey	Owner	Position at Finish
CORTOLVIN *by Chicken or Cheerful Horn*	br. g.	a.	11–13	J. Page	Duke of Hamilton	1
FAN	b. m.	5	10–3	Thorpe	Mr. Barber	2
SHANGARRY (H. B.)	br. h.	a.	10–13	Mr. Thomas	Mr. Studd	3
GLOBULE	b. g.	a.	11–7	G. Holman	Mr. T. V. Morgan	4
LIGHTHEART			11–1	E. Jones	Mr. A. W. Clayton	5
REVOLVER			11–1	Igoe	Mr. T. Jackson	6
SHAKSPERE			11–1	Mr. Goodman	Mr. Carew	7
TENNYSON (H. B.)			10–10	G. Stevens	Lord Coventry	8
SILVER STAR			10–9	G. Waddington	Mr. S. J. Welfitt	9
GENIEVRE			10–3	Mr. Edwards (carried 10–5)	Lord Poulett	10
ASTROLABE			12–7	Cassidy	Baron Finot	K. O.
HALL COURT			12–3	Owner	Capt. Brown	F.
BANKER			11–10	T. Abbott	Mr. J. Dally	
THOMASTOWN			11–3	Murphy	Mr. J. Doyle	P. U.
MILLER			11–1	Mr. Lawrence (carried 11-4)	Mr. W. Smith	
MARENGO			11–1	Owner	Mr. C. Fermin	K. O.
LITTLE FRANK			10–13	Knott	Mr. Vallender	K. O.
WHITEHALL			10–13	Mr. Milward	Mr. P. Herbert	K. O.
PLINLIMMON			10–13	J. Holman	Capt. Parkinson	
SEA KING			10–11	G. Barry	Mr. E. Brayley	
KING ARTHUR			10–3	Capt. Harford	Capt. Brabazon	P. U.
HAVELOCK (late CLAXTON)			10–3	Jarvis	Mr. J. Wood	F.
LITTLE WIDEAWAKE			10–3	J. Rickaby	Mr. Schwartz	K. O.

STARTING PRICES

5–1 King Arthur	100–7 Shangarry	25–1 Silver Star, Thomastown, Little Frank
7–1 Shakspere	100–6 Cortolvin	30–1 Little Wideawake
8–1 Fan	20–1 Astrolabe	40–1 Whitehall, Lightheart
12–1 Sea King	20–1 Genievre	50–1 Hall Court, Tennyson
100–8 Globule		

1868

Going: HEAVY   *Starters:* 21   *Time:* NOT TAKEN
Weather: CLEAR BUT WINDY   *Date:* MARCH 4

Horse	Colour and Sex	Age	Weight	Jockey	Owner	Position at Finish
THE LAMB by Zouave	gr. h.	6	10–7	Mr. Edwards	Lord Poulett	1
PEARL DIVER	b. g.	a.	10–12	Tomlinson	Mr. E. Brayley	2
ALCIBIADE	ch. h.	a.	11–10	Col. Knox	Mr. B. J. Angell	3
CAPTAIN CROSSTREE	b. g.	a.	10–5	W. Reeves	Mr. R. Herbert	4
ASTROLABE	ch. m.	a.	12	A. French	Mr. E. Bournet	5
HELEN	b. m.	a.	10 (carried 10–1)	Mr. Goodman	Mr. Barber	6
HALL COURT			11–4	B. Land	Capt. J. M. Browne	7
BUSZKE			12	Count Szapary	Count Carolyi	P. U.
CHIMNEY SWEEP			12	J. Adams	Lord Coventry	B.L.,DES·
DAISY			11–7	Mr. Thomas	Mr. W. R. H. Powell	P. U.
THE NUN			11–6 (incl. 10 lbs. extra)	Wheeler	Mr. E. Green	F.
GARUS			10–12	J. Page	Duke of Hamilton	
KINGSWOOD			10–12	Gilroy	Mr. W. Forbes	F.
HUNTSMAN'S DAUGHTER		a.	10–12	G. Holman	Mr. T. V. Morgan	P. U.
THE PLOVER			10–10	The Owner	Mr. R. Walker	
MOOSE			10–7	W. White	Mr. E. Brayley	P. U.
FAN			10–6	Thorpe	Mr. Barber	REF.
MENTMORE			10–4 (carried 10–6)	Hyland	Mr. W. Forbes	F.
CHARMING WOMAN			10	Terratta, Jr.	Mr. J. Willing	
SLIEVE CARNE			10	Mr. Pritchard	Mr. G. H. Moore	REF.
THALASSIUS			10	Mr. Crawshaw	Lord Stamford	F.

NOTE: Mr. Brayley declared to win with Moose, and Mr. Barber with Helen.

STARTING PRICES

7–1 Chimney Sweep
8–1 Moose
9–1 Pearl Diver
10–1 The Lamb, Fan, Helen

11–1 Daisy
100–6 The Nun, Huntsman's Daughter, Alcibiade
25–1 Astrolabe

33–1 Garus, Capt. Crosstree
40–1 Thalassius, Buszke
50–1 Slieve Carne, Hall Court

1869

Going: AVERAGE *Starters:* 22 *Time:* 11 MIN.
Weather: CLEAR *Date:* MARCH 3

Horse	Colour and Sex	Age	Weight	Jockey	Owner	Position at Finish
THE COLONEL *by Knight of Kars— Boadicea (h.b.)*	br. h.	6	10–7	G. Stevens	Mr. Weyman	1
HALL COURT	b. g.	a.	10–12	Capt. Tempest	Capt. Brown	2
GARDENER	br. g.	a.	10–7	Ryan	Capt. Machell	3
ALCIBIADE	ch. h.	a.	11–2	Col. Knox	Mr. B. J. Angell	4
Q. C.			10–9	Griffiths	Mr. Lynton	5
DESPATCH (H. B.)			10–8	Mr. Edwards	Mr. Studd	6
GLOBULE			10–12	G. Holman	Mr. T. V. Morgan	7
THE ROBBER			11–2	Mr. P. Merton	Mr. Doncaster	8
HARCOURT			10–10	Capt. Harford	Mr. Eaton	9
PEARL DIVER			12–7	W. Reeves	Mr. E. Brayley	F.
THE NUN (H. B.)			11–9	Mr. Thomas	Mr. E. Green	F.
FORTUNATUS			11–4	J. Page	Mr. E. Brayley	P. U.
ORME			11–2	W. White	Mr. T. Wadlow	K. O.
HAVELOCK			11	Wheeler	Mr. J. Wood	F.
BARBARIAN			10–10	G. Waddington	Mr. S. J. Welfitt	P. U.
(incl. 10 lbs. extra)						
HUNTSMAN'S DAUGHTER			10–8	J. Holman	Mr. T. V. Morgan	P. U.
FAN			10–6	Thorpe	Mr. J. Barber	REF.
KNAVE OF TRUMPS			10–6	Mr. Martin	Mr. T. Golby	F.
BISHOPSTON			10–4	Potter	Mr. F. G. Hobson	K. O.
GUY OF WARWICK			10	Mr. Crawshaw	Mr. Dixon	REF.
PLUM CAKE			10	Mr. Spofford	Mr. Yates	F.
DICK TURPIN			10	J. Knott	Mr. Foulkes	F.

NOTE: Mr. Brayley declared to win with Fortunatus, and Mr. Morgan with Globule.

STARTING PRICES

100–30 Fortunatus	20–1 Alcibiade, Knave of Trumps, Q.C.	40–1 Harcourt, Dick Turpin, Huntsman's Daughter
5–1 Despatch	25–1 The Nun, Globule	50–1 Orme
11–2 Fan	33–1 Havelock	66–1 Hall Court, Gardener
13–1 The Colonel		100–1 Plum Cake The Robber
14–1 Pearl Diver		

1870

Going: VERY GOOD   *Starters:* 23   *Time:* 10 MIN. 10 SEC.
Weather: CLEAR   *Date:* MARCH 9

Horse	Colour and Sex	Age	Weight	Jockey	Owner	Position at Finish
THE COLONEL *by Knight of Kars— Boadicea (h.b.)*	br. h.	a.	11–12	G. Stevens	Mr. M. Evans	1
THE DOCTOR *by The Cure— Margaret of Anjou*	br. g.	a.	11–7	G. Holman	Mr. V. St. John	2
PRIMROSE *by Bonny Fido— Rosebud*	ch. m.	6	10–12	Owner	Mr. W. R. Brockton	3
SURVEY	b. g.	a.	10–4	R. I'Anson	Mr. J. Nightingall	4
KEYSTONE (H. B.)			10–12	Mr. R. Walker	Mr. G. Nelson	5
GARDENER			10–12	Ryan	Capt. Machell	6
Q. C.			10–10	Mr. A. Yates	Mr. May	7
ALCIBIADE			10–12	Capt. Harford	Mr. B. J. Angell	8
PEARL DIVER			12–7	J. Page	Mr. E. Brayley	
MOOSE			11–7	A. French	Mr. E. Brayley	
HALL COURT			10–12	Mr. Thomas	Capt. J. M. Browne	
TATHWELL			10–12	G. Waddington	Mr. S. J. Welfitt	
SCARRINGTON (H. B.)			10–12	R. Wheeler	Mr. T. Wilkinson	
MIDDLETON			10–12	Mr. T. Kirk	Mr. Yardley	
PRETENTAINE II			10–8	Mumford	Mr. R. Hennessy	
GUY OF WARWICK			10–8	Mr. Edward	Mr. E. Weever	
THE ELK			10–7	B. Land	Mr. Rose	P. U.
CENNA			10–7	Count	Baron Finot	
CRISTAL			10–6	Mr. Crawshaw	Duke of Hamilton	P. U.
TRAVELLER			10–4	Napier	Lord Eglinton	F.
CASSE TETE			10	J. Rudd	Mr. Brayley	
FAN			10	H. Taylor	Mr. Lawrence	REF.
KARSLAKE (H. B.)			10	Owner	Capt. Tempest	

NOTE: Seventeen horses finished. Mr. Brayley declared to win with Pearl Diver.

STARTING PRICES

4–1 The Colonel	100–6 Pearl Diver, Guy of Warwick	40–1 Hall Court
5–1 The Doctor		50–1 Karslake
10–1 Primrose	20–1 Survey, Tathwell, Cristal, Gardener	66–1 Fan, The Elk
100–7 Q.C.	33–1 Alcibiade, Cenna	1000–5 Keystone, Middleton Scarrington

1871

Going: PERFECT
Weather: SUNNY

Starters: 25
Date: MARCH 21

Time: 9 MIN. 35¾ SEC.

Horse	Colour and Sex	Age	Weight	Jockey	Owner	Position at Finish
THE LAMB *by Zouave—dam by Arthur (h.b.)*	g. h.	a.	11–4	Mr. Thomas	Lord Poulett	1
DESPATCH (H. B.)		a.	10	G. Waddington	Mr. Studd	2
SCARRINGTON (H. B.)		a.	11–4	Cranshaw	Mr. J. Wilkinson	3
THE COLONEL (H. B.)		a.	12–8	G. Stevens	Baron C. Oppenheim	4
PEARL DIVER		a.	11–5	J. Page	Mr. E. Brayley	5
TUSCULANUM		a.	11	Capt. Smith	Capt. W. H. Cooper	6
RUFUS		a.	11–4	Ryan	Mr. J. F. Montgomery	7
SOUVENANCE		6	11–2	Rickaby	Duke of Hamilton	8
THE DOCTOR		a.	11–13	Mr. Crawshaw	Duke of Hamilton	P. U.
SNOWSTORM		a.	11–7	Mr. R. Walker	Mr. J. N. Leighton	
PHILOSOPHER		a.	10–12	H. Ellison	Mr. Gardener	F.
WILD FOX		6	10–12	Murphy	Capt. Ainstie	
LORD RAGLAN		a.	10–10	Daniels	Mr. O. Perry	B.L.,DES.
PURLBROOK		6	10–10	Marsh	Mr. W. Bingham	
MAGNUM BONUM		a.	10–10	Mr. J.M.Richardson	Capt. Machell	
SCALTHEEN		6	10–10	G. Grey	Lord Eglinton	
CASSE TETE		6	10–10	J. Rudd	Mr. E. Brayley	
LADY GERALDINE		5	10–6	Cunningham	Capt. Haworth	
CECIL		6	10–6	R. I'Anson	Mr. Etcher	K. O.
SCOTS GREY		a.	10–5	Welsh	Maj. Browne	
ST. VALENTINE		6	10–4	J. Adams	Lord Anglesey	F.
BOGUE HOMA		6	10–4	Tomlinson	Lord Anglesey	
ALCIBIADE		a.	10–4	Walters	Mr. B. J. Angell	
INON		5	10–4	Capt. Harford	Capt. Pigott	
DOG FOX		a.	10	J. Potter	Mr. Mannington	

NOTE: Lord Anglesey declared to win with St. Valentine, and Mr. Brayley with Pear
Diver.

STARTING PRICES

4–1 Pearl Diver
5–1 The Lamb
8–1 The Colonel
10–1 The Doctor, Despatch, Cecil

25–1 Souvenance, Purlbrook, Dog Fox
40–1 Snowstorm, St. Valentine
50–1 Tusculanum, Magnum Bonum, Bogue Homa

60–1 Scarrington, Lord Raglan, Lady Geraldine, Casse Tete, Inon
100–1 Philosopher, Alcibiade

1872

Going: VERY HARD   Starters: 25   Time: 10 MIN. 14½ SEC.

Weather: CLEAR   Date: MARCH 21

Horse	Colour and Sex	Age	Weight	Jockey	Owner	Position at Finish
CASSE TETE *by Trumpeter— Constance, by Spirus*	ch. m.	a.	10	J. Page	Mr. E. Brayley	1
SCARRINGTON (H.B.) *by Martext*	br. g.	a.	11–2	R. I'Anson	Mr. T. Wilkinson	2
DESPATCH (H. B.) *by Dough*	br. g.	a.	10–4	G. Waddington	Mr. E. Studd	3
THE LAMB (H. B.)	gr. h.	a.	12–7	Mr. Thomas	Baron Oppenheim	4
FLEURISTE			10–10	Rickaby	Duke of Hamilton	5
MASTER MOWBRAY			10–12	G. Holman	Mr. J. Goodliffe	6
OURAGAN II			10	A. Holman	Mr. P. Merton	7
SCOTS GREY			10–11 (incl. 7 lbs. extra)	Mr. G. Moore	Maj. Browne	8
SCALTHEEN			10–4	J. Murphy	Lord Eglinton	9
HARVESTER			12	Owner	Mr. A. Yates	P. U.
MARIN			11–10	Cassidy	Baron Finot	F.
PRIMROSE			11–9	Owner	Mr. W. R. Brockton	B.B., DES
SNOWSTORM			11–9 (incl. 7 lbs. extra)	Thorpe	Mr. Chaplin	
SCHIEDAM			11–4	Mr. J. M. Richardson	Lord Eglinton	
RUFUS			11–4	Patter	Capt. Montgomery	
NUAGE			11–2	Harding	Mr. Doncaster	F.
RHYSWORTH			10–12	Boxall	Mr. Chaplin	F.
FRANC LURON			10–7	J. Cannon	Lord Aylesford	F.
CINDERELLA			10–7	J. Adams	Lord Anglesey	F.
ACTON			10–7	J. Rudd	Mr. Finchley	F.
PHILOSOPHER			10–6	Gray	Mr. W. Murray	F.
ROYAL IRISH FUSILIER			10–6	T. Andrews	Baron Oppenheim	P. U.
SAUCEBOX (late THREATENER)			10–4	Whiteley	Mr. H. Ellison	
DERBY DAY			10	Marsh	Lord Conyngham	F.
HALL COURT			10	Mr. Brown	Capt. Browne	

NOTE. Mr. Chaplin declared to win with Rhysworth.

STARTING PRICES

4–1 Despatch
100–15 Nuage and Cinderella
10–1 Schiedam
100–8 The Lamb
100–6 Primrose and Franc Luron

20–1 Casse Tete
25–1 Harvester, Marin, Rufus, Master Mowbray
33–1 Scots Grey
40–1 Fleuriste

50–1 Acton, Snowstorm, Derby Day
66–1 Saucebox
100–1 Royal Irish Fusilier, Philosopher, Hall Court

1873

Going: GOOD   *Starters:* 28   *Time:* WATCH STOPPED BY ACCIDENT

Weather: PERFECT   *Date:* MARCH 27

Horse	Colour and Sex	Age	Weight	Jockey	Owner	Position at Finish
DISTURBANCE *by Commotion— Polly Peachum*	b. h.	6	11–11	Mr. J. M. Richardson	Capt. Machell	1
RHYSHWORTH	a.		11–8	Boxall	Mr. H. Chaplin	2
COLUMBINE	a.		10–9	Harding	Mr. W. H. P. Jenkins	3
MASTER MOWBRAY	a.		10–7	G. Holman	Mr. J. Goodliffe	4
ALICE LEE	a.		10–3	Waddington	Mr. Studd	5
STAR AND GARTER		6	10–7	Capt. Smith	Mr. Vyner	6
REVIRESCAT	a.		11–8 (incl. 9 lbs. extra)	Mr. W. H. Johnstone	Mr. J. H. Maxwell	
FOOTMAN		6	11–5	R. Marsh	Mr. Moreton	F.
RED NOB	a.		11–8	Mr. J. Goodwin	Mr. Sankey	K. O.
CASSE TETE	a.		11–8	J. Page	Mr. E. Brayley	P. U.
CURRAGH RANGER	a.		11–3	Ryan	Capt. F. J. Montgomery	
ACTON	a.		11–1	R. I'Anson	Mr. Jones	
LINGERER		6	10–13	Mr. Mumford	Mr. W. Burton	K. O.
REUGNY		5	10–13	J. Cannon	Lord Aylesford	
TRUE BLUE	a.		10–13	Owner	Marquis of Queensferry	F.
LOUSTIC		6	10–13	Mr. Bembridge	Col. Byrne	
CINDERELLA		6	10–13	J. Adams	Lord Anglesey	
ISMAEL	a.		10–13	Daniels	Mr. W. Wilson	REF.
CRAWLER		6	10–10	Mr. A. Yates	Mr. Lynton	
CONGRESS	a.		10–10	Mr. E. P. Wilson	Mr. H. Wilson	
CECIL	a.		10–9	Wyatt	Mr. G. Etches	K. O.
CHARLIE	a.		10–9	Gregory	Mr. Horwood	
SOLICITOR		6	10–8	Owner	Mr. G. Dalglish	K. O.
HUNTSMAN		6	10–7	Owner	Mr. H. Ellison	K. O.
NEW YORK		5	10–6	W. Reeves	Lord Stamford	K. O.
BROADLEA		6	10–5	Mr. Thomas	Lord Poulett	F.
SARCHEDON		5	10–3	Pope	Mr. W. H. Powell	
RICHARD I		5	10–3		Capt. McAlmont	

STARTING PRICES

100–15 Footman	12–1 Master Mowbray, Broadlea	30–1 Acton
8–1 Rhyshworth	14–1 Alice Lee	33–1 Loustic, Red Nob,
100–12 Cinderella	20–1 Disturbance	Reugny
10–1 Casse Tete, Cecil	25–1 Curragh Ranger, Sarchedon	40–1 Richard I
		50–1 Others

1874

Going: AVERAGE | *Starters:* 22 | *Time:* 10 MIN. 4 SEC.
Weather: CLEAR | *Date:* MARCH 26

Horse	Colour and Sex	Age	Weight	Jockey	Owner	Position at Finish
REUGNY *by Minos—Reine Blanche*	ch. h.	6	10–12	Mr. J. M. Richardson	Capt. Machell	1
CHIMNEY SWEEP	bl. g.	a.	10–2	J. Jones	Lord M. Beresford	2
MERLIN	br. g.	a.	10–7	J. Adams	Capt. Thorold	3
DEFENCE			11–13	Mr. Rolly	Capt. Machell	4
MASTER MOWBRAY			10–5	A. Holman	Mr. Jno. Goodliffe	5
DISTURBANCE			12–9	J. Cannon	Capt. Machell	6
COLUMBINE			10–6	Harding	Mr. W. H. P. Jenkins	7
OURAGAN II			10–5	Mr. G. Mulcaster	Mr. J. Fearon	8
FURLEY			11–10	Mr. A. Yates	Mr. H. Baltazzi	
EUROTAS			11–8	Mr. Thomas	Mr. Chaston	
CONGRESS			11–4	Mr. E. P. Wilson	Mr. W. Wilson	
CASSE TETE			11	H. Day	Mr. Brayley	F.
DEWICKE			10–12	R. I'Anson	Lord M. Beresford	
DAYBREAK			10–11 (incl. 9 lbs. extra)	Holt	Mr. H. Houldsworth	
FANTOME			10–10	J. Page	Duke of Hamilton	F.
HERAUT D'ARMES			10–8	Capt. Smith	Mr. W. Forbes	
DAINTY			10–7	Mr. Hathaway	Mr. S. Davies	K. O.
VINTNER			10–3	Mr. Crawshaw	Sir R. B. Harvey	F.
LAST OF THE LAMBS			10	Mr. Dalglish	Mr. H. Houldsworth	REF.
BRETBY			10	W. Daniels	Mr. B. J. Angell	
LORD COLNEY			10	Rickards	Capt. Boynton	F.
PALADIN			10–3	J. Rugg	Capt. Rising	F.

STARTING PRICES

5–1	Reugny	14–1	Eurotas	40–1	Last of the Lambs, Merlin
100–15	Casse Tete	16–1	Congress		
7–1	Vintner	20–1	Fantome	50–1	Master Mowbray, Ouragan II
12–1	Columbine, Furley	25–1	Defence, Dewicke	66–1	Dainty

1875

Going: VERY DEEP Starters: 19 Time: 10 MIN. 22 SEC.
Weather: CLEAR Date: MARCH 18

Horse	Colour and Sex	Age	Weight	Jockey	Owner	Position at Finish
PATHFINDER (late KNIGHT) *by Mogador, dam's pedigree unknown*	b. g.	a.	10–11	Mr. Thomas	Mr. H. Bird	1
DAINTY *by Loyola—Tit Bit*	b. m.	a.	11	Mr. Hathaway	Mr. S. Davis	2
LA VENIE *by Ventre St. Gris— Valeriane*	ch. f.	5	11–12	J. Page	Baron Finot	3
JACKAL *by Caterer—Maggiore*	ch. g.	a.	11–11	R. Marsh	Mr. H. Baltazzi	4
MARMORA			11–2	Jones	Capt. R. Thorold	5
VICTOIRE			10–13	Mr. Barnes	Mr. Bracher	6
SPARROW			11–2	Gregory	Mr. Percival	7
CONGRESS			12–4	Mr. E. P. Wilson	Mr. Gomm	8
FURLEY			12–2	Mr. J. Goodwin	Mr. H. Baltazzi	REF.
CLONAVE			12–1	Gavin	Sir W. Nugent	F.
DUC DE BEAUFORT			11–13	Capt. Smith	Mr. Vyner	
LABURNUM			11–12	Jewitt	Capt. Machell	
MISS HUNGERFORD			11–10	Mr. Rolly	Mr. F. Bennett	F.
ST. AUBYN			11–7	J. Pickett	Mr. C. A. Egerton	F.
SAILOR			11–7	Fleming	Capt. S. Gubbins	F.
MESSAGER			11–7	Whiteley	Mr. Percival	F.
BAR ONE			11–4	Owner	Mr. L. Nicholson	
FLEURISTE			11	R. I'Anson	Mr. Granger	
NEW YORK			10–13	Mr. Dalglish	Mr. F. Platt	F.

STARTING PRICES

6–1 La Venie, Jackal
7–1 Congress
9–1 Clonave

100–8 Duc de Beaufort, Sailor, Marmora
100–7 Sparrow
100–6 Pathfinder

20–1 Laburnum, Hungerford
25–1 Dainty
33–1 Fleuriste, Messager
40–1 St. Aubyn

1876

Going: GOOD   *Starters:* 19   *Time:* 11 MIN. 14 SEC.
Weather: CLEAR   *Date:* MARCH 24

Horse	Colour and Sex	Age	Weight	Jockey	Owner	Position at Finish
REGAL by Saunterer—Regalia	bl. g.	5	11–3	J. Cannon	Capt. Machell	1
CONGRESS	b. g.	a.	11–3	Mr. E. P. Wilson	Mr. Gomm	2
SHIFNAL	br. h.	a.	10–3 (incl. 10 lbs. extra)	R. I'Anson	Mr. J. Nightingall	3
CHIMNEY SWEEP			10–8	Jones	Lord M. Beresford	4
RYE			10	G. Waddington	Mr. W. Weston	5
JACKAL			11	Marsh	Mr. H. Baltazzi	6
MASTER MOWBRAY			11–11	G. Holman	Mr. John Goodliffe	7
DEFENCE			11–11	Mr. Thomas	Mr. H. Baltazzi	P. U.
CHANDOS			11–7	Jewitt	Capt. Machell	F.
CLONAVE			11–5	Gavin	Sir W. Nugent	REF.
PHRYNE			11–3	Mr. J. Goodwin	Mr. C. B. Brookes	
PATHFINDER			11	W. Reeves	Mr. H. Bird	
PALM			11	Mr. Barnes	Mr. G. Brown	REF.
GAMEBIRD			10–12	Owner	Mr. Appleton	F.
THE LIBERATOR			10–11	T. Ryan	Mr. C. E. Hawkes	F.
ZERO			10–10	Mr. Rolly	Mr. J. M. Richardson	F.
GAZELLE			10–9	Mr. Flutter	Mr. T. Smyth	REF.
THYRA			10–6	W. Daniels	Mr. J. Robinson	REF.
SPRAY			10–2	T. Cunningham	Capt. Bayley	REF.

STARTING PRICES

100–30 Chandos
100–8 Defence, Master Mowbray, Palm, Jackal

20–1 Phryne, Zero, Thyra, Pathfinder
22–1 Clonave
25–1 Congress, Regal, Chimney Sweep, Rye

100–3 Shifnal
40–1 Gamebird, The Liberator, Gazelle

1877

Going: GOOD   *Starters:* 16   *Time:* 10 MIN. 10 SEC.

Weather: CLEAR   *Date:* MARCH 23

Horse	Colour and Sex	Age	Weight	Jockey	Owner	Position at Finish
AUSTERLITZ	ch. h.	5	10–8	Owner	Mr. F. G. Hobson	1
by Rataplan—Lufra						
CONGRESS	b. g.	a.	12–7	J. Cannon	Lord Lonsdale	2
THE LIBERATOR		a.	10–12	Mr. Thomas	Mr. Moore	3
CHIMNEY SWEEP		a.	10–13	J. Jones	Lord M. Beresford	4
DAINTY		a.	10–4	Mr. J. Goodwin	Mr. S. Davis	5
SHIFNAL		a.	11–5	R. I'Anson	Sir M. Crofton	6
CITIZEN		6	10–5	W. Reeves	Sir J. L. Kaye	7
REGAL		6	12–2	Jewitt	Lord Lonsdale	F.
REUGNY		a.	11–6	Mr. E. P. Wilson	Mr. Gomm	P. U.
PRIDE OF KILDARE		6	11–4	Canavan	Capt. Bates	F.
ZERO		a.	11–2	Sherrington	Lord C. Beresford	REF.
			(incl. 7 lbs. extra)			
LANCET		a.	11	Daniels	Mr. J. Johnson	P. U.
GAMEBIRD		a.	10–11	Mr. Appleton	Mr. Moore	F.
SULTANA		a.	10–11	Mr. Beasley	Mr. A. Crofton	P. U.
			(incl. 7 lbs. extra)			
EARL MARSHAL		6	10–10	Mr. Rolly	Lord Downe	F.
ARBITRATOR		6	10–6	Mr. Crawshaw	Sir C. F. Rushout	F.

STARTING PRICES

100–15 Reugny	12–1 Citizen, Pride of Kildare	25–1 Gamebird, The
7–1 Chimney Sweep	14–1 Arbitrator	Liberator
100–14 Shifnal	15–1 Austerlitz	33–1 Lancet
8–1 Regal	20–1 Congress, Dainty	50–1 Zero, Sultana

1878

Going: AVERAGE Starters: 12 Time: 10 MIN. 23 SEC.
Weather: CLEAR Date: MARCH 29

Horse	Colour and Sex	Age	Weight	Jockey	Owner	Position at Finish
SHIFNAL *by Saccharometer— Countess Amy*	br. h.	a.	10–12	J. Jones	Mr. John Nightingall	1
MARTHA *by Coroner—Martha*	b. m.	a.	10–9 (incl. 7 lbs. extra)	Mr. T. Beasley	Capt. A. Crofton	2
PRIDE OF KILDARE *by Plum Pudding or Canary—Hibernia*	ch. m.	a.	11–7	Mr. J. Moore	Mr. Moore	3
JACKAL			10–12	Jewitt	Capt. Machell	4
MISS LIZZIE			10–7	Hunt	Capt. Davison	5
CURATOR			10–5	Mr. E. P. Wilson	Lord Lonsdale	6
BOYNE WATER			10–12	J. Adams	Mr. J. Jessop	7
VERITY			10–10 (incl. 7 lbs. extra)	Gregory	Mr. J. Hefford	F.
HIS LORDSHIP			10–5 (carried 10–7)	R. I'Anson	Mr. G. Brown	K. O.
THE BEAR			10–4	R. Marsh	Duke of Hamilton	K. O.
NORTHFLEET			10–3	C. Lawrence	Mr. T. J. Clifford	F.
TATTOO			10–3	W. Canavan	Mr. J. G. Blake	F.

STARTING PRICES

9–2 His Lordship
5–1 Boyne Water
6–1 Pride of Kildare

100–15 Shifnal
12–1 Jackal
100–8 The Bear
100–7 Northfleet

20–1 Verity, Martha
100–3 Tattoo
25–1 Miss Lizzie

1879

Going: AVERAGE   *Starters:* 18   *Time:* 10 MIN. 12 SEC.
Weather: CLEAR   *Date:* MARCH 28

Horse	Colour and Sex	Age	Weight	Jockey	Owner	Position at Finish
THE LIBERATOR *by Daniel O'Connell— Mary O'Toole*	b. g.	a.	11–4	Owner	Mr. G. Moore	1
JACKAL *by Caterer—Maggiore*	ch. g.	a.	11 (incl. 7 lbs. extra)	J. Jones	Lord M. Beresford	2
MARTHA *by Coroner—Martha*	b. m.	a.	10–13	Mr. Beasley	Capt. Crofton	3
WILD MONARCH			11–7	Andrews	Marquis de Sauveur	4
BOB RIDLEY			10–9	Mr. E. P. Wilson	Mr. T. D'Arcy Hoey	5
REGAL			11–10	Jewitt	Capt. Machell	6
ROSSANMORE			10–7	Toole	Mr. James Conolly	7
LORD MARCUS			10–9	Mr. W. Beasley	Mr. P. M. V. Saurin	8
TURCO			10–9	Mr. H. Beasley	Mr. R. Stackpoole	9
BRIGAND			10–10	Count Metternich	Count Festetic, Jr.	10
QUEEN OF KILDARE			11–5	J. Doucie	Mr. P. Doucie	F.
BACCHUS			11–1	J. Cannon	Mr. Dunlop	F.
HIS LORDSHIP			10–12	Levitt	Mr. Russell	REF.
MARSHAL NIEL			10–12	Gavin	Sir J. L. Kaye	F.
VICTOR II			10–12	Mr. J. Beasley	Mr. Denny	P. U.
BELLRINGER			10–7 (incl. 7 lbs. extra)	Mr. A. Coventry	Mr. Vyner	F.
THE BEAR			10–7 (incl. 5 lbs. extra)	R. Marsh	Duke of Hamilton	REF.
CONCHA			10–2	Mr. W. B. Morris	Sir T. Hesketh	P. U.

STARTING PRICES

5–2 Regal	100–8 Victor II and Marshal Niel	20–1 Wild Monarch
5–1 Liberator		40–1 Queen of Kildare
10–1 Bacchus and The Bear	100–6 Turco and Bellringer	50–1 Martha, Concha, Brigand, Rossanmore
	1000–65 Jackal	

1880

Going: GOOD   *Starters:* 14   *Time:* 10 MIN. 20 SEC.
Weather: CLEAR   *Date:* MARCH 19

Horse	Colour and Sex	Age	Weight	Jockey	Owner	Position at Finish
EMPRESS *by Blood Royal—Jeu des Mots*	ch. m.	5	10–7	Mr. T. Beasley	Mr. P. Ducrot	1
THE LIBERATOR *by Dan O'Connell—Mary O'Toole*	b. g.	a.	12–7	Owner	Mr. G. Moore	2
DOWNPATRICK *by Master Bagot—Lady Wilde*	gr. g.	6	10–7	Gavin	Col. Lloyd	3
JUPITER TONANS			10–5	Owner	Mr. J. F. Lee-Barber	4
WOODBROOK			11–7	Mr. H. Beasley	Capt. Kirkwood	5
WILD MONARCH			11–11	R. I'Anson	Count de St. Sauveur	6
VICTOR II			10–7	Mr. Morris	Mr. E. Will	7
VICTORIA			10–7	Mr. J. Beasley	Mr. J. Schawell	8
SHIFNAL			11–11	Capt. Smith	Mr. John Nightingall	9
DAINTY			10–2	Darling	Mr. S. Davis	10
REGAL			11–11	J. Cannon	Lord Aylesford	F.
GUNLOCK			10–5	Davis	Mr. P. Aaron	REF.
SLEIGHT OF HAND			10–4	Childs	Mr. C. Howard	REF.
ST. GEORGE			10–2	Levitt	Mr. Greenall	REF.

STARTING PRICES

5–1 Regal	8–1 Empress	100–3 Gunlock
11–2 The Liberator, Wild Monarch	100–7 Victoria	50–1 JupiterTonans,Sleight of Hand, Victor II
100–15 Downpatrick	20–1 Shifnal	
	25–1 Woodbrook, St. George	66–1 Dainty

1881

Going: VERY BAD   *Starters:* 13   *Time:* 11 MIN. 50 SEC.
Weather: RAIN AND SNOW   *Date:* MARCH 25

Horse	Colour and Sex	Age	Weight	Jockey	Owner	Position at Finish
WOODBROOK *by The Lawyer—Doe*	ch. g.	a.	11–3	Mr. T. Beasley	Capt. Kirkwood	1
REGAL	bl. g.	a.	11–12	Jewitt	Capt. Machell	2
THORNFIELD	b. h.	5	10–9	R. Marsh	Mr. Leopold de Rothschild	3
NEW GLASGOW			10–7	Capt. Smith	Mr. A. Peel	4
THE SCOT			10	F. Webb	Capt. Machell	5
ABBOT OF ST. MARY'S			10–9 (incl. 7 lbs. extra)	J. Adams	Sir George Chetwynd	6
CROSS QUESTION			10	J. Jones	Mr. R. Carington	7
MONTAUBAN			10–7	Mr. A. Coventry	Mr. T. G. Baird-Hay	8
THE LIBERATOR			12–7	Owner	Mr. G. Moore	9 (REM.)
FAIR WIND			10–13	Mr. H. Beasley	Capt. Ducrot	F.
LITTLE PRINCE			10–8	S. Canavan	Mr. C. G. Way	REF.
FABIUS			10	Hunt	Mr. Vyner	REF.
BURIDAN			10	Childs	Mr. A. Yates	REF.

STARTING PRICES

6–1 Woodbrook	11–2 Thornfield	100–7 Montauban, Fair Wind
100–15 The Liberator	8–1 Abbot of St. Mary's	25–1 The Scot, Fabius
Cross Question	11–1 Regal, New Glasgow	40–1 Little Prince

1882

Going: VERY BAD   *Starters:* 12   *Time:* 10 MIN. 42 SEC.

Weather: RAIN AND SNOW   *Date:* MARCH 24

Horse	Colour and Sex	Age	Weight	Jockey	Owner	Position at Finish
SEAMAN *by Xenophon— Lena Rivers*	b. g.	6	11–6	Owner	Lord Manners	1
CYRUS *by Xenophon, dam by Newton-le-Willows*	b. g.	5	10–9	Mr. T. Beasley	Mr. John Gubbins	2
ZOEDONE *by New Oswestry— Miss Honiton*	ch. f.	5	10	Capt. Smith	Mr. Clayton	3
THE LIBERATOR			12–7	J. Adams	Mr. W. H. Moore	F.
THE SCOT			11–8	Jewitt	Mr. J. B. Leigh	F.
WILD MONARCH			10–12	Andrews	Mr. C. Cunningham	DES.
EAU DE VIE			10–8	Mr. D. Thirlwell	Duke of Hamilton	R. O.
MONTAUBAN			10–7	G. Waddington	Mr. T. G. Baird-Hay	P. U.
MOHICAN			10–7	Mr. H. Beasley	Mr. Bunbury	F.
FAY			10–7	Mr. E. P. Wilson	Capt. Machell	F.
IGNITION			10–5	Sensier	Mr. H. Rymill	REF.
BLACK PRINCE			10	F. Wynne	Mr. P. George	F.

STARTING PRICES

100–30	Mohican	10–1	Seaman	20–1	The Liberator
9–2	Cyrus	100–8	Eau de Vie	20–1	Zoedone
5–1	The Scot	100–7	Wild Monarch	50–1	Ignition

1883

Going: VERY HEAVY   Starters: 10 (smallest in Grand National history)

Weather: CLEAR   Date: MARCH 30   Time: 11 MIN. 39 SEC.

Horse	Colour and Sex	Age	Weight	Jockey	Owner	Position at Finish
ZOEDONE	ch. m.	6	11	Owner	Count C. Kinsky	1
by New Oswestry—						
Miss Honiton						
BLACK PRINCE	a.		10–4	Canavan	Mr. P. George	2
DOWNPATRICK	a.		10–7	Mr. T. Widger	Col. J. Lloyd	3
ZITELLA		5	11–2	Mr. T. Beasley	Mr. J. Gubbins	4
MONTAUBAN	a.		10–9	Mr. E. P. Wilson	Lord Yarborough	5
EAU DE VIE	a.		11–10	Mr. D. Thirlwell	Duke of Hamilton	6
MOHICAN		6	12–1	Mr. H. Beasley	Maj. Bunbury	F.
ATHLACCA	a.		11–4	J. Adams	Mr. T. McGoudal	P. U.
CORTOLVIN		6	10–5	Barker	Lord Rossmore	F.
JOLLY SIR JOHN		6	10–5	Mr. A. Coventry	Mr. Davis	REF.

STARTING PRICES

3–1 Zitella	9–1 Mohican, Athlacca,	100–7 Downpatrick
9–2 Eau de Vie	Montauban	100–3 Cortolvin, Black
100–12 Jolly Sir John	100–8 Zoedone	Prince

Going: HEAVY   *Starters:* 15   *Time:* 10 MIN. 5 SEC
Weather: THICK MIST   *Date:* MARCH 28

Horse	Colour and Sex	Age	Weight	Jockey	Owner	Position at Finish
VOLUPTUARY *by Cremorne— Miss Evelyn*	b. g.	6	10–5	Mr. E. P. Wilson	Mr. H. F. Boyd	1
FRIGATE *by Gunboat— Fair Maid of Kent*	b. m.	6	11–3 (incl. 7 lbs. extra)	Mr. H. Beasley	Mr. A. Maher	2
ROQUEFORT *by Winslow— Cream Cheese*	br. g.	5	10–5	J. Childs	Capt. Fisher	3
ZOEDONE			12–2	Owner	Count Kinsky	4
CYRUS			11–12	J. Jewitt	Mr. J. B. Leigh	5
BLACK PRINCE			10–11	Mr. T. Widger	Mr. P. George	6
ZITELLA			12	Mr. T. Beasley	Mr. J. Gubbins	
REGAL			11–6	W. Hunt	Capt. Machell	P.U.
THE SCOT			11–3	J. Jones	H.R.H. The Prince of Wales	F.
ALBERT CECIL			11–2	Owner	Mr. R. Sheriffe	
IDEA			10–12 (incl. 5 lbs. extra)	Mr. W. H. Moore	Mr. Oehlschlaeger	
SATELLITE			10–5	Mr. J. Beasley	Mr. E. W. Tritton	
TOM JONES			10–4	Capt. Lee-Barber	Sir W. Eden	F.
CORTOLVIN			10	Capt. Smith	Lord Rossmore	
TERRIER			10	Mr. D. Thirlwell	Duke of Hamilton	

Winner trained by Mr. T. Wilson, Jr., Herrington, Warwickshire.

The data on this race is very incomplete because the mist was so thick that no one really knew what was happening a good deal of the time.

STARTING PRICES

6–1 The Scot	10–1 Frigate, Voluptuary	25–1 Tom Jones
8–1 Satellite	100–7 Zoedone, Zitella	33–1 Terrier
100–12 Cortolvin	100–6 Idea	50–1 Others
9–1 Roquefort, Cyrus	20–1 Regal	

1885

Going: GOOD   Starters: 19   Time: 10 MIN. 10 SEC.

Weather: CLEAR   Date: MARCH 27

Horse	Colour and Sex	Age	Weight	Jockey	Owner	Position at Finish
ROQUEFORT *by Winslow— Cream Cheese*	b. g.	6	11	Mr. E. P. Wilson	Mr. A. Cooper	1
FRIGATE *by Gunboat— Fair Maid of Kent*	b. m.	a.	11–10	Mr. H. Beasley	Mr. Maher	2
BLACK PRINCE *by Warden of Galway—Empress*	bl. g.	a.	10–5	T. Skelton	Capt. Machell	3
REDPATH			10–3	Mr. A. Coventry	Mr. Zigomala	4
AXMINSTER			10–7	Sayers	Mr. J. Rutherford	5
ALBERT CECIL			10–9	J. Childs	Mr. R. Sheriffe	6
DOG FOX			10–3	Capt. Lee-Barber	Mr. C. Ascher	7
LIONESS			11–7	Mr. G. Lambton	Mr. Hungerford	8
RED HUSSAR			10–7	Owner	Capt. Armitage	9
ZOEDONE	ch. m.		11–11	Owner	Count Ch. Kinsky	POIS., F
KILWORTH			11–6	Owner	Capt. E. R. Owen	F.
CANDAHAR			10–12	W. Hunt	Mr. H. B. Craig	P.U.
JOLLY SIR JOHN			10–12	W. Ningtingall	Mr. Dane	
BELMONT			10–11	W. D. Canavan	Mr. James Daly	P.U.
LANG SYNE			10–8 (incl. 5 lbs. extra)	T. Hall	Mr. H. de Windt	
BEN MORE			10–7	Mr. W. H. Moore	Mr. H. T. Barclay	F.
HARLEQUIN			10	D. Sensier	Duke of Hamilton	F.
GAMECOCK			10	W. E. Stephens	Mr. E. Jay	F.
DOWNPATRICK			10	Capt. W. B. Morris	Col. J. Lloyd	

Winner trained by Swatton.

STARTING PRICES

100–30 Roquefort	100–6 Belmont	33–1 Black Prince
5–1 Zoedone	20–1 Redpath, Down-	50–1 Red Hussar, Harle-
7–1 Frigate	patrick, Albert Cecil	quin, Jolly Sir John,
10–1 Kilworth	25–1 Candahar, Dog Fox,	Gamecock
100–8 Ben More	Axminster	

1886

Going: AVERAGE   Starters: 23   Time: 10 MIN. 14⅗ SEC.
Weather: CLEAR   Date: MARCH 26

Horse	Colour and Sex	Age	Weight	Jockey	Owner	Position at Finish
OLD JOE by Barefoot—Spot	b. g.	a.	10–9	T. Skelton	Mr. Douglas	1
TOO GOOD by Ingomar or Uncas—Mary Hyland	br. g.	a.	11–12	Mr. H. Beasley	Count Erdody	2
GAMECOCK by Revolver—Lightning	b. g.	a.	10–12	W. E. Stephens	Mr. E. Jay	3
MAGPIE by Pell Mell—Sister to Hazeldene	bl. g.	a.	10–5 (carried 5 lbs. extra)	Mr. W. Woodland	Mr. E. Woodland	4
THE BADGER			10–3	A. Nightingall	Baron C. de Tuyll	5
CORONET			10–7	Capt. Lee-Barber	Mr. J. G. Muir	6
CORTOLVIN			11–2	W. Dollery	Mr. Abington	7
LADY TEMPEST			10–5	Mr. W. Beasley	Mr. P. M. V. Saurin	8
ROQUEFORT			12–3	Mr. E. P. Wilson	Mr. A. Cooper	F.
FRIGATE			11–13	Mr. J. Jones	Mr. Broadwood	F.
REDPATH			11–7	Mr. G. Lambton	Mr. P. J. Zigomala	
JOLLY SIR JOHN			11–6	Mr. C. W. Waller	Mr. F. Gibhard	F.
BLACK PRINCE			10–12	Mr. Nightingall	Capt. Machell	
BILLET DOUX			10–11	J. Behan	M. Zborowski	P.U.
THE LIBERATOR			10–10	Mr. S. Woodland, Jr.	Mr. E. Woodland	F.
BELMONT			10–10	Westlake	Mr. J. Daly	F.
HARRISTOWN			10–7	Owner	Mr. J. Purcell	
FONTENOY			10–4	J. Page	Mr. Iquique	REF.
SINBAD			10–3	A. Hall	Mr. L. de Rothschild	F.
SAVOYARD			10–3	G. Kirby	Baron W. Schroeder	F.
LIMEKILN			10–2	W. Brockwell	M. Zborowski	F.
AMICIA			10	F. W. Cotton	Mr. H. Wood	
CONSCRIPT			10	H. Escott	Capt. Child	F.

STARTING PRICES

3–1 Coronet
5–1 Roquefort
7–1 Too Good
9–1 Frigate
100–6 Redpath

22–1 Lady Tempest, Savoyard
25–1 Sinbad, Amicia, Old Joe, Badger
33–1 Belmont
40–1 Jolly Sir John

50–1 Gamecock, Cortolvin, Black Prince
66–1 Harristown
100–1 The Liberator, Conscript, Billet Doux
200–1 Magpie, Fontenoy

1887

Going: GOOD   Starters: 16   Time: 10 MIN. 10⅕ SEC.
Weather: CLEAR   Date: MARCH 25

Horse	Colour and Sex	Age	Weight	Jockey	Owner	Position at Finish
GAMECOCK *by Revolver—* *Lightfoot*	b. g.	a.	11	W. Daniells	Mr. E. Jay	1
SAVOYARD *by New Oswestry—* *Solferino*	ch. g.	a.	10–13	T. Skelton	Baron W. Schroeder	2
JOHNNY LONGTAIL *by Polardine—* *Debonnaire*	ch. g.	a.	10–6	Childs	Lord Wolverton	3
CHANCELLOR			10–12	Mr. W. Moore	Capt. Foster	4
CHANCERY			11–6	Dollery	Mr. Popham	5
TOO GOOD			12	Mr. H. Beasley	Count G. Erdody	6
MAGPIE			10–10	Mr. W. Woodlands	Mr. E. Woodlands	7 DIS.
ROQUEFORT			12–8	Mr. E. P. Wilson	Mr. James Lee	F.
OLD JOE			11–10	Mr. C. J. Cunningham	Mr. A. J. Douglas	
FRIGATE			11–5	Mr. Lawrence	Mr. F. E. Lawrence	
BELLONA			10–10	Owner	Mr. George Lambton	F.
SPECTRUM			10–10	Grimes	Sir G. Chetwynd	F.
SPAHI			10–10	Mr. T. Beasley	Mr. J. Gubbins	F.
BALLOT BOX			10–5	Capt. Owen	Mr. P. Nickalls	F.
SINBAD			10–3	W. Nightingall	Mr. J. Percival	
HUNTER			10	Mr. W. Beasley	Lord Cholmondeley	F.

Winner trained by Jordan.

STARTING PRICES

9–2 Spahi	100–8 Old Joe	35–1 Spectrum
7–1 Roquefort	100–7 Too Good	40–1 Johnny Longtail
100–14 Savoyard	20–1 Gamecock, Chancellor	50–1 Hunter
10–1 Magpie	22½–1 Sinbad	100–1 Chancery
100–9 Frigate, Bellona	33–1 Ballot Box	

1888

Going: GOOD   Starters: 20   Time: 10 MIN. 12 SEC.

Weather: CLEAR   Date: MARCH 23

Horse	Colour and Sex	Age	Weight	Jockey	Owner	Position at Finish
PLAYFAIR by Rippenden—dam by Rattlebones—Drayton	bl. g.	a.	10–7	Mawson	Mr. E. W. Baird	1
FRIGATE by Gunboat—Maid of Kent	b. m.	a.	11–2	Mr. W. Beasley	Mr. Maher	2
BALLOT BOX by Candidate—Susan	br. g.	a.	12–4	W. Nightingall	Mr. P. Nickall	3
RINGLET by Highborn—Ladywell	bl. m.	a.	11–11	T. Skelton	Lord Rodney	4
ALADDIN			11	Mr. C. W. Waller	Mr. L. de Rothschild	5
JEANIE			10–6	H. Barker	Mr. Abington	6
GAMECOCK			12–4	Capt. E. R. Owen	Mr. E. Benzon	7
MAGIC			10–12	A. Hall	H.R.H. The Prince of Wales	8
THE BADGER			11–1	A. Nightingall	Baron C. de Tuyll	9
USNA			12–7	Mr. H. Beasley	Mr. J. Gubbins	D.S.
SAVOYARD			12–4	Mr. G. Lambton	Baron W. Schroeder	F.
JOHNNY LONGTAIL			12 (incl. 7 lbs. extra)	Dollery	Mr. A. Yates	
BELLONA			11–12 (incl. 5 lbs. extra)	Mr.C.J.Cunningham	Mr. T. B. Miller	F.
SPAHI			11–9	T. Kavanagh	Mr. J. Gubbins	REF.
OLD JOE			11–9	W. Daniells	Mr. A. J. Douglas	
CHANCELLOR			11–5	Mr. W. H. Moore	Mr. E. Wardour	
KINFAUNS			10–10	J. Page	Mr. T. Brinckman	REF.
THE FAWN			10–6	Mr. E. P. Wilson	Lord Cholmondeley	F.
TRAP			10–6	G. Lowe	Mr. Churtin	F.
CORK			10–6	Mr. W. Woodland	Mr. Adrian	F.

STARTING PRICES

7–1 Usna
8–1 Chancellor
10–1 The Badger
100–9 Ringlet
100–8 Frigate

100–6 Bellona
18–1 Old Joe
20–1 Gamecock, Trap, The Fawn
25–1 Ballot Box, Savoyard, Magic

33–1 Spahi and Aladdin
40–1 Johnny Longtail, Playfair
100–1 Kinfauns, Cork
1000–5 Jeanie

1889

C O N D I T I O N S same as usual, except that the race became a steeplechase of 1,500 sovs.

Going: GOOD *Starters:* 20 *Time:* 10 MIN. 1 ⅕ SEC.
Weather: CLEAR *Date:* MARCH 29

Horse	Colour and Sex	Age	Weight	Jockey	Owner	Position at Finish
FRIGATE *by Gunboat— Fair Maid of Kent*	b. m.	a.	11–4	Mr. T. Beasley	Mr. M. A. Maher	1
WHY NOT *by Castlereagh— Twitter*	b. g.	a.	11–5	Mr.C.J.Cunningham	Mr. B. J. Jardine	2
M. P. *by Minstrel—dam of Blood Royal*	ch. g.	a.	10–9	A. Nightingall	Mr. Rutherford	3
BELLONA			11–2	Mr. C. W. Waller	Mr. Abington	4
MAGIC			10–9	Jones	H.R.H. The Prince of Wales	5
THE SIKH			10–9	Mr. D. Thirlwell	Lord Dudley	6
THE FAWN			10–10	Mr. W. Beasley	Lord Cholmondeley	7
RINGLET			11–12	Walsh	Mr. Neol Fenwick	8
			(incl. 7 lbs. extra)			
BATTLE ROYAL			10–8	Mr. H. Beasley	Mr. W. Fulton	9
GAMECOCK			11–12	Dollery	Mr. Strong	10
BALLOT BOX	br. g.		12–7	W. Nightingall	Mr. P. Nickalls	F.
ROQUEFORT			12	Mr. E. P. Wilson	Mr. Abington	F.
SAVOYARD			11–11	Mr. G. Lambton	Baron W. Schroeder	K.O.
VOLUPTUARY			11–3	T. Skelton	Mr. H. F. Boyd	F.
KILWORTH			10–13	Capt. E. R. Owen	Lord Dudley	REF.
ET CETERA			10–13	G. Morris	Count N. Esterhazy	F.
GLENTHORPE			10–10	Mr. W. H. Moore	Mr. O. H. Jones	
MERRY MAIDEN			10–7	Capt. Lee-Barber	Capt. Childe	REF.
HETTIE			10–5	A. Hall	H.R.H. The Prince of Wales	F.
GREAT PAUL			10	Ellis	Mr. B. W. J. Alexander	

STARTING PRICES

6–1 Roquefort	20–1 Ballot Box, M. P.,	33–1 Gamecock
8–1 Et Cetera and Frigate	Bellona	40–1 Kilworth
10–1 Glenthorpe	25–1 Savoyard, Magic,	66–1 Ringlet, Merry
100–9 Why Not, The Sikh	Battle Royal,	Maiden, Hettie
100–6 Voluptuary	The Fawn	200–1 Great Paul

1890

Going: AVERAGE   Starters: 16   Time: 10 MIN. 41⅘ SEC.
Weather: CLEAR   Date: MARCH 28

Horse	Colour and Sex	Age	Weight	Jockey	Owner	Position at Finish
ILEX *by Rostrevor— Rostrum's dam*	ch. g.	a.	10–5	A. Nightingall	Mr. G. Masterman	1
PAU *by Ambergris—Elf*	b. h.	a.	10–3	Halsey	Mr. E. Woodland	2
M. P. *by Minstrel—dam of Blood Royal*	ch. g.	a.	11–5	Mr. W. H. Moore	Mr. J. Rutherford	3
BRUNSWICK			10–4	Mawson	Mr. Lancashire	4
WHY NOT			12–5	Mr. C. J. Cunningham	Mr. D. J. Jardine	5
EMPEROR			11–1	Mr. D. Thirlwell	Capt. Machell	6
FRIGATE			12–7	Mr. T. Beasley	Mr. M. A. Maher	F.
GAMECOCK			12–6 (incl. 7 lbs. extra)	Dollery	Mr. Swan	REM.
BLOOD ROYAL			11–13	Mr. Wildman	Mr. Fulton	F.
BELLONA			11–9	H. Barker	Mr. Abington	F.
VOLUPTUARY			11–7	T. Skelton	Mr. H. F. Boyd	F.
BRACEBOROUGH			10–13	Owner	Mr. F. E. Lawrence	F.
FETICHE			10–12	V. Baker	M. M. Euphrussi	
HETTIE			10–11	Mr. E. P. Wilson	H.R.H. The Prince of Wales	REM.
BACCY			10–8	Mr. W. Woodland	Mr. R. Woodland	F.
FIREBALL			10–4	D. Comer	Mr. H. Holmes	F.

Winner trained by Nightingall.

STARTING PRICES

4–1 Ilex	10–1 Voluptuary	20–1 Gamecock
11–2 Bellona	100–8 Battle Royal	25–1 Fetiche and Hettie
8–1 M. P.	100–7 Frigate	100–1 Others
100–9 Why Not	100–6 Emperor	

1891

Going: VERY GOOD   Starters: 21   Time: 9 MIN. 58 SEC.
Weather: CLEAR   Date: MARCH 20

Horse	Colour and Sex	Age	Weight	Jockey	Owner	Position at Finish
COME AWAY by Cambuslang— Larkaway	b. g.	a.	11–12	Mr. H. Beasley	Mr. W. G. Jameson	1
CLOISTER by Ascetic—Grace II	b. g.	a.	11–7	Capt. E. R. Owen	Lord Dudley	2
ILEX by Rostrevor— Rostrum's dam	ch. g.	a.	12–3	A. Nightingall	Mr. G. Masterman	3
ROQUEFORT by Winslow— Cream Cheese	b. g.			Guy	Mr. A. Yates	4
CRUISER			10–8	Mr. T. Beasley	Maj. Bunbury	5
GAMECOCK			12–4	Dollery	Mr. Swan	6
WHY NOT			12–4	Mr. Cunningham	Mr. C. Perkins	F.
ROMAN OAK			12	Escott	Mr. Leetham	K.O.
VOLUPTUARY			11–3	Mr. E. P. Wilson	Mr. H. F. Boyd	P.U.
EMPEROR			11–3	W. Nightingall	Capt. Machell	P.U.
CHOUFLEUR			11–3	T. Kavanagh	Lord Zetland	F.
VEIL			10–13	Mr. W. H. Moore	Sir James Miller	F.
DOMINION			10–13	Thornton	Mr. W. H. Russell	P.U.
GRAPE VINE			10–7	J. Hoysted	Mr. G. H. Archer	F.
JEANIE			10–4	H. Barker	Mr. Abington	F.
BRUNSWICK			10–4	Mawson	Mr. H. W. Lancashire	F.
FLOWER OF THE FOREST			10–4	P. Clark	Mr. Charter	F.
YOUNG GLASGOW			10–3	R. Mitchell	Mr. W. Gordon Canning	F.
FIREBALL			10	Halsey	Mr. H. Holmes	P.U.
ADELAIDE			10	Mr. Ripley	Mr. E. H. Wolton	P.U.
NASR ED DIN			10	H. Brown	Mr. F. Gallane	F.

Winner trained in Ireland.

STARTING PRICES

4–1 Come Away
5–1 Ilex
7–1 Cruiser
9–1 Grape Vine
100–9 Roman Oak, Why Not

20–1 Cloister
25–1 Choufleur, Veil, Emperor
40–1 Young Glasgow, Roquefort, Brunswick

50–1 Flower of the Forest, Nasr ed Din
66–1 Voluptuary, Dominion, Jeanie, Gamecock
100–1 Fireball
200–1 Adelaide

1892

Going: GOOD   *Starters:* 25   *Time:* 9 MIN. 48 ⅕ SEC.

Weather: THICK FOG   *Date:* MARCH 25

Horse	Colour and Sex	Age	Weight	Jockey	Owner	Position at Finish
FATHER O'FLYNN *by Retreat—Kathleen*	b. g.	a.	10–5	Capt. E. R. Owen	Mr. C. G. Wilson	1
CLOISTER *by Ascetic—Grace II*	b. g.	a.	12–3	Mr. J. C. Dormer	Mr. C. Duff	2
ILEX *by Rostrevor—Rostrum's dam, by Master Bagot*	ch. g.	a.	12–7	A. Nightingall	Mr. G. Masterman	3
ARDCARN			10–10	T. Kavanagh	Maj. Kirkwood	4
FLYING COLUMN			10–7	Mr. W. Beasley	Capt. Peel	5
HOLLINGTON			10–9	G. Williamson	Capt. A. E. Whitaker	6
CRUISER			11–7	Mr. W. P. Cullen	Capt. J. Byron	7
RELIANCE			10–8	Mr. J. C. Cheney	Mr. W. Whitehead	8
ULYSSES			10–10	Mr. G. B. Milne	Lord E. Talbot	9
FAUST			10–5	Mr. Lushington	Gen. Beresford	10
BAGMAN			10–7	Mr. F. H. Hassall	Capt.R.W.Ethelstone	11
THE MIDSHIPMITE			11–6	Mr. Atkinson	Mr. H. Powell	F.
TENBY			11–2	C. Gregor	Mr. A. M. Singer	F.
PARTISAN			11–1	Barker	Sir H. de Trafford	K.O.
LORD OF THE GLEN			11	Mr. C. W. Waller	Mr. C. Waller	
THE PRIMATE			10–13	Capt. Bewicke	Mr. J. Bald	P.U.
MELDRUM			10–12	Lathom	Mr. B. Goodall	F.
JASON			10–12	G. Mawson	Mr. Abington	P.U.
PAUL PRY			10–12 *(incl. 7 lbs. extra)*	T. Adams	Mr. F. E. Lawrence	R.O.
LORD ARTHUR			10–7	Capt. Lee-Barber	Mr. H. T. Barclay	
NAP			10–7	Mr. H. Woodland	Mr. E. Woodland	F.
SOUTHAM			10–7	Dollery	Mr. F. Swan	
ROLLESBY			10–5	H. Brown	Mr. P. Vincent-Turner	P.U.
BILLEE TAYLOR			10–3	Mr. H. Beasley	Maj. Kearsley	R.O.
BRUNSWICK			10–2	Mr. Levenston	Mr. H. W. Lancashire	

Winner trained privately.

STARTING PRICES

11–2 Cloister	20–1 Ilex and Father O'Flynn	50–1 Ulysses, Southam,
100–14 The Primate	25–1 Billee Taylor, Lord	Flying Column,
10–1 Ardcarn	Arthur, The Midship-	Rollesby
100–9 Hollington	mite, Cruiser	100–1 Brunswick, Faust,
100–8 Jason	33–1 Lord of the Glen	Meldrum
100–7 Tenby	40–1 Partisan	200–1 Reliance, Nap, **Bag-man**, Paul Pry

1893

Going: VERY HARD AND DRY   Starters: 15   Time: 9 MIN. 32⅖ SEC.

Weather: SUNNY AND HOT   Date: MARCH 24   (RECORD TIME)

Horse	Colour and Sex	Age	Weight	Jockey	Owner	Position at Finish
CLOISTER *by Ascetic—Grace II*	b. g.	a.	12–7	Dollery	Mr. C. G. Duff	1
AESOP *by Chippendale—Fable*		a.	10–4	H. Barker	Capt. Michael Hughes	2
WHY NOT *by Castlereagh—Twitter*	b. g.		11–12	A. Nightingall	Mr. C. H. Fenwick	3
TIT FOR TAT			10	G. Williamson	Col. A. S. Lucas	4
THE MIDSHIPMITE			12–3	Sensier	Mr. H. L. Powell	5
FATHER O'FLYNN			11–11	Mr. G. B. Milne	Mr. G. C. Wilson	6
ROMAN OAK			11–9	Mr. W. P. Cullen	Sir H. de Trafford	7
FAUST			10–6	Capt. Yardley	Gen. Beresford	8
FIELD MARSHAL			11–4	Capt. Crawley	Mr. Eustace Loder	P.U.
THE PRIMATE			11–3	Mr. Bewicke	Mr. F. Dald	F.
LADY HELEN			11–1	R. Nightingall	Capt. Dundas	F.
CHOULEUR			10–13	Kavanagh	Mr. T. Toynbee	P.U.
JOAN OF ARC			10–4	G. Morris	Capt. H. T. Fenwick	F.
GOLDEN GATE			10–2	G. Mawson	Capt. E. W. Baird	P.U.
GOLDEN LINK			10	N. Behan	Mr. J. Dowling	REF.

Winner trained by Swatton.

STARTING PRICES

9–2 Cloister
5–1 Why Not
100–15 The Midshipmite
100–12 Aesop
100–9 Father O'Flynn

100–7 The Primate
25–1 Tit for Tat
28–1 Field Marshal
33–1 Golden Gate, Faust
40–1 Roman Oak

50–1 Lady Helen, Joan of Arc
100–1 Choufleur, Golden Link

1894

Going: GOOD   Starters: 14   Time: 9 MIN. 45⅖ SEC.

Weather: CLEAR   Date: MARCH 30

Horse	Colour and Sex	Age	Weight	Jockey	Owner	Position at Finish
WHY NOT *by Castlereagh— Twitter*	b. g.	a.	11–13	A. Nightingall	Capt. C. H. Fenwick	1
LADY ELLEN II *by Prince George— Lady Helen*	b. m.	6	9–10	T. Kavanagh	Mr. J. McKinley	2
WILD MAN FROM BORNEO *by Decider—Wild Duck*	ch. g.	6	10–9	Mr. Jos. Widger	Mr. John Widger	3
TROUVILLE *by Beaupaire*	ch. m.	6	10–6 (incl. 4 lbs. extra)	Mr. J. C. Cheney	Duke of Hamilton	4
AESOP			10–12 (incl. 8 lbs. extra)	Mawson	Capt. Michael Hughes	5
MUSICIAN			9–10	F. Hassall	Mr. Mark Firth	6
CARROLLSTOWN			10–13	Williamson	Lord Shaftesbury	7
SCHOONER			9–12	W. Taylor	Mr. M. A. Maher	8
VARTEG HILL			9–10	D. Davies	Mr. Lort Phillip	9
FATHER O'FLYNN			11–3	Owner	Mr. C. Grenfell	F.
ARDCARN			10–12	Mr. Bewicke	Mr. Grant	F.
NELLY GRAY			9–12	Escott	Mr. F. B. Atkinson	F.
CALCRAFT			9–10	Mr. A. H. Ripley	Mr. J. C. Leslie	F.
DAWN			9–7	G. Morris	Mr. E. Storey	F.

Winner trained by Collins.

STARTING PRICES

5–1 Nelly Gray, Why Not
11–2 Ardcarn
6–1 Aesop
100–7 Father O'Flynn

25–1 Schooner, Musician, Lady Ellen II, Dawn, Trouville

40–1 Wild Man from Borneo
50–1 Varteg Hill, Carrollstown
100–1 Calcraft

1895

Going: HEAVY Starters: 19 Time: 10 MIN. 32 SEC.
Weather: FOG Date: MARCH 29

Horse	Colour and Sex	Age	Weight	Jockey	Owner	Position at Finish
WILD MAN FROM BORNEO *by Decider—Wild Duck*	ch. g.	a.	10–11	Mr. Jos. Widger	Mr. John Widger	1
CATHAL *by Cassock or Hominy—Daffodil*	b. g.	6	10–9	H. Escott	Mr. J. B. Atkinson	2
VAN DER BERG *by Dutch Skater—Yurata*	b. g.	a.	9–13	Dollery	Maj. A. Crawley	3
MANIFESTO			11–2	T. Kavanagh	Mr. H. M. Dyas	4
WHY NOT			12	Mr. E. Guy Fenwick	Capt. C. H. Fenwick	5
LEYBOURNE			10–3	G. Williamson	Capt. Gordon	6
FATHER O'FLYNN			11–1	Owner	Mr. C. A. Grenfell	7
LADY PAT			10–13	Shanahan	Mr. F. D. Leyland	8
DALKEITH			9–12	J. Knox	Mr. W. Murray-Thriepland	9
FIN MA COUL II			10–5	W. Canavan	Mr. J. Arnold	10
MOLLY MAGUIRE			9–9	W. Taylor	Mr. J. T. Hartigan	11
HORIZON			12–2	Mawson	Mr. G. W. Greswolde-Williams	K.O.
PRINCE ALBERT			10–12	Mr. W. P. Cullen	Mr. Roden	F.
SARAH BERNHARDT			10–10	E. Matthews	Mr. C. D. Rose	F.
ARDCARN			10–10	Mr. C. Thompson	Mr. E. Clarke	
AESOP			10–8	A. Nightingall	Capt. Michael Hughes	F.
ROYAL BUCK			10–4	W. Slinn	Mr. G. W. Greswolde-Williams	F.
COCK OF THE HEATH			10–2	Hoysted	Mr. H. M. Dyas	
CAUSTIC			10–1	Mr. A. Gordon	Mr. B. Benson	

Winner trained by Gatland.

STARTING PRICES

5–1 Aesop
100–14 Horizon
10–1 Wild Man From Borneo
100–8 Cathal, Leybourne, Manifesto

100–7 Father O'Flynn
100–6 Cock of the Heath
25–1 Lady Pat, Van der Berg, Molly Maguire
33–1 Dalkeith
40–1 Fin Ma Coul II

50–1 Sarah Bernhardt, Royal Buck, Prince Albert, Ardcarn, Why Not
100–1 Caustic

1896

CONDITIONS the same, except added money was 2,500 sovs.

Going: AVERAGE
Weather: CLEAR

Starters: 28
Date: MARCH 27

Time: 10 MIN. 11 ⅕ SEC.

Horse	Colour and Sex	Age	Weight	Jockey	Owner	Position at Finish
THE SOARER *by Skylark, dam by Lurgan*	b. g.	a.	9–13	Mr. D. G. M. Campbell	Mr. W. H. Walker	1
FATHER O'FLYNN *by Retreat—Kathleen (h. b.)*		a.	10–12	Owner	Mr. C. Grenfell	2
BISCUIT *by Barnaby—Reversion*	b. m.	a.	10	Matthews	Mr. W. C. Keeping	3
BARCALWHEY *by Barcaldine—Junket*	bl. h.	6	9–8	Hogan	Capt. Whitaker	4
WHY NOT			11–5	A. Nightingall	Mr. E. G. Fenwick	5
RORY O'MORE			10–9	R. Nightingall	Mr. C. Hibbert	6
KESTREL			9–10	H. Smith	Mr. W. Lawson	7
CATHAL			11–13	Owner	Mr. Reginald Ward	8
VAN DER BERG			10–9	G. Mawson	Mr. W. Pritchard Gordon	9
WILD MAN FROM BORNEO			12	Mr. T. J. Widger	Mr. J. W. Widger	F.
MARCH HARE			11–7	R. Chaloner	Mr. F. C. Stanley	R.O.
THE MIDSHIPMITE			11–4	Hewitt	Mr. H. L. Powell	F.
MANIFESTO			11–4	Gourley	Mr. H. M. Dyas	F.
MORIARTY			11–2	Acres	Mr. J. Hale	
ARDCARN			11–1	G. Williamson	Mr. Egerton Clarke	F.
WATERFORD			10–13	Mr. Joe Widger	Mr. F. E. Irving	K.O.
SWANSHOT			10–13	Anthony	Capt. J. H. Orr-Ewing	F.
REDHILL			10–12	Mr. G. S. Davies	Capt. Aiken	K.O.
DOLLAR II			10–11	Halsey	Mr. J. A. Miller	
ST. ANTHONY			10–10	Owner	Capt. Ricardo	F.
ALPHEUS			10–10	Mr. A. Gordon	Mr. Vyner	
EMIN			10–8 (incl. 4 lbs. extra)	H. Brown	Sir S. Scott	K.O.
FLEETWING			10–6	Mr. Parsons	Mr. M. J. Corbally	P.U.
CLAWSON			10–4	Mr. W. H. Bissill	Mr. A. Jolland	
MISS BARON			10	T. Kavanagh	Mr. W. Widger	K.O.
PHILACTERY			9–11	E. Driscoll	Sir Samuel Scott	P.U.
WESTMEATH			9–7 (carried 9–8)	G. Morris	Mr. F. D. Leyland	
CAUSTIC			9–7	H. Mason	Mr. W. B. Benison	F.

Winner trained by Collins.

STARTING PRICES

7–1 Rory O'More
8–1 Ardcarn
100–12 Waterford
100–9 Cathal
100–7 Caustic, Why Not, Manifesto
100–6 March Hare

20–1 Alpheus, Swanshot, Van der Berg
25–1 Biscuit, Redhill
33–1 Barcalwhey
40–1 The Soarer, Father O'Flynn, Moriarty,

40–1 *(Cont.)* Wild Man From Borneo
50–1 Dollar, Emin
66–1 Clawson, Miss Baron, The Midshipmite
100–1 Others

1897

Going: GOOD			*Starters:* 28		*Time:* 9 MIN 49 SEC.	
Weather: CLOUDY			*Date:* MARCH 26			

Horse	Colour and Sex	Age	Weight	Jockey	Owner	Position at Finish
MANIFESTO *by Man of War— Væ Victis*	b. g.	a.	11–3	T. Kavanagh	Mr. H. M. Dyas	1
FILBERT *by Regent, dam by Double X*	b. g.	a.	9–7	Mr. C. Beatty	Mr. G. R. Powell	2
FORD OF FYNE *by Studley,*	br. g.	6	10–7	Mr. Withington	Maj. J. A. Orr-Ewing	3
PRINCE ALBERT *by Althotos—Bessie*	b. g.	a.	10–8	Mr. G. S. Davies	Mr. J. S. Forbes	4
LOTUS LILY			9–7	Mr. A. W. Wood	Capt. R. W. Ethelston	5
TIMON			9–10	Tervit	Mr. R. W. Brown	6
FAIRY QUEEN			9–7	Mr. E. H. Lord	Mr. G. S. Davies	7
SEAPORT II			10–7	C. James	Mr. H. White	8
NELLY GRAY			11–3	G. Morris	Maj. J. A. Orr-Ewing	9
ARGONAUT			10–12	R. Woodland	Mr. J. A. Miller	10
WESTMEATH			11–4	W. Taylor	Mr. F. D. Leyland	F.
CLAWSON			10–10	Mr. W. Bissill	Mr. Jolland	P.U.
NORTON			10–7	J. Hickey	Mr. Spencer Gollan	F.
DAIMIO			12–6	H. Escott	Mr. C. Gibson	P.U.
CATHAL			11–10	Owner	Mr. R. Ward	F.
WILD MAN FROM BORNEO			11–5	Mr. T. J. Widger	Miss Norris	P.U.
THE SOARER			11–4	Mr. D. G. M. Campbell	Mr. W. H. Walker	F.
BALLYOHARA			10–3	Denby	Lord Shrewsbury	P.U.
GOLDEN CROSS			10–2	G. Wilson	Mr. E. P. Wilson	F.
BARCALWHEY			10–1	C. Hogan	Capt. A. E. Whitaker	F.
RED CROSS			10–1	H. Taylor	Count Zech	F.
THE CONTINENTAL			10	H. Brown	Mr. A. H. Hudson	F.
CHEVY CHASE			9–13	Anthony	Mr. F. F. McCabe	P.U.
GREENHILL			9–10	E. Matthews	Mr. C. D. Rose	K.O.
MEDIATOR			9–8	Grosvenor	Lord Coventry	F.
LITTLE JOE			9–8	Bland	Mr. R. T. Bell	K.O.
GOLDFISH			9–7	T. Fitton	Mr. E. C. Smith	F.
GAUNTLET			11–13	Capt. W. H. Johnstone	Mr. F. D. Leyland	F.

Winner trained by Mr. Auliffe.

STARTING PRICES

6–1 Manifesto	25–1 Ford of Fyne, Greenhill, Prince Albert, Barcalwhey	40–1 Daimio
7–1 Cathal		50–1 Fairy Queen, Seaport II
9–1 Wild Man From Borneo		
10–1 Norton	28–1 Chevy Chase	66–1 Gauntlet, Goldfish
100–6 The Soarer	33–1 Argonaut Clawson, Golden Cross	100–1 Others
20–1 Nelly Gray, Timon		

1898

Going: VERY HEAVY AND BAD *Starters:* 24 *Time:* 9 MIN. 43⅗ SEC.
Weather: BLINDING SNOWSTORM *Date:* MARCH 25

Horse	Colour and Sex	Age	Weight	Jockey	Owner	Position at Finish
DROGHEDA *by Cherry Ripe— Eglantine*	b. g.	6	10–12	Gourley	Mr. C. G. Adams	1
CATHAL *by The Cassock or Hominy—Daffodil*	b. g.	a.	11–5	Owner	Mr. R. Ward	2
GAUNTLET *by Gallinule— Lady Louisa*	ch. g.	a.	10–13	W. Taylor	Mr. F. D. Leyland	3
FILBERT			9–12	Mr. C. Beatty	Mr. G. R. Powell	4
DEAD LEVEL			10–7	Anthony	Mr. G. Hamilton	5
FORD OF FYNE			11	Mr. Withington	Maj. J. H. Orr-Ewing	6
GRUDON			11–5	Hickey	Mr. B. Bletsoe	7
BARSAC			9–12	Mr. M. B. Bletsoe	Mr. C. A. Brown	8
PRINCE ALBERT			11	Mr. G. S. Davies	Mr. J. S. Forbes	9
GREENHILL			10–3	C. Hogan	Mr. C. D. Rose	10
THE SOARER			11–5	A. Nightingall	Mr. W. H. Walker	F.
NEPCOTE			10–9	Dollery	Mr. Lincoln	P.U.
SWANSHOT			10–7	Owner	Mr. H. de Mont- morency	P.U.
BARCALWHEY			10–6	R. Chalmer	Capt. A. E. Whitaker	F.
ATHELFRITH			10–4	W. Hoysted	Mr. A. Coats	P.U.
SURPLICE			10–1	Lathom	Mr. Reid Walker	F.
KINGSWORTHY			10	Acres	Mr. F. R. Hunt	P.U.
SHERIFF HUTTON	b. g.		10	J. Morrell	Mr. H. B. Singleton	F.
CRUISKEEN II			10	T. Kavanagh	Mr. Sadleir-Jackson	P.U.
ST. GEORGE			9–11	J. Walsh, Jr.	Mr. John Widger	K.O.
HOBNOB			9–11	H. Bax	Mr. A. Stedall	F.
ELECTRIC SPARK			9–11	A. Waddington	Mr. R. Wright	P.U.
CUSHALU MAVOURNEEN			9–11	H. Smith	Mr. G. R. Powell	P.U.
HALL IN			9–7 (carried 9–8)	L. Bland	Mr. W. Ward	F.

STARTING PRICES

11–2 Ford of Fyne
7–1 Cathal
8–1 Prince Albert
100–12 Gauntlet

100–7 The Soarer, Barcalwhey
20–1 Kingsworthy
25–1 Drogheda, Dead Level, Filbert, Barsac, Nep- cote, Grudon

28–1 Little Joe
40–1 Hobnob, St. George
50–1 Sheriff Hutton
100–1 Others

1899

Going: GOOD Starters: 19 Time: 9 MIN. 49⅘ SEC.
Weather: CLEAR Date: MARCH 24

Horse	Colour and Sex	Age	Weight	Jockey	Owner	Position at Finish
MANIFESTO by Man of War— Væ Victis	b. g.	a.	12–7	G. Williamson	Mr. J. G. Bulteel	1
FORD OF FYNE by Studley—	br. g.	a.	10–10	E. Matthews	Maj. J. A. Orr-Ewing	2
ELLIMAN by Melton—Recovery	b. h.	a.	10–1	Piggott	Mr. Audley Blyth	3
DEAD LEVEL by Isobar—Paragon			10–6	Mason	Mr. Gavin Hamilton	4
BARSAC			9–12	Mr. H. M. Ripley	Mr. C. A. Brown	5
WHITEBOY II			9–10	A. Banner	Mr. R. Barke	6
AMBUSH II			10–2	W. Anthony	H.R.H. The Prince of Wales	7
ELECTRIC SPARK			9–11	A. Waddington	Mr. R. Wright	8
MUM			10–5	W. Hoysted	Mr. J. G. Mosenthal	9
FAIRY QUEEN			9–11	Oates	Mr. Saunders Davies	10
CORNER			9–7	D. Read	Mr. W. Harris	11
GENTLE IDA			11–7	W. Taylor	Mr. Horatio Bottomley	F.
XEBEE			11–4	Mr. A. W. Wood	Mr. R. C. B. Cave	F.
THE SAPPER			10–11	Mr. G. S. Davies	Maj. J. A. Orr-Ewing	F.
TRADE MARK			10–2	Knox	Mr. A. Alexander	P.U.
PISTACHE			9–13	Owner	Count de Geloes	F.
LOTUS LILY			9–12	W. Latham	Capt. Ethelston	F.
SHERIFF HUTTON			9–10	C. Hogan	Mr. F. W. Greswolde-William	P.U.
LITTLE NORTON			9–7	C. Clack	Mr. G. R. Powell	F.

Winner trained by Collins.

STARTING PRICES

4–1 Gentle Ida	100–7 Sheriff Hutton	40–1 Ford of Fyne
5–1 Manifesto	20–1 Elliman, Electric Spark	100–1 Pistache, Mum, Fairy Queen
100–12 Ambush II	25–1 Trade Mark, Barsac	200–1 Others
10–1 The Sapper	33–1 Xebee, Dead Level	
00–8 Lotus Lily		

Going: GOOD   *Starters:* 16   *Time:* 10 MIN. 1⅖ SEC.
Weather: CLEAR   *Date:* MARCH 30

Horse	Colour and Sex	Age	Weight	Jockey	Owner	Position at Finish
AMBUSH II *by Ben Battle— Miss Plant*	b. g.	6	11–3	Anthony	H.R.H. The Prince of Wales	1
BARSAC *by Barcaldine— Stillwater*	ch. h.	a.	9–12	W. Halsey	Mr. C. H. Brown	2
MANIFESTO *by Man of War— Væ Victis*	b. g.	a.	12–13	G. Williamson	Mr. J. G. Bulteel	3
BREEMONT'S PRIDE *by Kendal— Mavourneen*	b. m.	a.	11–7	Mr. G. S. Davies	Mr. G. Edwardes	4
LEVANTER			9–8	McGuire	Capt. Scott	5
GRUDON			10–5	Mr. M. B. Bletsoe	Mr. B. Bletsoe	6
EASTER OGUE			9–13	C. Hogan	Lord William Beresford	7
LOTUS LILY			9–10 (carried 1 lb. extra)	Mr. A. W. Wood	Capt. R. W. Ethelston	8
SISTER ELIZABETH			10	C. Clack	Mr. Arthur James	9
MODEL			10–7	P. Woodland	Mr. E. Woodland	10
ELLIMAN			10–1	E. Driscoll	Mr. Audley Blyth	11
HIDDEN MYSTERY			12	Mr. H. Nugent	Col. Gallwey	K.O.
COVERT HACK			11	F. Mason	Capt. Eustace Loder	F.
ALPHEUS			10–10	A. Waddington	Mr. Vyner	F.
BARCALWHEY			10	T. Lane	Mr. J. Cannon	F.
NOTHING			9–7	W. Hoysted	Mr. G. R. Powell	R.O.

Winner trained in Ireland.

STARTING PRICES

75–20 Hidden Mystery
4–1 Ambush II
6–1 Manifesto
100–7 Elliman

100–6 Covert Hack
20–1 Breemont's Pride, Barcalwhey
25–1 Barsac, Lotus Lily

40–1 Sister Elizabeth, Grudon, Alpheus
50–1 Levanter
66–1 Easter Ogue, Model
100–1 Nothing

Going: VERY DEEP—COURSE WHITE WITH SNOW *Starters:* 24 *Time:* 9 MIN. 47⅘ SEC.

Weather: BLINDING SNOWSTORM *Date:* MARCH 29

Horse	Colour and Sex	Age	Weight	Jockey	Owner	Position at Finish
GRUDON *by Old Back—Avis*	br. h.	a.	10	A. Nightingall	Mr. B. Bletsoe	1
DRUMCREE *by Ascetic— Witching Hour*	b. g.	a.	9–12 (including 2lbs. extra)	Mr. H. Nugent	Mr. O. J. Williams	2
BUFFALO BILL *by Master Bill—Etna*	ch. g.	a.	9–7	H. Taylor	Mr. J. E. Rogerson	3
LEVANTER			9–13	F. Mason	Maj. J. D. Edwards	4
FANCIFUL			11–6	Mr. W. P. Cullen	Mr. T. Tunstall-Moore	5
CURAGH HILL			9–9	C. Hagan	Mr. J. Lonsdale	6
COVERT HACK			11–4	Anthony	Capt. Eustace Loder	7
PRINCE TUSCAN			10–6	Owner	Mr. H. Hunt	8
MODEL			11–4	Owner	Mr. W. H. Pawson	
CUSHENDEN			11–2	Mr. J. G. Davies	Capt. H. H. Johnstone	
SUNNY SHOWER			10–6 (carried 10–8)	Mr. J. T. Widger	Mrs. J. Widger	
COOLGARDIE			10–6	A. Waddington	Mr. R. Davy	
THE SAPPER			10–5	W. Halsey	Mr. W. H. Pawson	
MAYO'S PRIDE			10–5	Mr. Phillips	Mr. W. W. Lewison	
HOMPOOL			10–5	Acres	Mr. B. Wade	
GREYSTONE II			10–1	J. H. Stainton	Mr. J. Herdman	
TRUE BLUE			9–13	P. Woodland	Mr. V. A. Parnell B.L., DES.	
BARSAC			9–13	Mr. H. M. Ripley	Mr. C. H. Brown	
CHIT CHAT			9–13 (carried 10–2)	C. Clack	Capt. Machell	
CROSSET			9–13	Mr. F. Hartigan	Mr. H. Barnato	
PAWNBROKER			9–7	J. O'Brien	Mr. R. C. Dawson	
ZODIAC			9–7	A. Banner	Mr. F. Bibby	
PADISHAH			10	A. Birch	Mr. A. Gorman	
GOSSIP			9–7	J. Polletti	Mr. F. Keene	

Winner trained by T. Holland.

Just what happened to the various horses in this race is very indefinite. Eight finished in the order indicated above; but the weather conditions were so impossible that neither spectators nor jockeys could get any detailed idea of the race.

STARTING PRICES

5–1 Levanter	100–8 Fanciful, The Sapper	40–1 Model, Coolgardie
100–14 Barsac	100–6 Pawnbroker	66–1 Hompool, True Blue
9–1 Grudon	20–1 Cushenden, Crosset	Padishah
10–1 Covert Hack, Drumcree	25–1 Chit Chat, Curagh Hill	100–1 Others
	33–1 Buffalo Bill, Prince Tuscan	

1902

Going: HEAVY
Weather: CLEAR

Starters: 21
Date: MARCH 21

Time: 10 MIN. 3⅗ SEC.

Horse	Colour and Sex	Age	Weight	Jockey	Owner	Position at Finish
SHANNON LASS *by Butterscotch— Mazurka*	b. or br. m.	a.	10–1	D. Read	Mr. A. Gorham	1
MATTHEW *by Tacitus— Golden Locks*	ch. g.	6	9–12	W. Morgan	Mr. John Widger	2
MANIFESTO *by Man of War— Væ Victis*	b. g.	a.	12–8	A. E. Piggott	Mr. J. G. Bulteel	3
DETAIL			9–9	A. Nightingall	Mr. White-Heather	4
LURGAN			10–12	F. Freemantle	Lord Cadogan	5
TIPPERARY BOY			11–6	T. Moran	Mr. T. B. Holmes	6
DRUMCREE			10–10	Mr. H. Nugent	Mr. J. S. Morrison	7
BARSAC			9–12	F. Mason	Mr. C. A. Brown	8
THE SAPPER			10–3 (incl. 2 lbs. extra)	H. Brown	Mr. W. H. Pawson	9
MISS CLIFDEN II			9–7	Mr. H. M. Ripley	Mr. F. W. Pole-hampton	10
STEADY GLASS			9–8	Mr. Longworth	Mr. R. Harding	11
DRUMREE			11–4	A. Anthony	Duke of Westminster	K. O.
HELMIN			10–10	Caley	Mr. S. W. Tinsley	
INQUISITOR				Mr. A. W. Wood	Lord Coventry	F.
ARNOLD			10–1	T. H. Bissill	Mr. J. A. Scorrer	
DIRKHAMPTON			10	Mr. J. Sharpe	Col.W.H.W.Lawson	F.
AUNT MAY			10	M. Walsh	Mr. B. W. Parr	
WHITEHAVEN			9–13	P. Woodland	Lord Denman	P. U.
FAIRLAND			9–7 (carried 9–10)	E. Acres	Mr. T. Bates	F.
ZODIAC			9–7	A. Banner	Mr. F. Bibby	P. U.
GOSSIP			9–7	H. Hewitt	Mr. Foxhall Keene	

Winner trained by Hackett.

STARTING PRICES

6–1 Drumree, Inquisitor
7–1 Barsac
10–1 Drumcree
100–8 Lurgan
100–8 Tipperary Boy

100–6 Manifesto
20–1 Shannon Lass, White-haven, Aunt May
25–1 Fairland, Detail
33–1 Arnold

40–1 The Sapper
50–1 Matthew, Miss Clif-den II, Helmin, Dirkhampton
100–1 Others

1903

Going: GOOD   *Starters:* 23   *Time:* 10 MIN. 9⅖ SEC.

Weather: PERFECT   *Date:* MARCH 27

Horse	Colour and Sex	Age	Weight	Jockey	Owner	Position at Finish
DRUMCREE *by Ascetic—Witching Hour*	b. g.	9	11–3	P. Woodland	Mr. J. S. Morrison	1
DETAIL *by Curly—Rosara*	b. g.	7	9–13	A. Nightingall	Mr. White-Heather	2
MANIFESTO *by Man of War—Væ Victis*	b. g.	15	12–3	G. Williamson	Mr. J. G. Bulteel	3
KIRKLAND *by Kirkham—Perigonius mare*		7	10–8	F. Mason	Mr. F. Bibby	4
AMBUSH II *by Ben Battle—Miss Plant*		9	12–7	A. Anthony	His Majesty The King	F.
FANCIFUL *by Hackler—Miss Fanny*		8	11–7	Mr. W. P. Cullen	Mr. H. Tunstall Moore	
DRUMREE *by Royal Meath—Comrie*		7	11–4	J. Phillips	Duke of Westminster	F.
INQUISITOR *by Cossack—Umpire mare*		8	10–13	R. Matthews	Lord Coventry	F.
FAIRLAND *by Ascetic—Far Away*		10	10–13	W. Morgan	Mr. T. Bates	F.
MARPESSA *by Marmeton—Grecian*		6	10–11	Mr. Persse	Maj. Loder	F.
CUSHENDON *by Timothy—Craftiness*		8	10–10	F. Cole	Mr. H. Bottomley	F.
KILMALLOO *by Torpedo—Andrea*		6	10–9	T. Moran	Mr. J. R. Cooper	F.
DEERSLAYER *by Hawkeye—Wallflower*		7	10–11	E. Piggott	Mr. J. G. Bulteel	F.
PRIDE OF MABESTOWN *by Ascetic—Witching Hour*		7	10–8	W. Dollery	Mr. Owen J. Williams	
PATLANDER *by Sir Patrick—Theodora II*		7	10–7	M. Walsh	Mr. W. Nelson	F.
MATTHEW *by Tacitus—Golden Lock*		7	10–7	Mr. J. W. Widger	Mr. John Widger	F.
EXPERT II *by Studey—Well Done*		6	10–5	J. Woodland	Mr. W. Haven	F.
AUNT MAY *by Ascetic—Mayo*		7	10	O. Read	Mr. B. W. Parr	
BENVENIR *by Bennithorpe—Souvenir*		7	9–12	Mr. Hayes	Mr. J. Moleady	
ORANGE PAT *by Ascetic—Orange Bitters*		7	9–10	R. Morgan	Mr. B. W. Parr	F.
PAWNBROKER *by Westmoreland— Uncertainty*		8	9–9	J. O'Brien	Mr. R. C. Dawson	
SAXILBY *by Carlton—Koza*		6	9–7	G. Goswell	Mr. G. C. Dobell	F.
GILLIE II *by Sweetheart— Mountain Queen*		11	9–7	A. Wilkins	Mr. C. D. Barron	F.

Winner trained by Sir Charles Nugent.

STARTING PRICES

13–2	Drumcree	100–6	Ambush II, Fanciful, Inquisitor
100–14	Detail		
10–1	Pride of Mabestown, Aunt May, Matthew	25–1	Marpessa, Manifesto, Drumree, Deerslayer
100–8	Kirkland	20–1	Fairland, Kilmalloo
40–1	Patlander, Expert II, Orange Pat		
50–1	Saxilby		
100–1	Others		

1904

Horse	Colour and Sex	Age	Weight	Jockey	Owner	Position at Finish
MOIFAA *by Natator—Denbigh*	br. g.	8	10–7	A. Birch	Mr. Spencer Gollan	1
KIRKLAND *by Kirkham— Perigonius mare*	ch. g.	8	10–10	F. Mason	Mr. F. Bibby	2
THE GUNNER *by Torpedo— Lady Windermere*		7	10–4	Mr. J. W. Widger	Mr. John Widger	3
SHAWN ABOO *by Chittaboo—Thelma*		6	10–1	A. Waddington	Maj. J. D. Edwards	4
ROBIN HOOD IV *by Red Prince II— dam's pedigree unknown*		6	10–3	A. Magee	Mr. E. E. Lennon	
BAND OF HOPE *by Enthusiast—Infula*		8	9–13	P. Cowley	Capt. Michael Hughes	
NAPILLAH *by Baliol—Little Nell*		8	9–9 (carried 9–11)	Mr. A. Wood	Mr. Morgan Crowther	
BENVENIR *by Bennithorpe—Souvenir*		8	9–10	P. Woodland	Mr. W. N. W. Gape	
AMBUSH II *by Ben Battle—Miss Plant*		10	12–6	A. Anthony	His Majesty The King	F.
MANIFESTO *by Man of War—Væ Victis*		16	12–1	H. Pigott	Mr. J. G. Bulteel	
THE PRIDE OF MABESTOWN *by Ascetic—Witching Hour*		8	11	Mr. A. Gordon	Mr. Owen J. Williams	F.
INQUISITOR *by Cassock—Umpire mare*				E. Acres	Lord Coventry	F.
PATLANDER *by Sir Patrick—Theodora II*		8	10–10	E. Matthews	Mr. W. E. Nelson	F.
DEERSLAYER *by Hawkeye—Wallflower*		8	10–10	J. Phillips	Prince Hatzfeldt	F.
DETAIL *by Curly—Rosara*				A. Nightingall	Mr. White-Heather	K. O.
CUSHENDON *by Timothy—Craftiness*		9	10–7	D. Morris	Mr.Horatio Bottomley	F.
KNIGHT OF ST. PATRICK *by Craig Royston— dam by Ireland Yet*		7	10–6	M. Walsh	Mr. A. Buckley, Jr.	
MAY KING *by May Boy—Katie Kendal*		8	10–5	W. Dollery	Mr. W. J. Compton	P. U.
COMFIT *by Butterscotch— Clan Ronald mare*		6	10–4	Mr. F. Hartigan	Mr. F. Bibby	F.
BIOLOGY *by St. Hilaire—Myrhh*		7	10–1	D. Read	Mr.Horatio Bottomley	F.
LOCH LOMOND *by Blairfinder—Yvette*		6	9–10	F. Freemantle	Mr. F. H. Wise	F.
RAILOFF *by Peterhoff—Railstorm*		7	9–9	R. Sullivan	Mr. K. Henry	F.
OLD TOWN *by Atheling—Carrollstown's dam*		13	9–7 (carried 9–8)	Mr. H. Ripley	Comte de Madre	P. U.
HONEYMOON II *by Monsieur—Moonrise*		9	9–7	W. Lynn	Mr. Barclay Walker	F.

1904—*Continued*

Horse	Age	Weight	Jockey	Owner	Position at Finish
KIORA *by Blue Mountain—May*	9	10–3	T. McGuire	Capt. Scott	F.
HILL OF BREE *by Ascetic—Au Revoir*	8	10–4	G. Goswell	Mr. W. Hall Walker	

STARTING PRICES

7–2 Ambush II	20–1 Benvenir, Manifesto	40–1 Band of Hope, Kiora
7–1 Patlander	25–1 May King, Moifaa,	50–1 Honeymoon II
100–14 Detail	Deerslayer, The Gunner	66–1 Pride of Mabestown,
9–1 Inquisitor	33–1 Comfit, Biology, Robin	Loch Lomond
100–7 Kirkland	Hood IV, Hill of Bree	100–1 Others

Q

Going: AVERAGE   *Starters:* 27   *Time:* 9 MIN. 48⅘ SEC.

Weather: CLEAR   *Date:* MARCH 31

Horse	Colour and Sex	Age	Weight	Jockey	Owner	Position at Finish
KIRKLAND by Kirkham (bred in Australia)—dam by Perigonius	ch. g.	9	11–5	F. Mason	Mr. F. Bibby	1
NAPPER TANDY by Ireland—Sweet Ethel	b. g.	8	10	P. Woodland	Capt. McLaren	2
BUCKAWAY II by Bennithorpe—Souvenir	br. g.	7	9–11	A. Newey	Mr. P. E. Speakman	3
RANUNCULUS by Quidnunc—Buttercup				C. Hollebone	Mr. T. Nolan	4
HERCULES II by St. Michal—Norrie		9	9–10	J. Dillon	Mr. D. Faber	
BAND OF HOPE by Enthusiast—Infula		9	9–11	W. Dowelly	Mr. W. M. G. Singer	
COTTENSHOPE by Enthusiast—Maidstone		9	9–11	D. Morris	Mr. C. Levy	
PHIL MAY by Milner—Sister May		6	11	R. Morgan	Mr. H. T. Fenwick	F.
MOIFAA by Natator—Denbigh		9	11–12	W. Dollery	His Majesty The King	F.
THE ACTUARY by Immune—dam by Cadet		7	10–9	E. Matthews	Mr. Leslie Rome	P. U.
AUNT MAY by Ascetic—Mayo			10–9	E. Sullivan	Mr. B. W. Parr	F.
MATTHEW by Tacitus—Golden Locks		9	10–9	W. Morgan	Mr. W. Bass	P. U.
DEERSLAYER by Hawkeye—Wallflower		9	10–8	Hon. A. Hastings	Prince Hatzfeldt	F.
LONGTHORPE by St. Serf—Orlet		8	10–7	P. Freemantle	Lord Sefton	REF.
SEAHORSE II by Nelson—Moon		7	10–7	D. O'Brien	Mr. Cotton	P. U.
DETAIL by Curly—Rosara		9	10–8	P. Cowley	Mr. White-Heather	F.
BUCHERON by Chalet—Bannerol		10	10–6	V. David	Count de Songeon	F.
TIMOTHY TITUS by Timothy—Precipice		7	10–5	E. Morgan	Mr. W. B. Partridge	F.
ASCETIC'S SILVER by Ascetic—Silver Lady	ch. h.	8	10–8	T. Dunn	Mr. P. J. Dunne	F.
ROYAL DRAKE by Royal Emperor—Manganese		7	10–4	A. Waddington	Sir P. Walker	F.
BIOLOGY by St. Hilaire—Myrrh			10–12	W. Woodland	Mr. H. Bottomley	F.
WHAT NEXT by Dictator or Quidnunc		7	10–2	Capt. Rasbotham	Mr. W. B. Black	F.
MISS CLIFDEN II by FitzClifden—King Fury's dam		9	9–13	F. Barter	Mr. D. Faber	F.
SAXILBY by Carlton—Koza		8	9–12	P. Heany	Mr. G. C. Dovell	

1905—*Continued*

Horse	Age	Weight	Jockey	Owner	Position at Finish
KIORA *by Blue Mountain—May*	10	9–11 (carried 10–5)	Owner	Mr. W. H. Pawson	F.
NEREUS *by Ocean Wave— Storm Witch*	7	9–10	G. Goswell	Mr. C. Bower Ismay	REF
HALLGATE *by New Barns*	6	9–7	Cole	Mr. Delagarde	F.

STARTING PRICES

4–1 Moifaa
6–1 Kirkland
7–1 Ranunculus
100–8 Aunt May
100–7 Detail

100–6 Timothy Titus, Deerslayer
20–1 Phil May, Seahorse II,
Royal Drake, Ascetic's
Silver
25–1 Napper Tandy
33–1 Hercules II, Longthorpe

40–1 Biology
50–1 What Next
66–1 Cottenshope, The
Actuary, Nereus,
Matthew, Saxilby
100–1 Others

1906

Going: GOOD   *Starters:* 23   *Time:* 9 MIN. 34⅖ SEC.
Weather: SUNNY   *Date:* MARCH 30

Horse	Colour and Sex	Age	Weight	Jockey	Owner	Position at Finish
ASCETIC'S SILVER *by Ascetic—Silver Lady*	ch. g.	a.	10–9	Hon. A. Hastings	Prince Hatzfeldt	1
RED LAD *by Red Prince II— Border Lassie*	ch. g.	6	10–2	C. Kelly	Mr. E. M. Lucas	2
AUNT MAY *by Ascetic—Mayo*	ch. m.	a.	11–2	Mr. H. Persse	Mr. B. W. Parr	3
CRAUTACAUN		a.	10–6	I. Anthony	Mr. J. W. Phillip	4
WOLF'S FOLLY		a.	10–6	T. Fitton	Mr. H. Gorham	5
OATLANDS		6	9–13	H. Aylin	Mr. C. T. Garland	6
GLADIATOR		6	9–9	E. Driscoll	Mr. G. Johnstone	7 (R.)
DRUMCREE *by Ascetic—Witching Hour*		a.	12–2	Mr. W. Bulteel	Mr. J. S. Morrison	8
PHIL MAY		7	11–5	J. Owens	Mr. Cotton	9 (R.)
JOHN M. P.		a.	11–10 (incl. 2 lbs. extra)	W. Taylor	Mr. J. S. Morrison	F.
ROMAN LAW		a.	11–5	J. Walsh, Jr.	Mr. H. Buckley, Jr.	K. O.
COMFIT *by Butterscotch— Clan Ronald mare*		a.	11	F. Mason	Mr. F. Bibby	
TIMOTHY TITUS *by Timothy—Precipice*		a.	11–12	E. Morgan	Mr. W. B. Partridge	F.
BUCKAWAY II *by Bennithorpe—Souvenir*		a.	10–4	A. Newey	Mr. P. E. Speakman	F.
DATHI		a.	10–4	A. Birch	Mr. T. Clyde	F.
KIORA *by Blue Mountain—May*		a.	10–4	G. Clancy	Mr. C. Bewicke	K. O.
DEERSLAYER *by Hawkeye—Wallflower*		a.	10–4	Mr. P. Whitaker	Prince Hatzfeldt	P. U.
HILL OF BREE *by Ascetic—Au Revoir*		a.	10–3	R. Chadwick	Mr. W. Hall Walker	K. O.
CANTER HOME		a.	9–13 (incl. 6 lbs. extra)	A. Aylin	Lord Sefton	F.
GLENREX		6	9–9	Mr. R. Walker	Mr. Barclay Walker	F.
ST. BOSWELLS		a.	9–7	D. Phelan	Mr. J. Bell-Irving	F.
PIERRE *by Pierrepoint—Little Go*		a.	9–7	J. Dillon	Mr. W. Paul	P. U.
HARD TO FIND		6	9–7	E. R. Morgan	Prince Hatzfeldt	F.

Winner trained by Hon. A. Hastings at Wroughton.

STARTING PRICES

7–2 John M.P.
9–1 Phil May
10–1 Comfit, Timothy Titus
100–7 Roman Law

100–6 Oatlands, Wolf's Folly, Gladiator, Crautacaun
20–1 Ascetic's Silver, Buck- away II
25–1 Aunt May, Dathi

33–1 Drumcree, Kiora, Pierre, Red Lad
50–1 Deerslayer
100–1 Glenrex
66–1 Others

T H E Grand National Steeplechase of 3,000 sovs, including a trophy value 125 sovs., second receives 300 sovs., the third 200 sovs., and the fourth 75 sovs. from the stakes; a handicap for five-year-olds and upwards; Grand National Course (about four miles 856 yards).

Going: GOOD   *Starters:* 23   *Time:* 9 MIN. 47½ SEC.
Weather: SUNNY   *Date:* MARCH 22

Horse	Colour and Sex	Age	Weight	Jockey	Owner	Position at Finish
EREMON *by Thurles—Daisy*	b. g.	7	10–1	A. Newey	Mr. Stanley Howard	1
TOM WEST *by Old Buck— Mother Shipton*	b. g.	8	9–12	H. Murphy	Mr. H. Hardy	2
PATLANDER *by Sir Patrick— Theodora II*	b. g.	11	10–7	J. Lynn	Mr. W. Nelson	3
RAVENSCLIFFE *by Ravensbury— Marie le Ragois*	b. g.	9	10–9	F. Lyall	Mr. R. J. Hannam	4
BARABBAS II *by Batt—Siberia*	br. h.	6	10–5 (carried 10–7)	R. Morgan	Mr. S. J. Unzue	5
ASCETIC'S SILVER *by Ascetic— Silver Lady*	ch.h.	10	12–7	Hon. A. Hastings	Prince Hatzfeldt	6
BUCKAWAY II *by Bennithorpe— Souvenir*	bl. g.	9	10–4	H. Aylin	Mr. P. E. Speakman	7
NAPPER TANDY *by Ireland— Sweet Ethel*	b. g.	10	10-13	Capt. Collis	Capt. McLaren	8
TIMOTHY TITUS *by Timothy— Precipice*	bl. g.	9	11–10	C. Kelly	Mr. W. B. Partridge	F.
DRUMCREE *by Ascetic— Witching Hour*	b. g.	a.	11–9	Mr. W. Bulteel	Mr. J. S. Morrison	F.
ROMAN LAW *by Tacitus— Lady Beatrice*	b. g.	9	11–7	A. Anthony	Mr. A. Buckley	P. U.
RED LAD *by Red Prince II— Border Lassie*	ch. g.	7	11–3	J. Dillon	Mr. C. Hibbert	F.
SEISDON PRINCE *by Dog Rose—Fudge*	b. g.	8	11	M. Phelan	Mr. T. Ashton	P. U.
RATHVALE *by Northampton or Ignis Fatuus—Secret*	ch. g.	6	10–13	E. Driscoll	Prince Hatzfeldt	F.
EXTRAVAGANCE *by Carlton Grange— Belle Demoiselle*	ch. g.	6	10–11	G. Goswell	Mr. G. Walmesley	F.
CENTRE BOARD *by Speed—Ballast*	b. g.	7	10–11	J. Cain	Lord Howard de Walden	REF.

Horse	Colour and Sex	Age	Weight	Jockey	Owner	Position at Finish
BOUCHAL OGUE *by Kentford—* *Spraight-in-Chint*	b. g.	11	10–7	C. Graham	Mr. J. Meynell-Knight	F.
YORK II *by Tostig—* *Conclusion*	ch. g.	8	10–6	T. Moran	Mr. Lionel Robinson	F.
KILTS *by Kilmarnock—* *Rockery mare*	br. g.	7	10–3	R. Harper	Mr. T. G. Arthur	F.
DETAIL *by Curly—Rosara*	b. g.	11	10	W. Payne	Mr. White-Heather	F.
LOOP HEAD *by Brayhead—* *Barberry*	ch. g.	8	9–12	A. Hogan	Mr. F. Bibby	F.
TEDDY III *by Warspite—* *Bayberry*	b. m.	9	9–13	Mr. O'B. Butler	Mr. W. P. Hanley	
FOREMAN *by Bend Or or* *Orme—Crusado*	b. g.	8	9–7	Lawn	Mr. T. Nolan	

Winner bred by Mr. Jas. Cleary; trained by Coulthwaite, at Hednesford.

STARTING PRICES

7–1 Red Lad, Ascetic's Silver	100–8 Timothy Titus	33–1 Napper Tandy
8–1 Eremon	100–7 Ravenscliffe	40–1 Detail, Buckaway II
10–1 Extravagance	100–6 Tom West, Kilts	50–1 Others
	20–1 Rathvale, Barabbas II, Centre Board, Drumcree	

Going: HEAVY			*Starters:* 24		*Time:* 10 MIN. 33 ⅕ SEC.	
Weather: SUNNY			*Date:* MARCH 27			

Horse	*Colour and Sex*	*Age*	*Weight*	*Jockey*	*Owner*	*Position at Finish*
RUBIO *by Star Ruby— La Toquera*	ch. g.	a.	10–5	H. Bletsoe	Maj. F. Douglas-Pennant	I
MATTIE MACGREGOR *by Evan Macgregor—Ju*	b. m.	6	10–6	W. Bissell	Mr. William Cooper	2
THE LAWYER III *by Broxton, dam by Solon*	ch. g.	a.	10–13	Owner	Mr. P. Whitaker	3
FLAXMAN *by Hackler—Circe*	b. g.	a.	9–12	A. Anthony	His Majesty The King	4
SPRINGBOK		a.	11–5	J. O'Brien	Col. R. L. Birkin	5
RED HALL		a.	10–1 (carried 10–8)	Owner	Mr. H. G. Farrant	6
KIRKLAND		a.	11–12	F. Mason	Mr. F. Bibby	7 (F., REM.)
CHORUS		a.	10–5	R. Chadwick	Mr. Foxhall Keene	8
MOUNT PROSPECT'S FORTUNE		6	11–11	R. Morgan	Mr. P. Nelke	F.
ROMAN LAW		a.	11–2	A. Newey	Mr. A. Buckley, Jr.	F.
SEISDON PRINCE		a.	11	M. Phelan	Mr. T. Ashton	F.
EXTRAVAGANCE		a.	10–12	H. Aylin	Mr. G. Walmsley	K. O.
LARA		a.	10–8	Mr. Bulteel	Capt. J. Foster	F.
NANOYA		6	10–7	J. Lynn	Mr. B. W. Parr	F.
TOM WEST		a.	10–7	H. Murphy	Mr. H. Hardy	F.
JENKINSTOWN		a.	10–5	F. Morgan	Mr. S. Howard	P. U.
YORK II		a.	10–4	W. Rollason	Mr. G. Walmsley	F.
PADDY MAHER		a.	10–3	Mr. O'B. Butler	Col. Kirkwood	F.
DATHIA		a.	10 (carried 10–2)	T. Anthony	Mr. J. W. Philipps	P. U.
PROPHET III		a.	10	J. Dillon	Mr. Foxhall Keene	F.
JOHNSTOWN LAD		a.	9–12	E. Driscoll	Mr. J. M. Kerne	F.
WEE BUSBIE		a.	9–11	D. Phelan	Mr. J. E. Rogerson	F.
ALERT III		a.	9–11	J. Harland	Mr. T. G. Paget	F.
WILD FOX III		6	9–9	Owner	Capt. W. A. Pallin	F.

Winner bred by Mr. J. B. Haggin, at Rancho del Paso Stud, California; trained by Costello, at Stockbridge.

STARTING PRICES

6–1 Kirkland	100–7 Roman Law, Mount Prospect's Fortune, Seisdon Prince, Extravagance, Lawyer III	25–1 Mattie Macgregor, Lara
8–1 Tom West, Springbok		33–1 Flaxman
10–1 Johnstown Lad		66–1 Rubio, and others
100–8 Paddy Maher		

1909

Going: GOOD   *Starters:* 32   *Time:* 9 MIN. 53⅕ SEC.

Weather: CLEAR   *Date:* MARCH 26

Horse	Colour and Sex	Age	Weight	Jockey	Owner	Position at Finish
LUTTEUR III	ch. h.	5	10–11	G. Parfrement	M. J. Hennessy	1
JUDAS *by Wild Monk—Little Alice*	b. g.	a.	10–10	R. Chadwick	Mr. B. W. Parr	2
CAUBEEN *by Chad—Revenue Cutter*	b. h.	a.	11–7	F. Mason	Mr. F. Bibby	3
TOM WEST		a.	10–9	H. Murphy	Mr. H. Hardy	4 (BLUN.)
HERCULES II		a.	9–13	Mr. A. Gordon	Mr. R. Faber	
LEINSTER		a.	11–7	Mr. J. Rogers	Sir T. Gallwey	
SHADY GIRL		a.	10–9	G. Clancy	Mr. P. Nelke	
CARSEY		6	10–8	Owner	Mr. J. M. Kerne	
ROBIN HOOD IV		a.	9–9	Mr. R. Walker	Capt. L. H. Jones	
PHAETON		a.	10–4	Mr. H. Ussher	Col. Kirkwood	
ASCETIC'S SILVER		a.	12–7	Hon. A. Hastings	Prince Hatzfeldt	
WEE BUSBIE		a.	9–12 (carried 9–13)	D. Phelan	Mr. J. E. Rogerson	
LOGAN ROCK		a.	10	H. Jackson	Mr. W. L. Longworth	
RATHVALE		a.	11–7	W. Morgan	Prince Hatzfeldt	
LORD RIVERS		a.	10–6	W. Bulteel	Baron de Forest	
WILD FOX III		a.	9–9	Owner	Capt. W. A. Pallin	REF.
BRINEOGE		a.	10–7	H. Smyth	Mr. C. F. K. Mainwaring	
COUNT RUFUS		a.	10	W. Payne	Mr. W. Charter	F.
RED HALL		a.	10–10 (carried 10–12)	Owner	Mr. H. G. Farrant	F.
RUSTIC QUEEN		a.	12	Mr. A. W. Wood	Mr. H. Hartland	F.
RUBIO		a.	11–9	W. Bissell	Maj. Douglas-Pennant	F.
MATTIE MACGREGOR		a.	11–4	R. Morgan	Mr. W. C. Cooper	REF.
DOMINO		a.	11–1	P. Cowley	Mr. H. M. Hartigan	F.
LORD CHATHAM		a.	11	J. McKenna	Mr. G. Aston	
WICKHAM		a.	10	Capt. Collis	Mr. F. Bibby	F.
PADDY MAHER		a.	10–9	Mr. O'B. Butler	Col. Kirkwood	
BLACK IVORY		a.	10–9 (carried 10–12)	Owner	Mr. A. Scott	P. U.
RED MONK		a.	10–6	E. Morgan	Mr. F. W. Greswolde-William	P. U.
DAVY JONES		6	10 (carried 10–2)	J. Anthony	Lord St. David	F.
BUCKAWAY II		a.	9–12 (carried 9–13)	B. Wall	Mr. S. F. Gilbert	P. U.
YOUNG BUCK		a.	9–12	H. B. Bletsoe	Mr. F. M. Freake	F.
THE LURCHER		a.	9–9	E. Piggott	Mr. T. Stacey	F.

Winner bred in France by M. Gaston Dreyfus; trained by H. Escott at Lewes.

STARTING PRICES

100–9 Lutteur III, Shady Girl
100–8 Domino
100–6 Tom West, Mattie Macgregor, Leinster, Davy Jones

20–1 Caubeen, Rubio, Ascetic's Silver
25–1 The Lurcher, Paddy Maher, Lord Rivers
33–1 Judas, Hercules II, Robin Hood IV

50–1 Wickham, Rustic Queen, Lord Chatham, Logan Rock, Count Rufus, Red Hall
100–1 Others

1910

Going: PERFECT *Starters:* 25 *Time:* 10 MIN. 44 ⅕ SEC.
Weather: SNOW STOPPED AT LAST MINUTE; CLEAR *Date:* MARCH 18

Horse	Colour and Sex	Age	Weight	Jockey	Owner	Position at Finish
JENKINSTOWN	b. g.	a.	10–5	R. Chadwick	Mr. Stanley Howard	1
by Hackler—Playmate						
JERRY M.	b. g.	a.	12–7	E. Driscoll	Mr. Assheton Smith	2
by Walmsgate, dam by						
Luminary—Quinine						
ODOR	ch. h.	a.	9–7	Owner	Mr. R. Hall	3
by Chevele d'Or—			(carried 9–8)			
Jessamine						
CARSEY		a.	10–7	G. R. Morgan	Prince Hatzfeldt	4
FETLAR'S PRIDE		a.	10–11	J. Walsh, Jr.	Mr. Law	5
CAUBEEN		a.	11–8	F. Mason	Mr. F. Bibby	F.
BLOODSTONE		a.	11–8	S. Walkington	Mr. Ismay	F.
SPRINGBOK		a.	11–5	W. Payne	Col. R. Birkin	P. U
JUDAS		a.	11–5	A. Anthony	Mr. W. Bailey	F.
RATHVALE		a.	11–1	R. Morgan	Prince Hatzfeldt	F.
LORD CHATHAM		a.	10–12	J. Dillon	Mr. G. Aston	F.
ALBUERA		a.	10–12	F. Lyall	Sir P. Walker	F.
WICKHAM		a.	10–11	W. Bulteel	Mr. F. Bibby	F.
PADDY MAHER		a.	10–9	Mr. R. H. Walker	Col. Kirkwood	F.
SHADY GIRL		a.	10–8	G. Clancy	Mr. P. Nelke	F.
PRECENTOR II		a.	10–7	W. Rollason	Mr. Foxhall Keene	P. U.
GLENSIDE		a.	10–4	R. Goswell	Mr. F. Bibby	F.
BRINEOGE		a.	10–4	Mr. F. A. Brown	Mr. C. F. K. Main-waring	REF.
GENERAL FOX		6	10–12	T. Wilmot	Lord Suffolk	F.
PHAETON		a.	10	F. Morgan	Col. Kirkwood	K. O.
			(carried 10–1)			
HERCULES II		a.	9–9	C. Hawkins	Mr. D. Faber	F.
THE LURCHER		a.	9–9	F. Dainly	Mr. Stacey	F.
CAPTAIN FARRELL		6	9–7	G. Brown	Sir John Smiley	REF.
			(carried 9–10)			
LOGAN ROCK		a.	9–7	H. Jackson	Mr. Longworth	K. O.
BUSHIDO		5	9–7	J. Hetherington	Mr. J. A. de Roths-child	K. O.

Winner bred by Mr. P. Leonard; trained by T. Coulthwaite, at Hednesford.

STARTING PRICES

6–1 Jerry M.	100–6 The Lurcher	33–1 Paddy Maher, Shady
13–2 Judas	20–1 Logan Rock	Girl
8–1 Caubeen	25–1 Glenside, Fetlar's	66–1 Wickham, Bushido,
100–8 Jenkinstown, Carsey	Pride, Springbok	Rathvale, General Fox
100–7 Bloodstone, Albuera		100–1 Others

1911

Going: VERY HEAVY   *Starters:* 26   *Time:* 10 MIN. 35 SEC.
Weather: RAIN   *Date:* MARCH 24

Horse	Colour and Sex	Age	Weight	Jockey	Owner	Position at Finish
GLENSIDE	b. g.	a.	10–3	Mr. J. Anthony	Mr. F. Bibby	1
RATHNALLY		6	11	R. Chadwick	Mr. O. H. Jones	2
by St. Pat—Alanna						
SHADY GIRL	br. m.	a.	10–5	G. Clancy	Mr. P. Nelke	3
by Le Noir—Gertie						
FOOLHARDY		a.	9–7	Owner	Mr. MacNeill	4
LUTTEUR III		a.	12–3	G. Parfrement	Mr. James Hennessy	F.
TRIANON III		6	11–8	R. Sauval	Mr. H. de Mumm	F.
JENKINSTOWN		a.	11–7	P. Woodland	Mr. S. Howard	P. U.
MOUNT PROSPECT'S FORTUNE		a.	11–6	E. Driscoll	Mr. P. Nelke	F.
RORY O'MOORE		a.	11–6	Owner	Mr. P. Whitaker	K. O.
CAUBEEN		a.	11–5	A. Newey	Mr. F. Bibby	F.
LORD RIVERS		a.	10–9	W. Payne	Baron de Forest	F.
FETLAR'S PRIDE		a.	10–7	J. Walsh, Jr.	Mr. C. Pearson	F.
CARSEY		a.	10–6	P. Cowley	Mr. C. Wildenberg	F.
VIZ		a.	10–5	H. Bletsoe	Mr. G. D'Arcy	F.
MONK V		a.	10–1	Mr. F. Drake	Mr. J. J. Astor	F.
SCHWARMER		a.	10	F. Damly	Mr. J. J. Astor	F.
SUHESCAN		a.	10 (carried 10–1)	A. V. Chapman	Mr. Charles De Gheest	F.
GREAT CROSS		6	9–13	Mr. Walwyn	Maj. J. Cliff	F.
CIRCASSIAN'S PRIDE		a.	9–12 (carried 9–13)	Isaac Morgan	Lady Torrington	K. O.
PRECENTOR II		a.	9–11	A. Aylin	Mr. Foxhall Keene	F.
BRIDGE IV		a.	9–9	Mr. P. Roberts	Mr. F. S. Francis	F.
CARDER		a.	9–7	B. Roberts	Mr. C. Luttrell	F.
FLAXEN		a.	9–7	Mr. A. Smith	Mr. G. L. Pirie	F.
ROMAN CANDLE		a.	9–7	T. Wilmot	Mr. W. Stratton	F.
HESPERUS MAGNUS		a.	9–7	W. Fitzgerald	Mr. D. Faber	P. U.
HERCULES II		a.	9–7 (carried 9–8)	Mr. R. W. Hall	Mr. D. Faber	P. U.

Winner bred by Mr. W. G. Peareth; trained by Captain Collis at Kinlet.

STARTING PRICES

7–2 Lutteur III
8–1 Caubeen, Rathnally
100–9 Carsey
100–7 Rory O'Moore, Jenkinstown
20–1 Glenside

25–1 Schwarmer, Circassian's Pride, Fetlar's Pride
28–1 Roman Candle
33–1 Shady Girl, Lord Rivers, Trianon III

50–1 Flaxen, Foolhardy, Viz, Suhescan, Carder, Hercules II
66–1 Mount Prospect's Fortune, Great Cross, Hesperus Magnus
100–1 Others

W. A. Rouch

Jerry M, who won in 1912. E. Piggot up.

W. A. Rouch

Poethlyn, E. Piggot up, winner in 1918 and 1919.

THE Grand National Steeplechase (handicap) of 3,500 sovs., including a trophy value 125 sovs., by subscription of 30 sovs. each, 20 forfeit, or 5 only if declared by Tuesday, January 30th to Messrs. Weatherby and Sons *only*; the second to receive 200 sovs., the third 100 sovs., and the fourth 70 sovs. from the race; for five-year-olds and upwards; weights published on January 25th, at noon: the lowest weight will be 10 stone. Grand National Course, about four miles and 856 yards.

The breeder of the winner will receive 100 sovs.

Going: AVERAGE *Starters:* 24 *Time:* 10 MIN. 13⅗ SEC.
Weather: CLEAR *Date:* MARCH 29

Horse	Colour and Sex	Age	Weight	Jockey	Owner	Position at Finish
JERRY M. *by Walmsgate— dam by Luminary*	b. g.	9	12–7	E. Piggot	Sir C. Assheton-Smith	1
BLOODSTONE *by Cherrystone— Royal Bride*	b. g.	10	11–6	F. Lyall	Mr. C. Bower Ismay	2
AXLE PIN *by Quidnunc— Hairpin*	br. g.	8	10–2	I. Anthony	Lord Derby	3
CARSEY *by Kersey—Fiction*	b. g.	9	10–13	Mr. H. T. Drake	Mr. C. H. Wildenburg	4
MOUNT PROSPECT'S FORTUNE *by St. Gris— Lady Childers*	g.	10	11–4	J. Kelly	Mr. P. Nelke	5
SIR HALBERT *by Hackler— Duchess II*	g.	9	10–6	Mr. A. Smith	Capt. F. D. Grissell	6
WHITELEG'S II *pedigree unknown*	ch. g.	8	10–2	J. Farrell	Mr. E. Brandon	7
RATHNALLY *by St. Pat—Alanna*	b. g.	7	11–11	R. Chadwick	Mr. O. H. Jones	F.
RORY O'MOORE *by Royal Meath— Vandala*	b. g.	11	11–7	F. Mason	Mr. P. Whitaker	
JENKINSTOWN *by Hackler— Playmate*	b. g	11	11–7	W. Payne	Mr. G. W. Blundell	
CAUBEEN *by Chad— Revenue Cutter*	b. h.	11	11–5	A. Newey	Mr. F. Bibby	
GLENSIDE *by Gris—Kilwinnie*	b. g.	10	11	Mr. H. Ussher	Mr. F. Bibby	F.
BALLYHACKLE *by Hackler— Ballymacarney*	g.	9	10–7	I. Morgan	Mr. K. F. Malcolmson	
KILKEEL *by Wiseman—Skit*	g.	7	10–7	R. Trudgill	Mr. Hunter Moore	

Horse	Colour and Sex	Age	Weight	Jockey	Owner
FETLAR'S PRIDE *by Fetlar—Monica II*	g.	11	10–7	G. Lyall	Mr. Clive Pearson
REGENT *by Diamond Jubilee—Western Flower*	g.	7	10–6	F. Morgan	Sir G. Bullough
BRIDGE IV *by Baddiley—Bridget*	g.	8	10–6	Mr. G. Poole	Mr. F. S. Francis
COVERTCOAT *by Hackler—Cinnamon*	b. g.	6	10–5	J. Walsh, Jr.	Sir C. Assheton-Smith
GREAT CROSS *by Rays Cross—Sedately*	g.	7	10–1	E. Lawn	Maj. H. M. Cliff
PRECENTOR II *by Chorister—Lady Invercauld*	g.	13	10	A. Aylin	Mr. Foxhall Keene
GOLD SEAL II *by Gold Reef—Seal Brown*	g.	12	10	J. Finn	Mrs. Croft
SANS PEUR *by Pierrepont—Timidity*	g.	13	10	J. Kay	Mr. William Wilson
FOOLHARDY *by Sainfoin—Retire*	g.	11	10	Owner	Mr. W. MacNeill
GLENFINDER *by Glenvannon, dam by Pathfinder*	g.	11	10	J. Foran	Capt. H. C. Higgins

Winner trained by Gore, second by Coulthwaite, third by Whitaker.

STARTING PRICES

4–1 Rathnally, Jerry M.	100–8 Carsey	33–1 Covertcoat
9–1 Rory O'Moore	100–7 Jenkinstown	40–1 Glenside, Great Cross
100–9 Caubeen	20–1 Axle Pin, Ballyhackle	Bloodstone
	25–1 Bridge IV	

1913

Going: AVERAGE   *Starters:* 23   *Time:* 10 MIN. 19 SEC.

Weather: CLEAR   *Date:* APRIL 4

Horse	Colour and Sex	Age	Weight	Jockey	Owner	Position at Finish
COVERTCOAT by Hackler—Cinnamon	b. g.	7	11–6	P. Woodland	Sir C. Assheton-Smith	1
IRISH MAIL by King's Messenger—Betsy Shannon	br. g.	6	11–4	Mr. O. Anthony	Mr. Tyrwhitt Drake	2
CARSEY by Kersey—Fiction	b. g.	10	12	Mr. H. Drake	Mr. C. H. Wildenburg	3 (F., REM.)
DYSART by Bealdberg, dam by Gay Reveller	g.	8	12–4	Capt. O'B. Butler	Capt. H. C. Higgins	
TRIANON III by Champaubert—Marie Antoinette	br. g.	8	12–3	W. O'Connor	M. H. de Mumm	
HIGHBRIDGE by Bridgewater—Duress	g.	7	12	F. Williams	Mr. J. R. Fell	
BALLYHACKLE by Hackler—Ballymacarney	b. g.	10	11–11	Mr. H. Ussher	Mr. K. F. Malcolmson	
THOWL PIN by Pilot—Hairpin	g.	8	11–9	I. Morgan	Capt. R. H. Collis	
JAMAGATA by Chislehurst—Win Some Money	g.	7	11–8	Owner	M. Bartosch	
REGENT by Diamond Jubilee—Western Flower	g.	8	11–7	Mr. J. R. Anthony	Sir G. Bullough	
THE MINER by Explorer—Diadem	g.	8	11–6	Mr. L. Brabazon	Mr. W. A. Wallis	
MELAMAR by Butterscotch, dam by Luminary	g.	7	11–6	W. Payne	Mr. W. R. Clarke	
BLACK PLUM by Persimmon—Princess Athenais	g.	9	11–5	R. Morgan	Mr. F. S. Watts	
AXLE PIN by Quidnunc—Hairpin	br. g.	9	11–4	Mr. P. Whitaker	Lord Derby	
BLOW PIPE by Bird of Paradise—Balista	g.	8	11–4	W. J. Smith	Mr. M. M. Henderson	
THE REJECTED IV by Toussaint—Katie Hermit	g.	10	11–3	Mr. G. Cotton	Mr. Eric Platt	
MERRY LAND by Chicago, dam by Buckingham	g.	9	11–3	Trudgill	Capt. H. C. Higgins	
FETLAR'S PRIDE by Fetlar—Monica II	g.	12	11	F. Morgan	Mr. C. Pearson	
FEARLESS VII by Red Prince II—Fancy Fair	g.	10	11	Mr. G. Pigot-Moodie	Mr. R. Whitehead	

Horse	Colour and Sex	Age	Weight	Jockey	Owner
WAVELET *by Wavelet's Pride—Mrs. Bowser*	g.	6	11	Alfred Newey	Mr. A. H. Straker
TOKAY *by Santoi—Sweet Muscat*	g.	7	11	M. Hopper	Mr. J. Langley
FOOLHARDY *by Sainfoin—Retire*	g.	11	11	Owner	Mr. W. MacNeill
BLOODSTONE *by Cherrystone—Royal Bride*	b. g.	11	12–7	F. Lyall	Mr. C. Bower Ismay

Winner trained by Gore, second by owner, third by Hon. Aubrey Hastings.

STARTING PRICES

5–1 Ballyhackle	20–1 Thowl Pin	50–1 Dysart, Tokay
100–9 Carsey, Highbridge, Wavelet, Covertcoat	25–1 Irish Mail, Blow Pipe	66–1 Regent, Black Plum
	33–1 Trianon III, Fetlar's Pride	100–1 The Miner, Fearless VII, Merry Land
100–8 Axle Pin, Melamar	40–1 The Rejected IV	
100–6 Bloodstone		200–1 Foolhardy

1914

Going: GOOD   *Starters:* 20   *Time:* 9 MIN. 58⅘ SEC.

Weather: CLEAR   *Date:* MARCH 27

Horse	Colour and Sex	Age	Weight	Jockey	Owner	Position at Finish
SUNLOCH *by Sundorne—Gralloch*	b. g.	8	9–7	W. J. Smith	Mr. T. Tyler	1
TRIANON III *by Champaubert—Marie Antoinette*	br. g.	9	11–9	C. Hawkins	M. H. de Mumm	2
LUTTEUR III *by St. Damien—Lausanne*	ch. g.	10	12–6	A. Carter	Mr. James Hennessy	3
RORY O'MOORE *by Royal Meath—Vandala*	b. g.	13	11–8	Owner	Mr. P. Whitaker	4
COVERTCOAT *by Hackler—Cinnamon*	b. g.	8	12–7	P. Woodland	Sir C. Assheton-Smith	
COUVREFEU II *by Curfew—Regime*	g.	10	11–7	Mr. J.R.Anthony	Sir W. Nelson	
GREAT CROSS *by Rays Cross—Sedately*	g.	9	11	Mr. O. Anthony	Maj. Cliff	
BAHADUR *by Nunthorpe—Azeeza*	g.	11	9–7	Mr. R. H. Hall	Mr. Gore Lambarde	
BALLYHACKLE *by Hackler—Ballymacarney*	b. g.	11	12	Mr. H. Ussher	Mr. K. F. Malcolmson	F.
ANOTHER DELIGHT *by General Symons—Annie's Delight*	g.	10	11–7	G. Brown	Capt. H. Wyndham	F.
BLOODSTONE *by Cherrystone—Royal Bride*	b. g.	12	11–7	F. Lyall	Mr. C. Bower Ismay	R. O.
JACOBUS *by Wavelet's Pride—Kendaline*	b. g.	7	11–2	E. Piggot	Mr. C. Bower Ismay	F.
REGENT *by Diamond Jubilee—Western Flower*	g.	9	10–12	Mr. H. Drake	Sir G. Bullough	B. D.
ILSTON *by Blankney—Lady Rufford*	g.	6	10–12	I. Anthony	Sir G. Bullough	F.
THOWL PIN *by Pilot—Hairpin*	g.	9	10–10	I. Morgan	Mr. F. Bibby	F.
ALL GOLD II *by Soleil d'Or, dam's pedigree unknown*	g.	a.	10–7	Capt. Stokes	Sir J. D. Tichborne	F.
DUTCH PENNANT *by Count Schomberg—Topsail Yard*	g.	8	10–5	Parnham	Capt. Crawshay	F.
BLOW PIPE *by Bird of Paradise—Balista*	g.	9	10–3	H. B. Bletsoe	Mr. Ambrose Shepherd	F.
FETLAR'S PRIDE *by Fetlar—Monica II*	g.	13	10–2	D. Dale	Mr. B. C. Pearson	REF.
DIPLOMATIST II *by First Consul—Alice, pedigree unknown*	g.	9	9–7	Owner	Mr. N. B. Davis	R. O.

Winner trained by owner, second horse trained in France, third horse trained by Escott.

1914—*Continued*

7–1 Covertcoat
10–1 Lutteur, Ilston
100–8 Trianon III
100–7 Ballyhackle

100–6 Sunloch, Jacobus, Bloodstone
20–1 Couvrefeu II, Rory O'Moore

25–1 Blow Pipe
33–1 Another Delight, Regent, Thowl Pin, Bahadur

1915

Going: GOOD   *Starters:* 20   *Time:* 9 MIN. 47⅘ SEC

Weather: CLEAR   *Date:* MARCH 26

Horse	Colour and Sex	Age	Weight	Jockey	Owner	Position at Finish
ALLY SLOPER *by Travelling Lad— Sally in Our Alley*	br. g.	6	10–5	Mr. J. R. Anthony	Lady Nelson	1
JACOBUS *by Wavelet's Pride— Kendaline*	b. g.	8	11	A. Newey	Mr. C. Bower Ismay	2
FATHER CONFESSOR *by St. Gris—Entrenous*	ch. g.	6	9–10	A. Aylin	Lord Suffolk	3
ALFRED NOBLE *by Garry Herrmann— Ethel Pace*	g.	10	10–12	T. Hulme	Mr. T. H. Barnard	4
BALSCADDEN *by Pilot, dam by Wellington—Erminie*	h.	8	11–8	F. Lyall	Mr. C. Bower Ismay	REM.
THOWL PIN *by Pilot—Hairpin*	g.	10	10–8	W. J. Smith	Mr. F. Bibby	
BLOW PIPE *by Bird of Paradise— Balista*	g.	10	10–4	W. Smith	Mr. A. Shepherd	
HACKLER'S BEY *by Kosmos Bey, dam by Hackler*	g.	8	10	Mr. H. S. Harrison	Sir T. R. Dewar	
SILVER TOP *pedigree unknown*	g.	8	10	S. Walkington	Mr. A. Browne	
IRISH MAIL *by King's Messenger— Betsy Shannon*	br. g.	8	11–12	Mr. L. Brabazon	Mr. Eric Platt	P. U.
BULLAWARRA *by Sir Simon— Nacrite*	g.	10	11–12	C. Hawkins	Mr. J. M. Niall	F.
BALLYHACKLE *by Hackler— Ballymacarney*	g.	12	11–9	S. Avila	Mr. K. F. Malcolmson	B. D.
ILSTON *by Blankney— Lady Rufford*	g.	7	11–8	I. Anthony	Sir G. Bullough	F.
DISTAFF *by Hackler—Circe*	g.	7	10–10	E. Piggot	Sir G. Bullough	P. U.
LORD MARCUS *by Walmsgate or Butter- scotch—Lady Rivers*	g.	7	10–3	G. Parfrement	Lord Lonsdale	F.
THE BABE *by Karma—Cute*	g.	7	10	R. Chadwick	Mr. F. Bibby	P. U.
ST. MATHURIN II *by St. Bris—Margot*	g.	10	9–10	T. Dunn	Mr. Adam Scott	F.
DENIS AUBURN *by General Peace or Denis Richard— Auburn's Pride*	g.	8	9–7	J. Reardon	Sir G. Bullough	F.
BACHELOR'S FLIGHT *by Flying Hackle— Lady Dern*	g.	8	9–7	H. Harty	Mr. F. Barbour	F.
BAHADUR *by Nunthorpe—Azeeza*	g.	12	9–7	Mr. P. Roberts	Mr. W. Gore Lambarde	F.

Winner trained by the Hon. Aubrey Hastings, second horse trained by Robinson, third horse trained by F. Hartigan.

R

1915—*Continued*

6-1 Irish Mail
7-1 Lord Marcus
9-1 Silver Top
10-1 Balscadden, Father Confessor

100-9 Bachelor's Flight
100-8 Ally Sloper
100-7 Bullawarra
25-1 Distaff, Alfred Noble, Jacobus

33-1 Denis Auburn, Ilston, Thowl Pin
40-1 Hackler's Bey

1916
(Run at Gatwick)

CONDITIONS the same as in the race when run at Aintree, but the race was called The Race Course Association Steeplechase, and was a handicap of 500 sovs.

Going: AVERAGE   *Starters:* 21   *Time:* 10 MIN. 22 SEC.
Weather: CLEAR   *Date:* MARCH 24

Horse	Colour and Sex	Age	Weight	Jockey	Owner	Position at Finish
VERMOUTH *by Barcadaile, dam by Bushey Park*	b. g.	6	11–10	J. Reardon	Mr. P. F. Heybourn	1
IRISH MAIL *by King's Messenger— Betsy Shannon*	br. g.	9	12–5	C. Hawkins	Mr. E. Platt	2
SCHOOLMONEY *by Silver Streak— Felstead*	b. g.	6	10–2	A. Saxby	Mr. H. C. Davey	3
JACOBUS *by Wavelet's Pride— Kendaline*	b. g.	11	12	A. Newey	Mr. C. Bower Ismay	4
COUVREFEU II *by Curfew—Regime*	g.	12	12–7	F. Dainty	Sir W. Nelson	
ALLY SLOPER *by Travelling Lad— Sally in Our Alley*	br. g.	7	11–13	Mr. J. R. Anthony	Lady Nelson	
LORD MARCUS *by Walmsgate or Butter- scotch—Lady Rivers*	g.	8	11–13	G. Parfrement	Lord Lonsdale	
MUNSTER VALE	g.	6	11	G. Calder	Mr. J. Ivall	
HACKLER'S BEY *by Kosmos Bey, dam by Hackler*	g.	9	11	Mr. H. S. Harrison	Sir T. Dewar	
THOWL PIN *by Pilot—Hairpin*	g.	11	10–12	C. Kelly	Mr. F. Bibby	
DENIS AUBURN *by General Peace or Denis Richard— Auburn's Pride*	g.	9	10–7	E. Driscoll	Sir G. Bullough	
BALLYNEETY	g.	a.	9–7	W. J. Smith	Mr. K. F. Malcolmson	
EUGENIST	g.	a.	11–10	H. Smyth	Mr. E. S. Wills	P. U.
LAMENTABLE	g.	a.	11–1	S. Walkington	Mr. F. C. Parker	P. U.
STRANGEWAYS	g.	a.	10–4	T. Dunn	Mr. F. W. Parnell	P. U.
LYNCH PIN	g.	a.	10	J. Dillon	Mr. W. H. Dixon	P. U.
HESPERUS MAGNUS	g.	a.	9–10	J. East	Mr. D. Faber	P. U.
DRUMLANE	g.	a.	9–10	J. Kelly	Sir W. W. Williams	P. U.
FLEUR-DE-LYS	g.	a.	9–7	W. Hives	Sir R. Wilmot	P. U.
BLIGH	g.	a.	9–7	B. Roberts	Mr. J. R. Heaton	P. U.
STAG'S HEAD	g.	a.	9–7	W. Smith	Mr. G. P. Sanday	F.

Only one horse fell.

STARTING PRICES

9–2 Ally Sloper	100–8 Hackler's Bey,	33–1 Schoolmoney
11–2 Lord Marcus	Vermouth	40–1 Couvrefeu II,
8·1 Thowl Pin, Denis	100–6 Jacobus, Eugenist	Munster Vale
Auburn	20–1 Irish Mail, Stag's Head	50–1 Ballyneety
	25–1 Lamentable	

1917

(Run at Gatwick)

CONDITIONS same, but name changed to The War National Steeplechase.

Going: HEAVY   *Starters:* 19   *Time:* 10 MIN. 12⅖ SEC.
Weather: RAIN   *Date:* MARCH 21

Horse	Colour and Sex	Age	Weight	Jockey	Owner	Position at Finish
BALLYMACAD *by Laveno— Ballymacarney*	b. g.	a.	9–12	E. Driscoll	Sir G. Bullough	1
CHANG *by Cupid—Threnody*	ch. h.	7	9–9	W. Smith	Mr. H. Trimmer	2
ALLY SLOPER *by Travelling Lad— Sally in Our Alley*	br. g.	8	11–10	I. Anthony	Lady Nelson	3
VERMOUTH *by Barcadaile— dam by Bushey Park*	b. g.	7	12–3	J. Reardon	Mr. P. F. Heybourn	4
FATHER CONFESSOR *by St. Bris— Entrenous*	ch. g.	8	11–7	A. Aylin	Lord Suffolk	
QUEEN IMAAL	m.	a.	11–3	A. Newey	Col. R. L. Birkin	
YELLOW CHAT	g.	6	11	G. Parfrement	Lord Lonsdale	
BLOW PIPE *by Bird of Paradise— Balista*	g.	12	10	E. Lancaster	Mr. G. H. Jones	
TEMPLEDOWNEY	g.	a.	12–7	T. Hulme	Maj. D. Dixon	F.
IRISH MAIL *by King's Messenger —Betsy Shannon*	br. g.	10	12–4	E. Piggot	Mr. E. Platt	P. U.
CARRIG PARK	g.	a.	11–6	C. Hawkins	Mr. Douglas Stuart	F.
LIMEROCK	g.	a.	11–5	W. J. Smith	Mr. E. W. Paterson	F.
HACKLER'S BEY *by Kosmos Bey mare by Hackler*	g.	10	10–10	Capt. D. Rogers	Sir T. Dewar	F.
KENIA	m.	a.	10–10	A. Saxby	Mr. R. B. Thorburn	F.
THOWL PIN *by Pilot—Hairpin*	g.	12	10–7	C. Kelly	Mr. F. Bibby	
CHARLBURY *by Succoth— May Hack*	g.	9	10–6	J. Dillon	Mr. H. Trimmer	P. U.
DENIS AUBURN *by General Peace or Denis Richards— Auburn's Pride*	g.	10	10–4	R. Burford	Sir G. Bullough	P. U.
FARGUE *by Fariman— Kitty Gallerte*	g.	7	9–7	Mr. H. A. Brown	Mr. P. S. Adams	F.
GRITHORPE	g.	a.	9–7	H. Smyth	Mr. E. S. Wills	F.

Winner trained by the Hon. Aubrey Hastings.

STARTING PRICES

7–2 Carrig Park	100–9 Ballamacad	25–1 Templedowney, Fargue,
11–2 Chang	100–7 Limerock	Queen Imaal, Irish Mail
100–12 Yellow Chat, Vermouth	20–1 Alley Sloper	33–1 Kenia

1918
(Run at Gatwick)

Going: GOOD   Starters: 17   Time: 9 MIN. 50⅖ SEC.

Weather: CLEAR   Date: MARCH 21

Horse	Colour and Sex	Age	Weight	Jockey	Owner	Position at Finish
POETHLYN *by Rydal Head Fine Champagne*	b. g.	8	11–6	E. Piggot	Mrs. Hugh Peel	1
CAPTAIN DREYFUS *by Santoi— Madame Dreyfus*	b. g.	a.	12–7	J. Reardon	Mr. F. R. Hunt	2
BALLYMACAD *by Laveno— Ballymacarney*	b. g.	a.	11–3	I. Anthony	Sir G. Bullough	3
BERNERAY	g.	a.	10–4	S. Avila	Mr. Barclay Walker	4
TOP HOLE	g.	a.	11–2	C. Hawkins	Mr. F. W. Parnell	
CLEAR MONEY	g.	5	11–2	Mr. Pepper	Col. H. P. Burnyeat	
SHAUN SPADAH *by Easter Prize— Rusialka*	b. g.	7	10–11	A. Stubbs	Mr. T. M. McAlpine	
QUEEN IMAAL	m.	a.	10–7	A. Newey	Mr. H. Denison	
SERGEANT MURPHY *by General Symons— Rose Graft*	ch. g.	8	10–7	S. Walkington	Mr. Douglas Stuart	
MARK BACK	g.	a.	10–5	H. Smyth	Mr. E. S. Wills	
CHANG *by Cupid—Threnody*	ch. h.	8	10–2	Mr. O. J. Casebourne	Mr. F. S. Watts	
SIMON THE LEPPER	g.	a.	10	R. Burford	Sir G. Bullough	
AWBEG	g.	a.	10	L. Jones	Mr. Horatio Bottomley	
CHARLBURY *by Succoth—May Hack*	g.	10	9–10	J. Dillon	Mr. H. Trimmer	
ALLY SLOPER *by Travelling Lad— Sally in Our Alley*	br. g.	9	11–9	J. Walsh	Lady Nelson	F.
WAVERTREE *by Wavelet's Pride— Kendal Lily*	g.	8	10–12	E. Driscoll	Capt. Brian Bibby	F.
VERMOUTH *by Barcadaile, dam by Bushey Park*	b. g.	8	11–13	Mr. J. R. Anthony	Mr. P. F. Heybourn	

Winner trained by Escott.

STARTING PRICES

5–1 Poethlyn, Watertree, Ally Sloper
7–1 Ballymacad
10–1 Shaun Spadah

100–8 Vermouth, Chang
100–7 Berneray
20–1 Captain Dreyfus
33–1 Charlbury

40–1 Mark Back, Sergeant Murphy
50–1 Simon the Lepper, Top Hole, Queen Imaal
100–1 Awbeg, Clear Money

Henceforth all races run at Aintree

Going: AVERAGE   Starters: 22   Time: 10 MIN. 8⅖ SEC.
Weather: CLEAR   Date: MARCH 28

Horse	Colour and Sex	Age	Weight	Jockey	Owner	Position at Finish
POETHLYN by Rydal Head— Fine Champagne	b. g.	9	12–7	E. Piggot	Mrs. Hugh Peel	1
BALLYBOGGAN by Frustrum— Gentle Annie	ch. g.	8	11–10	W. Head	Mr. E. W. Hope Johnstone	2
POLLEN by Picton— Folle Farine	ch. g.	10	11–4	A. Escott	Mr. J. L. Dugdale	3
LOCH ALLEN by Lochryan—Kirstie		8	10	J. J. Kelly	Mr. V. Stewart	4
PAY ONLY by Walmsgate— Teddie III		9	11–4	T. Hulme	Mr. W. P. Hanly	
ABOU BEN ADHEM by Roi Herode— Debris		8	12	A. Stubbs	Mr. J. Buchanan	
ALLY SLOPER by Travelling Lad— Sally in Our Alley	br. g.	10	11–3	I. Anthony	Lady Nelson	
SHAUN SPADAH by Easter Prize Rusialka	b. g.	8	11–2	R. Morgan	Mr. T. M. McAlpine	
VERMOUTH by Barcadaile— dam by Bushey Park	b. g.	9	10–12	G. Parfrement	Mr. P. F. Heybourn	
SERGEANT MURPHY by General Symons— Rose Graft	ch. g.	9	10–7	S. Walkington	Mr. Douglas Stuart	
ALL WHITE by White Eagle— Colonia	g.	5	9–10	T. Williams	Col. Hall Walker	
FARGUE by Fariman— Kitty Gallerte		9	9–9	W. Smith	Mr. G. P. Sanday	
CHANG by Cupid—Threnody	ch. h.	9	9–8	J. Reardon	Mr. F. S. Watts	
IRISH DRAGOON by Charles O'Malley or Orby—Lotus		5	9–8	H. B. Bletsoe	Mr. R. H. Edwards	
RUBINSTEIN by Star Ruby— Numeroet		12	11	W. Payne	Lt.-Col. F. Douglas-Pennant	F.
PICTURE SAINT by Picton— Wise Saint		7	10	F. McCabe	Col. Croft	F.
BALLINCARROONA by Uncle Mac or Santoi— Lizzie Kendal		11	9–13	Owner	Capt. Ian Straker	F.

Horse	Colour and Sex	Age	Weight	Jockey	Owner	Position at Finish
SCHOOLMONEY *by Silver Streak—* *Felstead*	b. g.	10	9–10	F. Cullen	Mr. P. R. L. Savill	F.
SUNLOCH *by Sundorne—* *Gralloch*	b. g.	13	9–10	E. Driscoll	Mr. T. Tyler	P. U.
THE TURK II *by Turk's Cap—* *Ethel's Darling*	br. g.	9	9–7	Mr. P. Roberts	Mr. C. L. Willcox	F.
CHARLBURY *by Succoth—* *May Hack*		11	9–7	P. Woodland	Mr. H. Trimmer	P. U.
SVETOI *by St. Martin—* *Seisdon Princess*		9	9–7	A. Saxby	Mr. W. E. Wren	F.

Winner trained by Escott, second by Fetherstonaugh, third by Escott.

STARTING PRICES

11–4 Poethlyn
7–1 Charlbury
9–1 Ballyboggan
100–7 Pollen, Pay Only
100–6 Ally Sloper

20–1 Ballincarroona, Vermouth
25–1 Sunloch, Sergeant Murphy
33–1 Loch Allen, Schoolmoney,
Shaun Spadah

40–1 Svetoi
50–1 Chang, Rubinstein,
Fargue
66–1 All White
100–1 Others

1920

Going: VERY HEAVY   *Starters:* 24   *Time:* 10 MIN. 20⅖ SEC.

Weather: RAIN   *Date:* MARCH 26

Horse	Colour and Sex	Age	Weight	Jockey	Owner	Position at Finish
TROYTOWN *by Zria—Diane*	br. g.	7	11–9	Mr. J. R. Anthony	Maj. Gerrard	1
THE TURK II *by Turk's Cap— Ethel's Darling*	br. g.	10	9–7	R. Burford	Mr. C. L. Willcox	2
THE BORE *by Ormondale— Betty Bramble*	b. g.	9	10–1	Owner	Mr. H. Brown	3
SERGEANT MURPHY *by General Symons— Rose Graft*	ch. g.	10	10	W. Smith	Mr. M. H. Benson	4
NEUROTIC *by Marcovil— Hari Kari*		9	9–7	Mr. F. B. Rees	Mr. T. Mile	5
GENERAL SAXHAM *by Saxham— Veldt Girl*	g.	7	9–7	Mr. P. Roberts	Mrs. J. Putnam	F.
POETHLYN *by Rydal Head— Fine Champagne*	b. g.	10	12–7	E. Piggot	Mrs. Hugh Peel	F.
SILVER RING *by Zria—Queen Silver*		8	11–4	G. Duller	Sir James Buchanan	F.
BALLYBOGGAN *by Frustrum— Gentle Annie*	ch. g.	9	11–3	Mr. C. Brabazon	Mr. E. W. Hope Johnstone	F.
WAVERTREE *by Wavelet's Pride— Kendal Lily*	g.	9	10–13	C. Kelly	Mr. F. Bibby	F.
CLONREE *by Atlas—Miss Eager*		6	10–10	E. R. Morgan	Mr. O. Toole	F.
TURKEY BUZZARD *by White Eagle— Therapia*	g.	7	10–7	W. Payne	Mrs. H. M. Hollins	F.
ARDONAGH *by Ardoon— Turkish Delight II*		7	10–6	Mr. P. Whitaker	Capt. C. P. Hanbury	F.
PICTURE SAINT *by Picton— Wise Saint*		8	10	Capt. G. H. Bennet	Col. Croft	F.
LOCH ALLEN *by Lochryan—Kirstie*		9	9–12	T. Hulme	Mr. V. Samuel	F.
ALL WHITE *by White Eagle— Colonia*	g.	6	9–10	R. Chadwick	Lord Wavertree	F.
GERALD L. *by Captivation— Lavenne*	ch. g.	6	9–7	F. Dainty	Maj. F. J. Scott Murray	F.
WAVEBEAM *by Wavelet's Pride— Princess Thera*		9	9–7	A. Aylin	Maj. Ian Straker	F.
IRISH DRAGOON *by Charles O'Malley or Orby—Lotus*		6	9–7	A. Escott	Mr. R. H. Edwards	F.

W. A. Rouch

Troytown, the 1920 winner, J. R. Anthony up.

W. A. Rouch

Sergeant Murphy, winner in 1923.   Capt. G. N. Bennet up.

1920—*Continued*

Horse	Age	Weight	Jockey	Owner	Position at Finish
DUNADRY *by Captivation—Glenavy*	7	9–7	S. B. Walkington	Mrs. Blain	F.
BONNY CHARLIE *by Stoccado—Prevoyance*	12	9–7	Mr. M. Blair	Capt. Willoughby Norrie	F.
LITTLE ROVER *by Highwayman—Bayberry*	14	9–7	Capt. Doyle	Mr. F. C. Romilly	F.
LUCY GLITTER'S II *by Clarionet, dam by Reduction*	8	9–7	L. B. Rees	Mr. H. J. Davis	F.
SQUARE UP *by Simon Square—Campana*	7	9–7	T. Wilmot	Mr. W. Read	F.

Winner trained in Ireland, second horse trained by the Hon. Aubrey Hastings, third by owner.

STARTING PRICES

3–1 Poethlyn
6–1 Troytown
10–1 Gerald L.

100–7 Ballyboggan, Sergeant Murphy, Turkey Buzzard, Silver Ring
25–1 Clonree

28–1 Neurotic, The Bore
33–1 Loch Allen, All White
40–1 Wavertree

1921

Going: HEAVY   Starters: 35   Time: 10 MIN. 26 SEC.
Weather: CLEAR   Date: MARCH 18

Horse	Colour and Sex	Age	Weight	Jockey	Owner	Position at Finish
SHAUN SPADAH *by Easter Prize—Rusialka*	b. g.	10	11–7	F. B. Rees	Mr. T. M. McAlpine	1
THE BORE *by Ormondale—Betty Bramble*	b. g.	10	11–8	Owner	Mr. H. A. Brown	2 (R.)
ALL WHITE *by White Eagle—Colonia*	g.	7	10–13	R. Chadwick	Lord Wavertree	3 (R.)
TURKEY BUZZARD *by White Eagle—Therapia*	g.	8	12–2	Capt.G.H.Bennet	Mrs. H. M. Hollins	4 (R.)
CLONREE *by Atlas—Miss Eager*		7	12	T. Hulme	Mrs. Blain	
OLD TAY BRIDGE *by Bridge of Earn—Broken Reed*	ch. g.	7	11–8	E. Piggot	Mr. W. H. Dixon	
GENERAL SAXHAM *by Saxham—Veldt Girl*	g.	8	11–4	W. Smith	Mrs. J. Putnam	
GARRYVOE *by Fugleman—Lesterlake*		7	11–2	I. Anthony	Mr. C. Bower Ismay	
LOCH ALLEN *by Lochryan—Kirstie*		10	11	J. J. Kelly	Mr. V. Samuel	
GLENCORRIG *by Kroonstad—Shinrone*		7	10–13	H. B. Bletsoe	Mr. K. Mackay	
DAYDAWN *by Bungebah—Princess Olga*		8	10–13	J. R. Anthony	Baron F. de Tuyll	
PRINCE CLIFTON *by Cliftonhall, dam by Red Prince II*		8	10–13	L. B. Rees	Mr. Lewis Pollock	
WHITE SURREY *by Nabot—Dejeuner*		9	10–12	A. Escott	Adm. Sir Hedworth Meux	
RATHER DARK *by Dark Donald—Jane Shore*		7	10–12	A. Gregson	Mr. W. H. Midwood	
BOBBYDAZZLER *by Marcovil—Vain Chick*		7	10–12	A. Stubbs	Sir F. C. Price	
SHORT KNOCK *by Servitor—Prize Cherry*		12	10–10	M. Halpin	Capt. E. Shirley	
HALSTON *by Bealderg—Chimura*		9	10–9	Mr. Frith	Maj. D. Dixon	
HILL OF CAMAS *by Simontault, dam by Walmsgate*		13	10–7	Capt. C. J. Delmege	Capt. W. Moloney	
WAVEBEAM *by Wavelet's Pride Princess Thera*		10	10–7	Mr. S. C. Lloyd	Mr. H. Kershaw	

Horse	Age	Weight	Jockey	Owner
PICTURE SAINT *by Picton—Wise Saint*	9	10–5	N. Hayes	Col. Croft
BALLYSAX *by Saxham—Silver Vixen*	7	10–5	G. Goswell	Mrs. J. Putnam
BONNIE CHARLIE *by Stoccado—Prevoyance*	13	10–4	Owner	Mr. M. C. Blair
EAMON BEAG *by Menander—Lady Olton*	8	10–4	M. Connors	Mr. Joseph Widger
BLAZERS *by Flying Hackle— Lady Blazes*	7	10–4	W. Watkinson	Maj. W. T. M. Buller
RUFUS XXI *pedigree unknown*	10	10	Capt. Doyle	Lt.-Col. Geoffrey Brooke
CUPID'S DART *by Target—Heart's Desire*	7	9–12	J. Hogan, Jr.	Mr. James Daly
LONG LOUGH *by Lochryan— Pride of Mabestown*	9	9–12	R. Trudgill	Mr. R. Power
WHITE COCKADE *by Uncle George—Proserpine*	8	9–10	H. Wicks	Mr. T. R. D. Longworth
FOREWARNED *by Foresight—Uneekah*	6	9–10	R. Burford	Mr. W. A. Bankier
GLENEFLY *by Convert—Katie Bush*	7	9–7	T. Willmot	Mr. S. Stewart
PROPSERITZ *by Uncle George—Proserpine*	7	9–7	W. Daly	Maj. Holliday
CHARLBURY *by Succoth—May Hack*	13	9–7	B. Ellis	Lord Denman
HACKAM *by Hackenschmidt—Seerdam*	6	9–7	G. Clancy	Mr. A. Humphrey
REDSTART V *by Hawfinch, dam by Rugby*	13	9–7	Owner	Maj. A. W. H. James
ANY TIME *pedigree unknown*	10	10–6	F. Wooton	Mr. G. W. Hands

Winner trained by Poole, second horse by owner, third by Fergusson.
Only four horses finished, and the winner was the only one that did not fall.

STARTING PRICES

9–1 The Bore	100–7 Daydawn	50–1 Halston, Forewarned
10–1 Eamon Beag	30–1 Blazers	Any Time, Glencorrig
100–9 Shaun Spadah, Turkey Buzzard, Garryvoe	33–1 Clonree, Rather Dark, All White, White Surrey	66–1 General Saxham, Hackham, Prince Clifton
100–8 Old Tay Bridge		

1922

Going: GOOD   *Starters:* 32   *Time:* 9 MIN 55⅘ SEC.
Weather: RAIN   *Date:* MARCH 24

Horse	Colour and Sex	Age	Weight	Jockey	Owner	Position at Finish
MUSIC HALL *by Cliftonhall—Molly*	b. g.	9	11–8	L. B. Rees	Mr. Hugh Kershaw	1
DRIFTER *by The Raft— Katie Darling*	br. g.	8	10	Watkinson	Mr. Joseph Widger	2
TAFFYTUS *by Eaves Dropper Faithful Lassie*	b. g.	9	11	T. Leader	Mr. J. C. Bulteel	3
SERGEANT MURPHY *by General Symons— Rose Graft*	ch. g.	12	11	C. Hawkins	Mr. Stephen Sanford	4 (R.)
A DOUBLE ESCAPE *by Swynford—Duma*	g.	8	10–3	Capt. G.H.Bennet	Mr. H. Adams	5 (R.)
SHAUN SPADAH *by Easter Prize— Rusialka*	b. g.	11	12–3	F. B. Rees	Sir M. McAlpine	
SOUTHAMPTON *by Southannan— Pink Lady*	g.	6	11–10	Mr. H. A. Brown	Lord Woolavington	
WAVERTREE *by Wavelet's Pride— Kendal Lily*	g.	11	11–10	H. Bletsoe	Mr. F. Bibby	
NORTON *by Leviathan—Bulmer*	g.	7	11–8	I. Morgan	Mr. V. T. Thompson	
CLONREE *by Atlas—Miss Eager*	g.	8	11–6	J. Mahoney	Mrs. A. Blain	
ST. BERNARD *by St. Monans— Lady May II*	g.	8	11–5	Mr. R. Pulford	Mrs. N. Brownlee	
CLASHING ARMS *by St. Martin— Glen Inch*	g.	7	11–3	J. R. Anthony	Col. W. S. Anthony	
ALL WHITE *by White Eagle— Colonia*	g.	8	11	R. Chadwick	Lord Wavertree	
THE TURK II *by Turk's Cap— Ethel's Darling*	br. g.	12	10–11	I. Anthony	Mr. T. A. Sutton	
ARRAVALE *by Ardoon—Lady Ina*	g.	7	10–10	Mr. P. Whitaker	Mr. C. R. Baron	
SUPER MAN *by Manwolf— Lady Superior*	g.	7	10–9	R. Burford	Mr. W. A. Bankier	
GENERAL SAXHAM *by Saxham— Veldt Girl*	h.	9	10–9	Mr. P. Dennis	Mrs. Putnam	
GAY LOCHINVAR *by Lochryan— Gaiety*	g.	6	10–8	F. Croney	Mr. G. E. Godson	
DUNADRY *by Captivation— Glenavy*	g.	9	10–7	J. Hogan, Jr.	Mrs. A. Blain	
ANY TIME *Pedigree unknown*	br. g.	11	10–5	G. Wall	Mr. G. W. Hands	

Horse	Colour and Sex	Age	Weight	Jockey	Owner	Position at Finish
SQUARE UP *by Simon Square— Campana*	h.	9	10–4	J. Rennison	Mr. W. A. Read	
MASK-ON *by Avidity, dam by Bergomask*	g.	9	10–2	J. Burns	Mr. T. A. O'Gorman	
ARABIAN KNIGHT *by Poor Boy—Shaft*	h.	6	10–2	R. Spares	Mr. J. P. Westlake	
SUDAN II *by Sundorne—Connie*	g.	13	10	G. Calder	Sir Reginald Rankin	
MASTERFUL *by Hastings— Madcap*	g.	9	10	Mr. M. Blair	Mr. Foxhall Keene	
VAULX *by Benvenuto— Bairgen breac*	g.	8	10	A. Escott	Mr. E. S. Patterson	
DUNSTANBURGH *by Sir Harry—Honey*	g.	10	10	H. Watkins	Mr. J. W. Burnett	
CONFESSOR *by Magic— Reverend Mother*	g.	8	10	R. Trudgill	Mr. T. Galletly	
THE INCA II *by Indian Runner— dam's pedigree unknown*	g.	8	10	F. Brookes	Capt.C.W.Brennand	F.,DES.
AWBEG *by Galgreina— Little Margery*	g.	11	10	Mr. A. Knowles	Mr. M. S. Thomson	DIED
GREY DAWN V *by Dandolo—dam's pedigree unknown*	g.	9	10	A. Newey	Mr. G. H. Edwards	
SUCH A SPORT *by Just Cause— Playmate IV*	g.	11	10	Capt.J.C.Delmege	Mr. R. Hardinge	

Winner trained by Owen Anthony, second horse by H. Harrison, third by T. Leader.

STARTING PRICES

100–12 Southampton	18–1 Drifter	40–1 A Double Escape, Norton
9–1 Clashing Arms	20–1 Square Up	
100–9 Music Hall	25–1 Wavertree, Grey Dawn V, Vaulx	50–1 Mask-On
100–8 Shaun Spadah		66–1 Taffytus, General Saxham, Dunadry, Masterful, St. Bernard
100–7 All White, Arravale	33–1 The Turk II, Clonree	
100–6 Sergeant Murphy		

1923

Going: VERY GOOD   Starters: 28   Time: 9 MIN. 36 SEC.

Weather: THICK FOG   Date: MARCH 23

Horse	Colour and Sex	Age	Weight	Jockey	Owner	Position at Finish
SERGEANT MURPHY by General Symons—Rose Graft	ch. g.	13	11–3	Capt.G.H.Bennet	Mr. Stephen Sanford	1
SHAUN SPADAH by Easter Prize—Rusialka	b. g.	12	12–7	F. B. Rees	Sir Malcolm McAlpine	2
CONJUROR II by Garb Or, dam by Juggler	b. g.	11	11	Mr. C. Dewhurst	Maj. C. Dewhurst	3
PUNT GUN by Fowling Piece—Permiller	g.	10	11–1	M. Tighe	Mrs. J. Putnam	4
DRIFTER by The Raft—Katie Darling	g.	9	10–10	W. Watkinson	Mr. J. Widger	
MAX by Zria—Bauble	g.	7	11–5	J. Hogan, Jr.	Mrs. Croft	
TURKEY BUZZARD by White Eagle—Therapia	h.	10	12–6	F. Brookes	Mrs. H. M. Hollins	F.
SQUARE DANCE by Simon Square—Flora Dance	h.	11	12	L. B. Rees	Mr. H. M. Curtis	F.
TAFFYTUS by Eaves Dropper—Faithful Lassie	g.	10	11–7	T. Leader	Mr. J. C. Bulteel	F.
TRENTINO by Frontino—Enchanted Queen	g.	9	11–7	Maj. J. Wilson	Maj.W.Howland Hillas	F.
DUETTISTE by Ethelbert—Dulcibella	g.	10	11–7	A. Escott	Mr. J. E. Widener	P.U.
FOREWARNED by Foresight—Uneekah	h.	8	11–5	J. R. Anthony	Mr. W. A. Bankier	F.
ARRAVALE by Ardoon—Lady Ina	h.	8	11–2	Capt.P.Whitaker	Mr. C. R. Baron	F.
MADRIGAL by Maiden Erlegh—Palm Tree	g.	6	10–12	D. Colbert	Mr. Harold Barry	P.U.
EUREKA II by Frustrum—Red Damsel	g.	6	10–10	A. Stubbs	Lord Woolavington	F.
MY RATH by Succoth—Bit of Thought	g.	11	10–8	Mr. C. Chapman	Mr. P. Ivall	F.
AMMONAL by Oppressor—Tippytoes	h.	6	10–7	I. Morgan	Mrs. F. M. Lloyd	F.
PENCOED by Creangate—Peahen	g.	8	10–3	Mr. D. Thomas	Lt.-Col. F. Lort-Phillips	P.U.
THE TURK II by Turk's Cap—Ethel's Darling	br. g.	13	10–2	C. Donnelly	Mr. T. Alan Arthur	F.
CINDERS II pedigree unknown	gr. g.	11	10	W. Williams	Mr. J. H. Betts	F.

Horse	Colour and Sex	Age	Weight	Jockey	Owner	Position at Finish
PAM NUT *by Pam—Broken Reed*	g.	10	10	S. Duffy	Capt. T. McDougal	P.U.
CANNY KNIGHT *by White Knight—Ceannacroc*	g.	9	10	A. Vause	Mr. Adam Scott	F.
CINZANO *by Dalmellington Yvonne de Feyrolles*	g.	6	10	F. Brown	Mr. James Kemp	REF.
MASTERFUL *by Hastings—Madcap*	g.	10	10	Mr. P. Roberts	Mr. Foxhall Keene	P.U.
NAVANA *by Master Magpie—dam by Tredennis*	m.	9	10	F. Mason	Mr. C. F. Kenyon	P.U.
GARDENRATH *by Pam—Punnet*	g.	8	10	J. Whelehan	Mr. J. T. Rogers	P.U.
LIBRETTO *by Brook—Bonne Espoir*	h.	8	10	G. Parfrement	Mr. A. Smith Cochran	P.U.
LIFFEYBANK *by Bergomask, dam by Gay Reveller*	g.	a.	10	Mr. K. Gibson	Maj. H. R. Cayzer	P.U.

Winner trained by Blackwell, second by Poole, third by Coulthwaite.

STARTING PRICES

11–2 Forewarned	
10–1 Arravale	
100–8 Libretto, Taffytus	
100–6 Sergeant Murphy	

100–6 Conjuror II, Square Dance
20–1 Shaun Spadah, Punt Gun, Drifter
25–1 Max
33–1 Turkey Buzzard

40–1 Duettiste, Eureka II, Ammonal
66–1 Trentino, My Rath, Gardenrath, Madrigal, Navana

1924

Going: GOOD   *Starters:* 30   *Time:* 9 MIN. 40 SEC.
Weather: CLEAR   *Date:* MARCH 28

Horse	Colour and Sex	Age	Weight	Jockey	Owner	Position at Finish
MASTER ROBERT *by Moorside II—Dodds*	ch. g.	11	10–5	R. Trudgill	Lord Airlie	1
FLY MASK *by Fly Fisher, dam by Bergomask, grandam by Ascetic*	b. g.	10	10–12	J. Moylan	Mr. T. K. Laidlaw	2
SILVO *by Minter—Ever True*	b. g.	8	12–2	G. Goswell	Mr. W. H. Midwood	3
DRIFTER *by The Raft—Katie Darling*	br. g.	10	10–5	G. Calder	Mr. S. Sanford	4
SERGEANT MURPHY *by General Symons—Rose Graft*	ch. g.	14	11–10	J. Hogan	Mr. S. Sanford	5
WAVETOWN *by Kroonstad—Waveoff*	g.	9	10–12	R. Lyall	Mr. A. Hood	6
SHAUN SPADAH *by Easter Prize—Rusialka*	b. g.	13	12–5	F. B. Rees	Sir M. McAlpine	7
BALLINODE *by Machakos—Celia*	m.	8	10–4	G. Fitzgibbon	Mr. J. C. Bentley	8
MUSIC HALL *by Cliftonhall—Molly*	ch. g.	11	12–7	J. R. Anthony	Mr. H. Kershaw	P.U.
GERALD L. *by Captivation—Lavenne*	ch. g.	10	12–6	I. Morgan	Maj. F. Scott Murray	P.U.
OLD TAY BRIDGE *by Bridge of Earn—Broken Reed*	ch. g.	10	11–13	Mr. H. M. Hartigan	Mrs. W. H. Dixon	F.
CHIN CHIN *by Santoi—Focus*	h.	8	11–7	A. Stubbs	Sir Francis Price	F.
EUREKA II *by Frustrum—Red Damsel*	g.	7	11–5	A. Robson	Lord Woolavington	F.
ARRAVALE *by Ardoon—Lady Ina*	h.	9	11–2	Mr. P. Whitaker	Mr. C. R. Baron	F.
CLONSHEEVER *by Avidity—Wise Gull*	g.	9	11–2	F. Brookes	Mr. J. E. Tyrrell	F.
CONJUROR II *by Garb Or, dam by Juggler*	b. g.	12	11	Mr. H. A. Brown	Maj. C. Dewhurst	K.O.
ALL WHITE *by White Eagle—Colonia*	g.	10	10–11	M. Tighe	Lord Wavertree	REF.
WINNALL *by Fowling-piece—Clayton*	g.	7	10–11	C. Donnelly	Mr. H. Liddell	F.
LIBRETTO *by Book—Bonne Espoir*	h.	9	10–8	W. O'Neill	Sir Edward Elgar	F.

Horse	Colour and Sex	Age	Weight	Jockey	Owner	Position at Finish
PENCOED *by Creangate—Peahen*	g.	9	10–6	Mr. D. Thomas	Lt.-Col. F. Lort-Phillips	P.U.
TAFFYTUS *by Eaves Dropper—Faithful Lassie*	b. g.	11	10–6	T. Leader	Mr. J. C. Bulteel	F.
JAMES PIGG *by Bealderg—Gweebarra*	g.	11	10–3	H. Morris	Mr. J. W. Corrigan	F.
A DOUBLE ESCAPE *by Swynford—Duma*	g.	10	10–3	G. Smith	Mr. H. Adams	F.
WINTER VOYAGE *by Torpoint—Mince Pie*	h.	7	10–2	C. Goswell	Mr. T. D. Oakshott	F.
AUCHINROSSIE *by Huon II—Campsie*	h.	8	10–2	E. Foster	Mr. Kincaid Lennox	P.U.
PALM OIL *by Coriander—Last Purchase*	g.	8	10	Mr. P. Roberts	Mr. H. E. Steel	F.
NEWLANDS *by Fugleman, dam by Wild Flower*	g.	10	10	R. Burford	Mr. C. Bower Ismay	P.U.
FAIRY HILL II *by Bright Bat—Cerf Agile*	g.	8	10	W. Watkinson	Maj. H. A. Wernher	F.
MAINSAIL *by Juggernaut—Dutch Pennant*	g.	8	10	Mr. Learmouth	Mr. S. C. Wells	REF.
GAY LOCHINVAR *by Lochryan—Gaiety*	g.	8	10	S. Duffy	Mr. G. E. Godson	F.

Winner trained by the Hon. Aubrey Hastings, second by Coulthwaite, third by Whitaker

STARTING PRICES

5–2 Conjuror II	25–1 Master Robert, Chin Chin, Auchin-rossie, Music Hall, Ballinode	40–1 (*Cont.*) Drifter, Old Tay Bridge, Pencoed
100–12 Taffytus		50–1 Gerald L.
100–7 Fly Mask, Silvo, Shaun Spadah		66–1 Palm Oil, Clonsheever Winter Voyage, New-lands, Mainsail
100–6 Eureka II, Sergeant Murphy	33–1 Fairy Hill II, Arravale	
	40–1 All White, Winnall	

1925

Going: AVERAGE *Starters:* 33 *Time:* 9 MIN. 42⅗ SEC.

Weather: CLEAR *Date:* MARCH 27

Horse	Colour and Sex	Age	Weight	Jockey	Owner	Position at Finish
DOUBLE CHANCE *by Roi Herode or Day Comet—Kelibia*	ch. g.	9	10–9	Maj. J. P. Wilson	Mr. D. Goold	1
OLD TAY BRIDGE *by Bridge of Earn— Broken Reed*	ch. g.	11	11–12	J. R. Anthony	Mrs. W. H. Dixon	2
FLY MASK *by Fly Fisher, dam by Bergomask, grandam by Ascetic*	b. g.	11	11–11	E. C. Doyle	Mr. T. K. Laidlaw	3
SPRIG *by Marco—Spry*	ch. g.	8	11–2	T. Leader	Mrs. M. Partridge	4
SILVO *by Minter—Ever True*	b. g.	9	12–7	F. B. Rees	Sir Edward Egar	5
DWARF OF THE FOREST *by The Giant— Blackbird*	g.	8	10–8	Owner	Mr. H. Kennard	6
JACK HORNER *by Cyllius— Melton's Guide*	ch. g.	8	10	Mr. M. D. Blair	Mr. K. Mackay	7
MAX *by Zria—Bauble*	g.	9	11–5	J. Hogan, Jr.	Mrs. Croft	8
DRIFTER *by The Raft— Katie Darling*	br. g.	11	10–3	W. Watkinson	Mr. S. Sanford	9
SERGEANT MURPHY *by General Symons— Rose Graft*	ch. g.	15	11–7	A. Escott	Mr. S. Sanford	REM.
ALCAZAR *by Yerres— Good Gracious*	h.	9	12–3	Squadron-Leader Ridley	Mr. R. McAlpine	F.
MUSIC HALL *by Cliftonhall—Molly*	ch. g.	12	12	L. B. Rees	Mr. H. Kershaw	REF.
BALLINODE *by Machakos—Celia*	m.	9	11–6	G. Fitzgibbon	Mr. J. C. Bentley	F.
WHITE SURREY *by Nabot—Dejeuner*	gr. g.	12	11–4	M. Tighe	Sir Hedworth Meux	F.
BEN CRUCHAN *by Ben Alder— Scotch Flower*	g.	11	11–2	Owner	Mr. W. H. Whitbread	F.
ARDEEN *by Evicted—Penryn*	g.	8	11–2	A. Lefebve	Sir Keith Fraser	F.
ARRAVALE *by Ardoon—Lady Ina*	h.	10	11	J. Meaney	Mr. C. R. Baron	P.U.
WINNALL *by Fowling-piece— Clayton*	g.	8	11	F. Gurney	Mr. H. Liddell	REF.
PATSEY V *by Lord Garvagh, dam by Walmsgate*	g.			Owner	Mr. B. Lemon	REF.
AMMONAL *by Oppressor— Tippytoes*	h.	8	10–10	R. Trudgill	Mr. J. W. Wood	P.U.

1925—*Continued*

Horse	Colour and Sex	Age	Weight	Jockey	Owner	Position at Finish
HIS LUCK *by His Majesty— Madame St. George*	g.	9	10–10	R. Burford	Capt. A. A. Bankier	F.
TAFFYTUS *by Eaves Dropper— Faithful Lassie*	b. g.	12	10–9	R. Lyall	Mr. J. C. Bulteel	REF.
THROWN IN *by Beau Bill— Va Largo*	ch. g.	9	10–8	J. Goswell	Mr. D. Faber	F.
GRACIOUS GIFT *by Minter — Simon's Lawn*	g.	10	10–8	W. Parvin	Mr. R. H. A. Gresson	F.
KEEP COOL *by Pam—Alexa*	b. g.	10	10–7	G. Green	Mr. W. H. Midwood	P.U.
MAINSAIL *by Juggernaut— Dutch Pennant*	g.	9	10–5	R. Prioleau	Mr. S. C. Wells	F.
PENCOED *by Creangate—Peahen*	g.	10	10–3	Mr. D. Thomas	Lt.-Col. F. Lort- Phillips	F.
BALLYMACRORY *by Wavelet's Pride, dam by Perth Medley*	g.	8	10–3	J. Moylan	Mr. R. C. Ross	F.
ROUSHAM *by Vedanta—Caspia*	g.	10	10	Mr. P. Dennis	Mr. H. Dyke Dennis	F.
ALL WHITE *by White Eagle— Colonia*	g.	11	10	J. Mason	Lord Wavertree	F
PETER THE PIPER *by The Page or Zria—Gelee*	g.	13	10	G. Turner	Sir Edward Egar	REF.
GARDENRATH *by Pam—Punnet*	g.	10	10	T. James	Mr. F. A. Waring	F.
JAMES PIGG *by Bealderg— Gweebarra*	g.			A. Robson	Mr. J. W. Corrigan	F.

Winner trained by F. Archer, second by F. Hartigan, third by Coulthwaite.

STARTING PRICES

9–1 Old Tay Bridge
10–1 Fly Mask, Silvo, Ballinode
100–9 Double Chance
20–1 Max, Drifter

25–1 Gracious Gift, Patsey V
28–1 Thrown In
28–1 Winnall, Ardeen
33–1 Keep Cool, Sergeant Murphy, Pencoed, Ballymacrory, Sprig

40–1 Peter The Piper, Ben Cruchan, Taffytus, Jack Horner
50–1 Alcazar, His Luck
66–1 Others

1926

Going: GOOD   *Starters:* 30   *Time:* 9 MIN. 36 SEC.
Weather: MIST   *Date:* MARCH 26

Horse	Colour and Sex	Age	Weight	Jockey	Owner	Position at Finish
JACK HORNER *by Cyllius— Melton's Guide*	ch. g.	9	10–5	W. Watkinson	Mr. A. C. Schwartz	1
OLD TAY BRIDGE *by Bridge of Earn— Broken Reed*	ch. g.	12	12–2	J. R. Anthony	Mrs. W. H. Dixon	2
BRIGHT'S BOY *by Soulouque— Divine Flower*	ch. g.	7	11–8	E. Doyle	Mr. S. Sanford	3
SPRIG *by Marco—Spry*	ch. g.	9	11–7	T. Leader	Mrs. M. Partridge	4
DARRACQ *by Littleton— Sea Pink*	b. g.	11	10–11	F. Gurney	Maj. F. R. Samson	5
GERALD L. *by Captivation— Lavenne*	ch. g.	12	12–2	F. Brookes	Mr. H. Kershaw	
THROWN IN *by Beau Bill— Va Largo*	ch. g.	10	10–11	Hon. H. Grosvenor	Lord Stallbridge	
RED BEE *by Honey Bee— Gate Change*	ch. g.	8	10–10	D. Behan	Maj. H. A. Wernher	
DWARF OF THE FOREST *by The Giant— Blackbird*	g.	9	10–10	Owner	Mr. H. Kennard	
MASTER BILLIE *by William Rufus— Octocide*	b. g.	7	10	E. Foster	Mr. W. Parsonage	
MISCONDUCT *by Ardoon— Lady Conway*	br. g.	7	10	W. Parvin	Maj. D. M. Methven	
POP AHEAD *by Devolution— Chatalja*	g.	8	10	S. Regan, Jr.	Mrs. Holroyd Smyth	
SILVO *by Minter—Ever True*	b. g.	10	12–7	F. B. Rees	Mr. W. H. Midwood	F.
ARDEEN *by Evicted—Penryn*	b. g.	9	11–9	R. Trudgill	Sir Keith Fraser	F.
MOUNT ETNA *by Harry Melton— Last Purchase*	b. g.	9	11–2	Mr. S. Dennis	Mr. S. Sanford	F., REM·
BEN CRUCHAN *by Ben Alder— Scotch Flower*	g.	12	11–2	Owner	Mr. W. H. Whitbread	F., REM.
KOKO *by Santoi—Persister*	b. g.	8	11–1	J. Hamey	Mr. F. Barbour	F.
KNIGHT OF THE WILDERNESS *by Knight of Kilcash— Barkaway*	g.	6	11	J. Meaney	Mr. G. White	F.
PATSEY V *by Lord Garvagh, dam by Walmsgate*	g.	12	10–9	Maj. Cavenagh	Mr. B. Lemon	F.

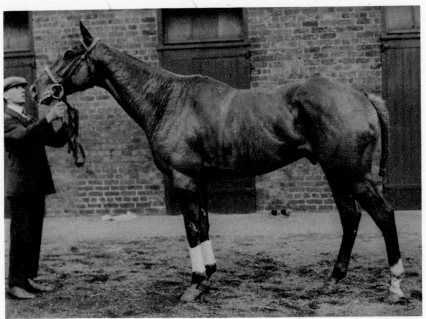

Jack Horner, winner in 1926.

The American-bred Billy Barton, second in 1928.

Horse	Colour and Sex	Age	Weight	Jockey	Owner	Position at Finish
UPTON LAD *by Benvenuto—Twang*	g.	11	10–8	Mr. W. Dutton	Mr. J. C. Paterson	F.
GRECIAN WAVE *by Prince Hermes— Wavelass*	b. m.	8	10–8	Maj. J. P. Wilson	Mr. W. Hume	F.
WHITE SURREY *by Nabot—Dejeuner*	gr. g.	14	10–7	Farragher	Sir Hedworth Meux	F.
LEE BRIDGE *by Sundawn— Lady Lee II*	g.	9	10–5	W. Stott	Mr. R. Shaw	F.
TEST MATCH *by Captivation—Test*	b. g.	8	10–5	P. L'Estrange	Mr. H. Mosenthal	F.
PENCOED *by Creangate— Peahen*	g.	11	10–2	Mr. D. Thomas	Lt.-Col. F. Lort-Phillips	F.
LONE HAND *by Call o' the Wild— Wine Gal*	g.	8	10	T. Morgan	Mr. A. W. Hedges	F., DIED
JOLLY GLAD *by Fariman— Dorfwych*	g.	9	10–1	Mr. P. Dennis	Capt. C. B. Petre	F.
SOLDIER BILL *by General Gough— Mollyroe*	g.	10	10	Mr. K. Goode	Mr. A. Hood	
WALLSEND *by Adam Bede— Broderie*	g.	6	10	Capt. H. Lumsden	Mrs. E. A. Cameron	F.
CASH BOX *by Just Cause— Mary Hughes*	g.	9	10	Mr. R. Read	Mr. R. Havelock-Allen	F.

Winner trained by H. Leader, second by F. Hartigan, third by Blackwell.

STARTING PRICES

5–1 Sprig	20–1 GrecianWave, LeeBridge	40–1 Darracq, Gerald L.
7–1 Silvo	Knight of the Wilderness,	50–1 Jolly Glad, Upton Lad
8–1 Old Tay Bridge	Master Billie	
100–8 Koko	25–1 Bright's Boy	66–1 Patsey V, Ben Cruchan, Lone Hand, Pop Ahead, Cash Box, Red Bee, Test Match, White Surrey
100–6 Mount Etna	28–1 Misconduct, Dwarf of the Forest	
25–1 Jack Horner	33–1 Ardeen, Thrown In	
		100–1 Others

1927

Going: HEAVY   *Starters:* 37   *Time:* 10 MIN. 20⅕ SEC.
Weather: VARIED FROM CLEAR TO   *Date:* MARCH 25
MISTY

Horse	Colour and Sex	Age	Weight	Jockey	Owner	Position at Finish
SPRIG *by Marco—Spry*	ch. g.	10	12–4	T. Leader	Mrs. M. Partridge	1
BOVRIL III *by Simonson—Bovril*	b. g.	9	10–12	Owner	Mr. G. W. Pennington	2
BRIGHT'S BOY *by Soulouque— Divine Flower*	ch. g.	8	12–7	J. R. Anthony	Mr. Stephen Sanford	3
DRINMOND *by Drinmore— Miss Desmond*	b. g.	10	10–13	Mr. J. B. Balding	Lord Queenborough	4
MASTER OF ARTS *by Pam—Juliet II*	g.	10	10–10	Maj. Cavenagh	Mr. M. D. Blair	5
WHITE PARK *by Redmond— Lady Alwine*	ch. g.	8	12–5	E. Foster	Maj. J. P. North	6 (R.)
BALLYSTOCKART *by Zria—Isle of the Blessed*	b. g.	8	11–1	Owner	Capt. R. E. Sassoon	7
GERALD L. *by Captivation— Lavenne*	ch. g.	13	12–5	L. B. Rees	Mr. H. Kershaw	
AMBERWAVE *by Wavelet's Pride— Ambergris*	br. g.	9	12	Mr. J. O'Brien	Lady Helen McCal- mont	BALKED
GRECIAN WAVE *by Prince Hermes— Waveless*	b. m.	9	11–12	J. Meaney	Mr. W. Hume	F.
MARSIN *by Sunder—St. Maria*	g.	9	11–12	P. Powell	Mr. Stephen Sanford	F.
THROWN IN *by Beau Bill— Va Largo*	ch. g.	11	11–10	Hon. H. Grosvenor	Lord Stallbridge	F.
KNIGHT OF THE WILDERNESS *by Knight of Kilcash —Barkaway*	g.	7	11–9	W. Gurney	Mr. W. P. Draper	F.
DWARF OF THE FOREST *by The Giant— Blackbird*	g.	10	11–4	Owner	Mr. H. Kennard	F.
SHAUN OR *by Radoilus— Turkey Hen*	ch. g.	8	11–3	W. Madden	Lord Glanely	F.
SILVER SOMME *by Royal Hackle II or General Gough— Lady Silver*	b. m.	10	11–3	M. Connors	Mr. H. Liddell	REF.
KEEP COOL *by Pam—Alesca*	g.	12	11–3	J. Goswell	Mr. W. H. Midwood	F.
RED BEE *by Honey Bee— Gate Change*	ch. g.			W. J. Payne	Maj. H. A. Wernher	F.

Horse	Colour and Sex	Age	Weight	Jockey	Owner	Position at Finish
HAWKER *by Ardoon, dam by Morganatic—Porzana*	g.	13	11–1	Owner	Capt. A. E. Grant	R.O.
TEST MATCH *by Captivation—The Test*	b. g.	9	11–1	R. Lyall	Mr. G. Redmond	F.
UNCLE JACK *by Juggernaut—Tzigane*	g.	8	11–1	T. O'Sullivan	Capt. A. Gollan	F.
TRUMP CARD *by Clarionet—Peggy Symons*	br. g.	9	11–1	Mr. S. H. Dennis	Mr. G. Newell Nairn	F.
MASTER BILLIE *by William Rufus—Octocide*	b. g.	8	10–13	F. B. Rees	Mr. W. Parsonage	F.
POP AHEAD *by Devolution—Chatalja*	g.	9	10–13	Owner	Mr. H. Fowler	F.
MISCONDUCT *by Ardoon—Lady Conway*	g.	8	10–12	W. Parvin	Mr. Gordon Selfridge	F.
SIR HUON *by Huon II—Lady Daffodil*	g.	13	10–12	M. Rayson	Mr. G. Gilbey	F.
CASH BOX *by Just Cause—Mary Hughes*	g.	10	10–12	G. Green	Mr. R. Havelock-Allen	F.
SNAPPER *by Snap Dragon—Dark Avis*	g.	9	10–10	Capt. M. Dennis	Maj. T. H. Sebag-Montefiore	F.
UPTON LAD *by Benvenuto—Twang*	g.	12	10–10	Mr. W. Dutton	Mr. J. C. Patterson	F.
EAGLE'S TAIL *by White Eagle—Addenda*	ch. g.	8	10–9	F. Brookes	Mr. J. A. Fairhurst	P.U.
GRAKLE *by Jackdaw—Lady Crank*	br. g.	5	10–9	J. Moloney	Mr. T. K. Laidlaw	F.
MR. JOLLY *by Cyllius—Manor Water*	g.	12	10–9	Mr. J. S. Wight	Lt.-Col. R. W. Tweedie	F.
CORAZON *by Charles O'Malley—Noramac*	g.	9	10–8	T. Morgan	Maj. Barret	F.
LISSETT III *by Bachelor's Lodge, dam by Otterton*	g.	11	10–5	J. Hamey	Lord Grimthorpe	F.
ALL WHITE *by White Eagle—Colonia*	g.	13	10–5	J. Mason	Lord Wavertree	P.U.
BLAENOR *by Courtesan II—Queen of the Rye*	g.	10	10–5	E. Doyle	Lord Marchamley	F.
MISS BALSCADDEN *by Balscadden—Wilkinstown*	m.	8	10–5	Owner	Mr. D. Thomas	F.

Winner trained by T. Leader, second by Cockton, third by Blackwell.

STARTING PRICES

8–1 Sprig
9–1 Grakle
100–8 Thrown In
100–7 Silver Somme, Bright's Boy
100–6 Shaun Or
20–1 Master Billie, White Park, Misconduct

20–1 (*Cont.*) Eagle's Tail, Amberwave
33–1 Knight of the Wilderness, Dwarf of the Forest, Trump Card, Blaenor, Keep Cool
40–1 Pop Ahead, Snapper

50–1 Grecian Wave, Test Match, Red Bee, Uncle Jack, Gerald L., Master of Arts
66–1 Marsin, Drinmond, Mr. Jolly, Hawker, Upton Lad
100–1 Others

1928

Horse	Colour and Sex	Age	Weight	Jockey	Owner	Position at Finish
TIPPERARY TIM *by Cipango—Last Lot*	b. g.	10	10	Mr. W. Dutton	Mr. H. S. Kenyon	1
BILLY BARTON *by Huon—* *Mary Le Bus*	b. g.	10	10–11	T. Cullinan	Mr. Howard Bruce	2 (R.)
SPRIG *by Marco—Spry*	ch. g.	11	12–7	T. Leader	Mrs. M. Partridge	F.
BRIGHT'S BOY *by Soulouque—* *Divine Flower*	ch. g.	9	12–7	M. Rayson	Mr. S. Sanford	F.
EASTER HERO *by My Prince—* *Easter Week*	ch. g.	8	12–5	P. Powell	Capt. A. Lowenstein	F.
KOKO *by Santoi—Persister*	b. g.	10	12–2	W. Gurney	Capt. the Hon. F. E. Guest	F.
THE COYOTE *by Sea Sick—* *Francisca*	b. g.	8	11–13	J. Hogan	Mr. Victor Emmanuel	F.
AMBERWAVE *by Wavelet's Pride—* *Ambergris*	br. g.	10	11–13	Mr. O'Brien	Lady Helen McCal- mont	F.
TRUMP CARD *by Clarionet—* *Peggy Symons*	br. g.	10	11–10	K. Piggot	Mr. G. Newell Nairn	F.
GREAT SPAN *by Bridge of Earn—* *Mullion*	b. g.	7	11–9	W. J. Payne	Mr.W.B.Duckworth	L.S.
THE ACE II *by Hollister—* *Foreshore*	b. g.	6	11–6	T. Morgan	Mr. R. B. Strassburger	F.
GRAKLE *by Jackdaw—* *Lady Crank*	br. g.	6	11–5	R. Lyall	Mr. C. R. Taylor	REF.
BALLYSTOCKART *by Zria—Isle of* *the Blessed*	b. g.	9	11–2	Owner	Capt. R. E. Sassoon	
DARRACQ *by Littleton—Sea Pink*	b. g.	13	11–2	J. Moloney	Mr. A. C. Schwartz	K.O.
ARDEEN *by Evicted—Penryn*	g.	11	11–2	J. Hamey	Sir Keith Fraser	
EAGLE'S TAIL *by White Eagle—* *Addenda*	ch. g.	9	11	E. Foster	Mr. J. A. Fairhurst	F.
RATHOWEN *by Drinmore—* *Avarine*	g.	8	11	Owner	Mr. H. Deterding	
FOXTROT *by Light Brigade—* *Flora Dance*	g.	12	10–13	Owner	Capt. H. Lumsden	
MAGUELONNE *by Ecouen—May Day*	ch. g.	6	10–13	Bedeloup	Comte P. de Jumilhac	F.
MAY KING *by Cherry Tree—* *Wigeon's Last*	g.	9	10–13	L. B. Rees	Lord Ednam	F.

Horse	Colour and Sex	Age	Weight	Jockey	Owner	Position at Finish
DRINMOND *by Drinmore—* *Miss Desmond*	b. g.	11	10–13	Owner	Mr. J. B. Balding	REF.
KEEP COOL *by Pam—Alexa*	g.	13	10–11	J. Goswell	Mr. W. H. Midwood	
SPEAR O'WAR *by Spearmint—* *Ortlinde*	g.	7	10–10	F. Brookes	Lord Queenborough	
CARFAX *by Drinmore—Zena*	b. g.	12	10–10	Owner	Mr. B. W. Ancil	
TEST MATCH *by Captivation—* *The Test*	b. g.	10	10–9	J. Maloney	Mr. G. L. Redmond	REF.
HERBERT'S CHOICE *by Aldegond—* *Mount Grace*	g.	7	10–8	F. Gurney	Miss D. Thomson	F.
MASTER BILLIE *by William Rufus—* *Octocide*	b. g.	9	10–8	F. B. Rees	Mr. W. Parsonage	REF.
BURGORIGHT *by Burgomaster—* *Ruby Right*	br. g.	13	10–7	Mr. F. A. Bonsal	Mr. B. L. Behr	REF.
MASTER OF ARTS *by Pam—Juliet II*	g.	11	10–6	Maj. Cavenagh	Mr. M. D. Blair	
RUDDYMAN *by Ruddygore, dam* *by Hermit II*	g.	9	10–4	W. Parvin	Mr. H. Gordon Selfridge	
SCOTCH EAGLE *by French Eagle,* *dam by Clanronald*	g.	12	10–3	Owner	Mr. Harold Fowler	
REDLYNCH *by Tracery—Glencree*	ch. g.	7	10–3	Mr. West	Mr. G. E. Strong	
THE GOSLING *by St. Petersburg—* *Vain Chick*	g.	8	10–3	Mr. S. Dennis	Lord Grimthorpe	
RATHORY *by Poet-Laureate—* *Helen Fenton*	b. g.	12	10–2	D. Williams	Maj. H. Lyon	F.
RATHMORE *by Drinmore—* *Avarine*	g.	11	10	Mr. Whitfield	Mr. J. Hylton	F.
ROSSIENY *by Rossendale—* *Crimea*	g.	9	10	Mr. Everett	Mrs. J. Putnam	F.
MELLERAY'S BELLE *by Melleray—* *Mountain Lily*	b. m.	9	10	J. P. Kelly	Mr. W. Wilson	P.U.
SOLDIER'S JOY *by Recruiting Officer—* *Lady Slavey*	g.	10	10	D. Quirke	Mr. S. G. R. Barrat	
DE COMBAT *by Atlas—* *Hors de Combat*	b. g.	11	10	F. Croney	Mr. C. Mulholland	F.
COMMONSIDE *by Be Very Wise—* *Silda*	g.	9	10	Mr. C. B. Harvey	Lt.-Col. G. Brooke	

Horse	Colour and Sex	Age	Weight	Jockey	Owner	Position at Finish
SCRAPTOFT	g.	11	10	Mr. M. Barry	Mr. W. Ross	
pedigree unknown						
SETI THE FIRST	g.	13	10		Mr. E. Craig Tanner	
by Pericles—Blair Anchor						

Winner trained by F. Dodd, second by the Hon. Aubrey Hastings.

This was the remarkable year in which Easter Hero stuck on the top of the fence at the Canal Turn and caused so many horses to refuse. The visibility was poor, and it is practically impossible to tell what happened to a great many of the horses who came to grief. Only two horses finished; even the official records in *Steeplechases Past*, published by Messrs. Weatherby & Sons, London, make no effort to say what happened to the various horses who did not finish. In cases covered by my personal knowledge, I have indicated the particular type of casualty which overtook the horse in question; in other cases I have left that part of the description blank.

STARTING PRICES

5–1 Master Billie
11–2 Trump Card
10–1 Amberwave
100–7 Easter Hero, Sprig
20–1 Maguelonne, Bright's Boy, Darracq, Koko
25–1 Carfax
33–1 Billy Barton, Great Span, Drinmond,

33–1 (*Cont.*) Rathowen, Rossieny, Grakle
40–1 The Coyote, Ardeen, Ballystockart, Seti the First
50–1 Eagle's Tail, Herbert's Choice, Spear o' War, Master of Arts, The Ace II

66–1 Keep Cool, Rathmore, Ruddyman, Test Match, Redlynch
100–1 De Combat, Foxtrot Scotch Eagle, May King, Rathory, Soldier's Joy, Tipperary Tim
200–1 Others

I N an effort to decrease the size of the fields that ran in the Grand National, the conditions were changed, and read this year as follows:

The Grand National Steeplechase (handicap) of 5 sovs. each, 50 sovs. extra if left in after January 22nd, an additional 25 sovs. if left in after March 12th, and 20 sovs. extra for starters with 5,000 sovs. (including a trophy value 200 sovs.) added, for five-year-olds and upwards; second to receive 700 sovs., third 400 sovs., and the fourth 150 sovs. from the stakes; weights published January 17th at noon; the highest weight not more than 12 stone 7 pounds, and the lowest weight not less than 10 stone. Grand National course, about four miles and 856 yards. Entries closed January 1st, 1929. The trainer of the winner will receive a cup value of 50 sovs., and the rider of the winner will receive a cup value of 25 sovs.

Going: AVERAGE				*Starters:* 66		*Time:* 9 MIN. 47 SEC.
Weather: SUNNY				*Date:* MARCH 22		
Horse	*Colour and Sex*	*Age*	*Weight*	*Jockey*	*Owner*	*Position at Finish*
GREGALACH *by My Prince— St. Germanie*	ch. g.	7	11–4	R. Everett	Mrs. M. A. Gemmell	1
EASTER HERO *by My Prince— Easter Week*	ch. g.	9	12–7	J. Moloney	Mr. J. H. Whitney	2
RICHMOND II *by Prince Philip— Thyme*	b. g.	6	10–6	W. Stott	Mr. R. McAlpine	3
MELLERAY'S BELLE *by Melleray— Mountain Lily*	b. m.	10	10	J. Mason	Mr. William Wilson	4
MAY KING *by Cherry King— Wigeon's Last*	b. g.	10	11–2	F. Gurney	Mrs. H. Mond	5
GRAKLE *by Jackdaw— Lady Crank*	br. g.	7	11–9	J. Hamey	Mr. C. R. Taylor	6
D. D. B. *by Wax Bullet, dam by Wavelet's Pride*	g.	9	10–11	Mr. R. Gubbins	Maj. A. W. Huntington	7
DELARUE *by St. Dunstan— Rose Amber*	g.	7	10–3	G. Wilson	Mr. J. B. Snow	8
KILBAIRN *by Kelso— Cottage Maiden*	g.	8	10	Mr. L. Parry	Mr. R. A. Parry	9
CAMPERDOWN *by Apprentice—dam's pedigree unknown*	g.	10	10	Mr. K. Goode	Mrs. E. Hutchinson	10(F.)

W. A. Rouch

Gregalach, R. Everett up, winner in 1929 and second in 1931.

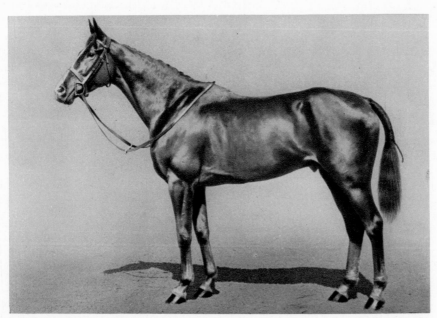

W. A. Rouch

Easter Hero, second in 1929.

Horse	Colour and Sex	Age	Weight	Jockey	Owner	Position at Finish
SPRIG *by Marco—Spry*	ch. g.	12	12–5	A. Escott	Mrs. M. Partridge	F.
BRIGHT'S BOY *by Soulouque— Divine Flower*	ch.g.	10	12–4	E. Foster	Mr. S. Sanford	F.
KOKO *by Santoi—Persister*	br. g.	11	12–3	S. Duffy	Capt. the Hon. F. E. Guest	F.
GREAT SPAN *by Bridge of Earn— Mullion*	b. g.	8	12	W. Payne	Mr. W. B. Duckworth	P. U.
TRUMP CARD *by Clarionet— Peggy Symons*	br.g.	11	11–12	T. Morgan	Mr. G. Newell Nairn	F.
MOUNT ETNA *by Harry Melton Last Purchase*	b. g.	12	11–7	T. Leader	Mr. S. Sanford	F.
KNIGHT OF THE WILNERNESS *by Knight of Kilcash— Barkaway*	g.	9	11–7	M. Keogh	Mr. F. Cundell	
BILLY BARTON *by Huon— Mary Le Bus*	b. g.	11	11–7	T. Cullinan	Mr. Howard Bruce	F.
LLOYDIE *by Vedanta— Lizzie Lane*	g.	7	11–4	F. B. Rees	Capt. R. F. H. Norman	F.
THE ACE II *by Hollister— Foreshore*	b. g.	7	11–3	Mr. G. Evans	Mr. R. B. Strassburger	F.
ARDEEN *by Evicted—Penryn*	g.	12	11–2	R. Lyall	Sir Keith Fraser	F.
CARFAX *by Drinmore—Zena*	g.	13	11–1	Mr. B. Ancil	Mr. B. W. Ancil	
BALLYSTOCKART *by Zria—Isle of the Blessed*	b. g.	10	11	Owner	Capt. R. E. Sassoon	
STORT *by Stortford—Winkie*	g.	10	11	T. Chisman	Mr. R. Wright	F., B. L.
LORDI *by Lormi— Santa Visto*	g.	8	11	Capt. Weber	Mr. A. M. Jones	F.
MASTER BILLIE *by William Rufus— Octocide*	b. g.	10	11	Mr. Rayson	Mr. W. Parsonage	P. U.
LE TOUQUET *by Marmouset— La Bourgevie*	g.	7	10–12	T. Teasdale	M. G. Watinne	F.
SKRUN PRINCE *by The Raft—Daisy*	g.	8	10–12	W. Gurney	Col. P. D. Stewart	F.
OVERDRAFT *by St. Tudwal—Draft*	g.	7	10–11	Mr. R. Bennet	Mrs. R. D. Cohen	
RAMPANT *by Don Juan— Red Rambler*	g.	9	10–11	Maj. Misa	Col. W. S. Anthony	
TIPPERARY TIM *by Cipango—Last Lot*	b. g.	11	10.10	Mr. W. Dutton	Mr. H. S. Kenyon	F.

Horse	Colour and Sex	Age	Weight	Jockey	Owner	Position at Finish
DARRACQ *by Littleton— Sea Pink*	b. g.	14	10–10	Mr. G. S. Poole	Mr. A. C. Schwartz	F.
K. C. B. *by The White Knight— Rill*	g.	7	10–10	J. Hogan	Mr. V. H. Smith	
ARDOON'S PRIDE *by Ardoon—Nancy*	g.	9	10–10	R. Thrale	Capt. T. H. Bird	F.
SANDY HOOK *by Santair—Pincurl*	b. g.	8	10–9	F. Fish	Mr. J. H. Hull	F.
HERBERT'S CHOICE *by Aldegond— Mount Grace*	g.	8	10–8	J. Farrell	Mr. J. Graeme Thomson	F.
DWARF OF THE FOREST *by The Giant— Blackbird*	g.	12	10–8	Owner	Mr. H. Kennard	F.
DRINMOND *by Drinmore— Miss Desmond*	b. g.	12	10–8	Owner	Mr. J. B. Balding	F.
UNCLE BEN *by Ben Alder— Frankfield*	g.	8	10–8	P. Powell	Mr. H. B. Brandt	
BEECHMARTIN *by Marten— Land Toll*	g.	8	10–7	L. B. Rees	Mr. David Faber	F.
RUDDYMAN *by Ruddygore—dam by Hermit II*	g.	10	10–5	W. Parvin	Mr. H. Gordon Selfridge	F.
HAWKER *by Ardoon, dam by Morganatic*	g.	15	10–5	Owner	Capt. A. E. Grant	
GAY DON II *by Jovial—Prudence*	g.	10	10–3	A. Birch	Sir Lindsay Parkinson	
DENBURGH *by Denis Richard— Poppy*	g.	10	10–3	G. Hardy	Mr. F. Usher	F.
SULTAN OF WICKEN *by St. Martin— Sultanina*	g.	10	10–3	T. James	Lady Penrhyn	F.
KILBRAIN *by Ardoon— Loo Bridge*	g.	9	10–3	V. Piggot	Mr. E. A. Longworth	F.
BALLYHANWOOD *by Cookhill—Crissy*	b. g.	8	10–2	J. Goswell	Mr. M. D. Blair	
SOLDIER'S JOY *by Recruiting Officer— Lady Slavey*	g.	11	10–2	Capt. Gossage	Mr. S. G. R. Barrat	
IRINA *by Irishman— Nehushta*	g.	7	10	J. Kelly	Mr. A. Heathorn	F.
DUKE OF FLORENCE *by Duke of Brandon —Florence*	g.	8	10	G. Turner	Mrs. Darby Rogers	
HAREWOOD *by Southannan— Daisy*	b. g.	7	10	D. Williams	Mr. M. L. Meyer	F.
MABESTOWN'S PRIDE *by General Gough— Pride of Mabestown*	g.	13	10	Mr. D. R. Daly	Brig.-Gen. C. Winser	K. O.

Horse	Colour and Sex	Age	Weight	Jockey	Owner	Position at Finish
RATHORY *by Poet Laureate— Helen Fenton*	b. g.	13	10	R. Burford	Maj. H. Lyons	
CLORINGO *by Jingo— Sweet Clorane*	g.	8	10	A. Wall	Mr. J. C. Paterson	F.
MERRIVALE II *by Rising Flour— The Vale*	b. g.	11	10	F. Brookes	Lord Westmorland	F.
MISS BALSCADDEN *by Balscadden— Wilkinstown*	m.	10	10	G. Bowden	Sir David Llewellyn	
ODD CAT *by Catmint—Odeon*	g.	8	10	J. Sinnot	Mr. J. B. D'Ardenne	
BEST HOME *by Dunholm— Best Birthday*	g.	8	10	Owner	Mr. G. Elliott	F.
BIG WONDER *by Sunningdale— Miss Bromfield*	g.	9	10	J. Bisgood	Mr. G. S. L. Whitelaw	REF.
FLEET PRINCE *by My Prince— May Fleet*	g.	11	10	Mr. F. R. Thackray	Mr. G. S. L. Whitelaw	F.
KWANGO *by Kwang-Su— Farcical*	g.	8	10	A. Waudby	Maj. R. Fenwick-Palmer	
MORE DIN *by Morena— Lady Dinneford*	g.	9	10	A. Harroway	Mr. H. S. Horne	F.
STAGE MANAGEMENT *by Boss— Pauline Chase*	g.	9	10	M. Doherty	Maj. C. W. M. Norrie	F.
THEOREM *by Bushido— Theobald's Park*	g.	12	10	T. Costello	Mr. H. M. Llewellyn	F.
TOY BELL *by Santoi—Clarebell*	g.	7	10	D. Morgan	Mrs. R. D. Cohen	F.
WILD EDGAR *by Edgar's Pet— dam by d'Arenberg*	g.	9	10	S. Regan	Mrs. E. A. Ryan	F.

Winner trained by T. Leader, second by J. R. Anthony, third by Poole.

This was the biggest field in the history of the race; 66 started and 10 finished.

STARTING PRICES

9–2 Easter Hero
100–6 Great Span
18–1 Grakle
20–1 Billy Barton, Master Billie
22–1 Skrun Prince, Lloydie
25–1 Bright's Boy, Ardeen
28–1 Mount Etna, Lordi
33–1 Trump Card

40–1 Darracq, Knight of the Wilderness, Carfax, Uncle Ben, Richmond II, Harewood
50–1 Beechmartin, Sprig, K.C.B., Drinmond, Ruddyman, Duke of Florence, Merrivale II, Big Wonder

66–1 Koko, The Ace II, May King, Ballystockart, Overdraft, D.D.B.
100–1 Rampant, Tipperary Tim, Sandy Hook, Ballyhanwood, Gregalach, Kilbrain, Stage Management, Toy Bell
200–1 Others

1930

Going: PERFECT   Starters: 41   Time: 9 MIN. 42⅖ SEC.
Weather: CLEAR   Date: MARCH 28

Horse	Colour and Sex	Age	Weight	Jockey	Owner	Position at Finish
SHAUN GOILIN sire's pedigree unknown —Golden Day	ch.g.	10	11–7	T. Cullinan	Mr. W. H. Midwood	1
MELLERAY'S BELLE by Melleray— Mountain Lily	b.m.	11	10	J. Mason	Mr. W. Wilson	2
SIR LINDSAY by Roi Herode— Polynetta	b. g.	9	10–6	D. Williams	Mr. J. H. Whitney	3
GLANGESIA by Le Souvenir— Mailline	gr.g.	10	10–4	J. Browne	Mr. R. K. Mellon	4
BALLYHANWOOD by Cookhill—Crissy	b. g.	9	10–4	E. Foster	Mr. M. D. Blair	5
ROYAL ARCH II by Righ Mor—Imaal	br. g.	9	10–2	Mr. Thackray	Mr. V. Emmanuel	6
GREGALACH by My Prince St. Germanie	ch. g.	8	12	R. Everett	Mrs. M. A. Gemmell	K.O. & P. U
GATE BOOK by Book—Flood Gate	gr. g.	9	11–8	T. Morgan	Marquis J. de San-Miguel	F.
DONZELON by Chaucer—Tortor	g.	9	11–7	R. Lyall	Col. G. Foljambe	F.
GRAKLE by Jackdaw— Lady Crank	br. g.	8	11–6	J. Piggot	Mr. C. R. Taylor	F.
NEWSBOY by Drinmore— Chattering Kit	g.	9	11–4	Owner	Capt. R. E. Sassoon	F.
DONEGAL by General Gough— The Jewess	g.	13	11–2	W. Speck	Mr. A. Bendon	F.
LORDI by Lormi— Santa-Visto	g.	9	11–2	W. Stott	Mr. A. M. Jones	K. O.
ALIKE by Southannan— The Very Same	m.	7	11	Mr. M. Barry	Lady Helen McCalmont	F.
IBSTOCK by Fowling-Piece— Marsore	bl. g.	10	10–12	Owner	Mr. K. Goode	P. U.
K. C. B. by The White Knight —Rill	g.	8	10–12	J. Moloney	Mr. V. H. Smith	K. O.
SANDY HOOK by Santair—Pincurl	b. g.	9	10–12	T. E. Leader	Mr. S. Sanford	F.
PEGGIE'S PRIDE by Tidal Wave— Magic Maid	g.	7	10–11	T. McCarthy	Mr. H. B. Brandt	F.
GUIDING LIGHT by Cyllius— Candle Fish	g.	9	10–11	Mr. C. W. Langlands	Mr. J. B. D'Ardenne	F.

W. A. Rouch

Shaun Goilin, who won in 1930.   T. Cullinan up.

W. A. Rouch

Grakle, the 1931 winner.

Horse	Colour and Sex	Age	Weight	Jockey	Owner	Position at Finish
BIG WONDER *by Sunningdale— Miss Broomfield*	g.	10	10–11	Capt.H.N.Weber	Mr.G.S.L.Whitelaw	REF.
SAVERNAKE *by Charles O'Malley— Goura*	g.	10	10–10	R. McCarthy	Mr. C. Anson	F.
MAY KING *by Cherry King— Wigeon's Last*	b.g.	11	10–9	G. Goswell	Mrs. H. Mond	F.
TOOTENHILL *by Poet Laureate— Think of Me*	g.			C. Wenham	Mrs. Boswall-Preston	F.
PARIS FLIGHT *by Rabelais— L'Adorable*	g.	10	10–7	E. Vinall	Mr. W. Harris	P. U.
DELARUE *by Sir Dunstan— Rose Amber*	g.	8	10–6	G. Wilson	Mr. J. B. Snow	K. O.
AGDEN *by Cyclops Too— Thelema*	g.	13	10–5	Mr.D.P.G.Moseley	Mr. O. G. Moseley	P. U.
TOY BELL *by Santoi—Clarebell*	br. g.	8	10–5	D. Morgan	Mrs. R. D. Cohen	F.
RUDDYMAN *by Ruddygore, dam by Hermit II*	g.	11	10–2	E. Brown	Mr.H.Gordon Selfridge	F.
BLENNERHASSET *by Ednam— Lady Liverton*	g.	11	10–2	Mr. W. Dutton	Mr. T. L. Parke	F.
MAY CRESCENT *by Marforio— Miller's Pride*	g.	8	10–2	G. Hardy	Mr. David Faber	F.
CRYPTICAL *by St. Gris, dam by The Crypt*	g.	15	10	J. Bisgood	Mr. F. H. Bowcher	P. U.
ANNANDALE *by Southannan— Lady Noggs*	g.	8	10	F. Gurney	Lady Glennap	F.
THE MONK *by Pommern— St. Maria*	g.	8	10	W. Parvin	Mr. F. J. Honour	P. U.
SOLDIER'S JOY *by Recruiting Officer— Lady Slavey*	g.	12	10	J. Farrell	Mr. S. G. R. Barrat	P. U.
CURTAIN RAISER *by Scene Shifter— Longestline*	g.	7	10	P. Powell	Mrs. E. W. B. Leake	P. U.
DERBY DAY II *by Irawaddy, dam by Travelling Lad*	g.	8	10	Mr. Stephenson	Mr. C. Nicholson	F. & D.
GAY DOG II *by Jovial—Prudence*	g.	10	10	W. Gurney	Sir Lindsay Parkinson	P. U.
MERRIVALE II *by Rising Flour— The Vale*	br. g.	12	10	F. Brookes	Lord Westmorland	F.

T

Horse	Colour and Sex	Age	Weight	Jockey	Owner	Position at Finish
THE GOSLING by St. Petersburg— Vain Chick	g.	10	10	A. Tannock	Maj. J. A. Coats	P. U.
HAREWOOD by Southannan Daisy	b. g.	8	10	J. Hamey	Mr. M. L. Meyer	F.
THEOREM by Bushido— Theobald's Park	g.	13	10	Mr. G. Owen, Jr.	Sir David Llewellyn	F.

Winner trained by *F. Hartigan, second by Easterby, third by J. R. Anthony.*

STARTING PRICES

100–12 Grakle
100–8 Shaun Goilin
100–7 Sir Lindsay
100–6 Gregalach
20–1 Melleray's Belle
22–1 K.C.B.

25–1 Donegal, Sandy Hook, May Crescent
28–1 Lordi, Alike
33–1 Peggie's Pride, Bally-hanwood, Tootenhill, Glangesia
40–1 May King, Merrivale II

50–1 Gate Book, Newsboy, Big Wonder, Agden, Royal Arch II
66–1 Donzelon, ToyBell, Blennerhasset, Gay Dog II
100–1 Others

1931

Going: PERFECT   Starters: 43   Time: 9 MIN. 32⅘ SEC.

Weather: BRIGHT SUN   Date: MARCH 27

Horse	Colour and Sex	Age	Weight	Jockey	Owner	Position at Finish
GRAKLE by Jackdaw— Lady Crank	br. g.	9	11–7	R. Lyall	Mr. C. R. Taylor	1
GREGALACH by My Prince— St. Germanie	ch. g.	9	12–0	J. Moloney	Mrs. M. A. Gemmell	2
ANNANDALE by Southannan— Lady Noggs	b. g.	9	10–7	T. Morgan	Lady Glennap	3
RHYTICERE by Ramrod— Cosmerops	b. g.	9	10–12	L. Niaudot	Mr. V. Emmanuel	4
BALLYHANWOOD by Cookhill— Crissy	b. g.	10	10–7	T. Isaac	Mr. M. D. Blair	5
SHAUN GOILIN Sire's pedigree unknown— Golden Day	ch. g.	11	12–4	M. Keogh	Mr. W. H. Midwood	6
GLANGESIA by Le Souvenir— Mailline	gr. g.	11	10–10	J. Browne	Mr. R. K. Mellon	7
MELLERAY'S BELLE by Melleray— Mountain Lily	b. m.	12	10–10	J. Mason	Mr. W. Wilson	8
GREAT SPAN by Bridge of Earn— Mullion	b. g.	10	11–0	G. Hardy	Mr. M. D. Blair	9
STARBOX by African Star— Pratebox	g.	8	10–10	Mr. K. Urquhart	Major J. B. Walker	10
HAREWOOD by Southannan— Daisy	b. g.	9	10–7	Mr. K. Goode	Mr. M. L. Meyer	11
ROYAL ARCH II by Righ Mor— Imaal	br. g.	10	10–7	J. Bedeloup	Mr. V. Emmanuel	12
EASTER HERO by My Prince— Easter Week	ch. g.	11	12–7	F. B. Rees	Mr. J. H. Whitney	F.
GIB by The Jabberwock— Bettyville	br. g.	8	12–5	E. Foster	Mr. B. D. Davis	F.
KAKUSHIN by Friar Marcus— Osaka	ch. g.	8	11–13	R. Everett	Mr. W. M. G. Singer	P.U.
DRINTYRE by Drinmore— Lady Longwood	br. g.	8	11–7	Owner	Capt. Brownhill	REF.
SIR LINDSAY by Roi Herode— Polynetta	b. g.	10	11–6	Mr. Thackray	Mr. J. H. Whitney	REF.
KILBUCK by Great Sport— Tredonna	g.	10	11–6	T. Chisman	Mr. E. R. Hartley	F.

Horse	Colour and Sex	Age	Weight	Jockey	Owner	Position at Finish
TRUMP CARD *by Clarionet— Peggy Symons*	br. g.	13	11–5	W. Gurney	Lord Stalbridge	F.
GYI LOVAM! *Oreg lak— Gyerunk Csak!*	b. g.	9	11–3	Owner	Capt. R. Popler	F.
THERAS *by Lomond— Thera H.*	g.	6	11–2	J. Walsh	Mr. Holford Harrison	F.
SWIFT ROWLAND *by Sir Rowland— Noble Queen*	br. g.	10	11–2	T. E. Leader	Mrs. C. Beatty	F. & D
DRIN *by Drinmore— dam by Balsamo*	br. g.	7	11–2	W. Speck	Mr. A. Bendon	F. & DES.
GUIDING LIGHT *by Cyllius— Candle Fish*	g.	10	11–0	Mr. McKeever	Mr. O. M. Smith	P.U.
BALLASPORT *by Drinmore— dam by Druce*	br. g.	7	11–0	D. Williams	Sir H. Wernher	F.
SANDY HOOK *by Santair— Pincurl*	b. g.	10	10–12	F. Fish	Mr. S. Sanford	F.
GEORGINATOWN *by Kroonstad— Georgina Mac*	m.	10	10–12	F. Maxwell	Mr. J. Wallace	F.
EASY VIRTUE *by Don Juan— Rusialka*	g.	8	10–12	P. Powell	Mr. W. P. Tyser	F.
BIG BLACK BOY *by Lorenzo— Miss Soliman*	br. g.	9	10–12	W. Payne	Major C. Stevens	F.
APOSTASY *by Cecilian— Faithless*	m.	10	10–12	F. Brookes	Lady Lindsay	F.
MAY KING *by Cherry King— Widgeon's Last*	ch. g.	12	10–10	Capt. Fanshawe	Lady Melchett	F.
ALIKE *by Southannan— The Very Same*	m.	8	10–10	Mr. Sclater	Mr. R. K. Mellon	F.
OXCLOSE *by Moorside II— Hampton Belle*	g.	7	10–10	F. Gurney	Mr. A. Hall Watt	F.
ASPIRANT *by Birk Gill— Mount Grace*	g.	8	10–10	W. Parvin	Mr. C. S. Green	F.
MOREKEEN *by Drinmore— Clonkeen*	g.	10	10–10	J. Cooke	Miss D. Robinson	F.
SOLANUM *by Pomme-de-terre— Speckled Agnes*	g.	6	10–8	J. Hamey	Miss D. Paget	F.

Horse	Colour and Sex	Age	Weight	Jockey	Owner	Position at Finish
RUDDYMAN *by Ruddygore— dam by Hermit II*	g.	12	10–8	E. C. Browne	Mr. H. G. Selfridge	F.
TAMASHA *by Santoi— Reception*	g.	10	10–7	Owner	Mr. G. Elliott	F.
PIXIE *by Battle-axe— Persimma*	ch. m.	6	10–7	Capt. Sassoon	Mrs. D. Fitzgerald	P.U.
MALLARD *by Fowling-piece— dam by Sheen*	b. g.	13	10–7	Mr. W. Carr	Mr. James Harrison	REF.
SOUTH HILL *by Southannan— Georgette*	g.	9	10–7	T. Cullinan	Mr. H. G. Blagrave	F.
TOY BELL *by Santoi— Clarebell*	br. g.	9	10–7	D. Morgan	Mrs. R. D. Cohen	F.
SLIEVE GRIEN *by By George!— Broidery*	g.	10	10–7	Owner	Capt. Moseley	F.

Winner trained by Coulthwaite, second by Woodland, third by Barret.

STARTING PRICES

5–1 Easter Hero
8–1 Melleray's Belle
100–6 Grakle, Ballasport
20–1 Drintyre, Drin,
  Georginatown
22–1 Kakushin
25–1 Sir Lindsay,

25–1 Gregalach
28–1 Swift Rowland, Alike
33–1 Gib, Shaun Goilin,
  Oxclose
40–1 Glangesia, Tamasha,
  Ballyhanwood, Sandy
  Hook, Apostasy

50–1 Kilbuck, Great Span,
  Rhyticere, Solanum,
  Ruddyman, South
  Hill, Harewood
66–1 Trump Card, Big
  Black Boy, Slieve
  Grien, Aspirant
100–1 Others

Won by one length and a half; ten lengths.

The Winners of the Grand National

Year	Horse	Colour and Sex	Age	Weight	Jockey	Odds
1839	LOTTERY *by Lottery—Parthenia*	br. g.	10	12	J. Mason	5–1
1840	JERRY *by Catterick*			12	Mr. Bretherton	12–1
1841	CHARITY *by Woodman*	b. m.		12	Mr. Powell	14–1
1842	GAYLAD *Brutandorf*			12	T. Olliver	7–1
1843	VANGUARD *by Belzoni*			11–10	T. Olliver	12–1
1844	DISCOUNT			10–12	Crickmere	5–1
1845	CURE-ALL *by Physician*	br. g.	a.	11–5	Loft	unquoted
1846	PIONEER *by Advance*	b. g.	6	11–12	Taylor	unquoted
1847	MATTHEW *by Vestris*		a.	10–6	D. Wynne	4–1
1848	CHANDLER *by Dr. Faustus*	br. g.	a.	11–12	Capt. Little	12–1
1849	PETER SIMPLE *by Patron*	b. g.	a.	11	Cunningham	20–1
1850	ABD EL KADER *by Ishmael—English Lass*	b. g.	a.	9–12	Green	unquoted
1851	ABD EL KADER *by Ishmael—English Lass*	b. g.	a.	10–4	Abbot	7–1
1852	MISS MOWBRAY *by Lancastrian—Norma*	b. m.	a.	10–4	Mr. A. Goodman	unquoted
1853	PETER SIMPLE *by Patron*	b. g.	a.	10–10	T. Olliver	9–1
1854	BOURTON *by Brayton*	b. g.	a.	11–12	Tasker	4–1
1855	WANDERER *by Verulam*	b. h.	a.	9–8	J. Hanlon	25–1
1856	FREETRADER *by The Sea*	br. h.	a.	9–6	G. Stevens	25–1
1857	EMIGRANT *by Drayton*	b. g.	a.	9–10	C. Boyce	10–1
1858	LITTLE CHARLEY *by Charles XII*	b. g.	a.	10–7	W. Archer	100–6
1859	HALF CASTE *by Morgan—Rattler*	br. h.	6	9–7	C. Green	7–1
1860	ANATIS *by King Dan—The Switcher's dam*	b. m.	a.	9–10	Mr. Thomas	7–2
1861	JEALOUSY *by The Cure*	br. m.	a.	9–12	Kendall	5–1
1862	THE HUNTSMAN *by Tupsley*	b. h.	a.	11	H. Lamplugh	3–1

NOTE: In 1839, 1840, 1841, 1842, all starters carried the same weight of 12 stone each. In 1843 the race became a handicap.

Year	Horse	Colour and Sex	Age	Weight	Jockey	Odds
1863	EMBLEM *by Teddington*	ch. m.	a.	10–10	G. Stevens	4–1
1864	EMBLEMATIC *by Teddington*	ch. m.	6	10–6	G. Stevens	10–1
1865	ALCIBIADE *by The Cossack*	ch. g.	5	11–4	Capt. H. Coventry	100–7
1866	SALAMANDER *by Fire-eater*	b. g.	a.	10–7	Mr. A. Goodman	40–1
1867	CORTOLVIN *by Chicken, or Cheerful Horn*	br. g.	a.	11–13	J. Page	100–6
1868	THE LAMB *by Zouave, dam by Arthur*	gr. h.	6	10–7	Mr. Edwards	10–1
1869	THE COLONEL *by Knight of Kars—Boadicea*	br. h.	6	10–7	G. Stevens	13–1
1870	THE COLONEL *by Knight of Kars—Boadicea*	br. h.	7	11–12	G. Stevens	4–1
1871	THE LAMB *by Zouave, dam by Arthur*	gr. h.	a.	11–4	Mr. Thomas	5–1
1872	CASSE TETE *by Trumpeter—Constance by Spirus*	ch. m.	a.	10	J. Page	20–1
1873	DISTURBANCE *by Commotion—Polly Peacham*	b. h.	6	11–11	Mr. J. M. Richardson	20–1
1874	REUGNY *by Minos—Reine Blanche*	ch. h.	6	10–12	Mr. J. M. Richardson	5–1
1875	PATHFINDER *by Mogador*	b. g.	a.	10–11	Mr. Thomas	100–6
1876	REGAL *by Saunterer—Regalia*	bl. g.	5	11–3	J. Cannon	25–1
1877	AUSTERLITZ *by Rataplan—Lufra*	ch. h.	5	10–8	Mr. F. G. Hobson	15–1
1878	SHIFNAL *by Saccharometer—Countess Amy*	br. h.	a.	10–12	J. Jones	100–15
1879	THE LIBERATOR *by Daniel O'Connell—Mary O'Toole*	b. g.	a.	11–4	Mr. G. Moore	5–1
1880	EMPRESS *by Blood Royal—Jeu des Mots*	ch. m.	5	10–7	Mr. T. Beasley	8–1
1881	WOODBROOK *by The Lawyer—Doe*	ch. g.	a.	11–3	Mr. T. Beasley	6–1
1882	SEAMAN *by Xenophon—Lena Rivers*	b. g.	6	11–6	Lord Manners	10–1
1883	ZOEDONE *by New Oswestry—Miss Honiton*	ch. m.	6	11	Count Charles Kinsky	100–8
1884	VOLUPTUARY *by Cremorne—Miss Evelyn*	b. g.	6	10–5	Mr. E. P. Wilson	10–1
1885	ROQUEFORT *by Winslow—Cream Cheese*	b. g.	6	11	Mr. E. P. Wilson	100–30
1886	OLD JOE *by Barefoot—Spot*	b. g.	a.	10–9	T. Skelton	25–1
1887	GAMECOCK *by Revolver—Lightfoot*	b. g.	a.	11	W. Daniells	20–1
1888	PLAYFAIR *by Rippenden, dam by Rattlebones—Drayton*	bl. g.	a.	10–7	Mawson	40–1
1889	FRIGATE *by Gunboat—Fair Maid of Kent*	b. m.	a.	11–4	Mr. T. Beasley	8 1

Year	Horse	Colour and Sex	Age	Weight	Jockey	Odds
1890	ILEX *by Rostrevor—Rostrum's dam*	ch. g.	a.	10–5	A. Nightingall	4–1
1891	COME AWAY *by Cambuslang—Larkaway*	b. g.	a.	11–12	Mr. H. Beasley	4–1
1892	FATHER O'FLYNN *by Retreat—Kathleen*	b. g.	a.	10–5	Capt. E. R. Owen	20–1
1893	CLOISTER *by Ascetic—Grace II*	b. g.	a.	12–7	Dollery	9–2
1894	WHY NOT *by Castlereagh—Twitter*	b. g.	a.	11–13	A. Nightingall	5–1
1895	WILD MAN FROM BORNEO *by Decider—Wild Duck*	ch. g.	a.	10–11	Mr. Jos. Widger	10–1
1896	THE SOARER *by Skylark, dam by Lurgan*	b. g.	a.	9–13	Mr. D. G. M. Campbell	40–1
1897	MANIFESTO *by Man of War—Væ Victis*	b. g.	a.	11–3	T. Kavanagh	6–1
1898	DROGHEDA *by Cherry Ripe—Eglantine*	b. g.	6	10–12	Gourley	25–1
1899	MANIFESTO *by Man of War—Væ Victis*	b. g.	a.	12–7	G. Williamson	5–1
1900	AMBUSH II *by Ben Battle—Miss Plant*	b. g.	6	11–3	Anthony	4–1
1901	GRUDON *by Old Buck—Avis*	br. h.	a.	10	A. Nightingall	9–1
1902	SHANNON LASS *by Butterscotch—Mazurka*	b. *or* br. m.	a.	10–1	D. Read	20–1
1903	DRUMCREE *by Ascetic—Witching Hour*	b. g.	a.	11–3	P. Woodland	13–2
1904	MOIFAA *by Natator—Denbigh*	br. g.	8	10–7	A. Birch	25–1
1905	KIRKLAND *by Kirkham—Perigonius mare*	ch .g.	a.	11–5	F. Mason	6–1
1906	ASCETIC'S SILVER *by Ascetic—Silver Lady*	ch. g.	a.	10–9	Hon. Aubrey Hastings	20–1
1907	EREMON *by Thurles—Daisy*	b. g.	7	10–1	A. Newey	8–1
1908	RUBIO *by Star Ruby—La Toquera*	ch. g.	a.	10–5	H. B. Bletsoe	66–1
1909	LUTTEUR III *by St. Damien—Lausanne*	ch. g.	5	10–11	G. Parfrement	100–9
1910	JENKINSTOWN *by Hackler—Playmate*	b. g.	a.	10–5	R. Chadwick	100–8
1911	GLENSIDE *by St. Gris—Kilwinnie*	b. g.	9	10–3	Mr. J. R. Anthony	20–1
1912	JERRY M. *by Walmsgate, dam by Luminary*	b. g.	9	12–7	E. Piggot	4–1
1913	COVERTCOAT *by Hackler—Cinnamon*	b. g.	7	11–6	P. Woodland	100–9
1914	SUNLOCH *by Sundorne—Gralloch*	b. g.	8	9–7	W. J. Smith	100–6
1915	ALLY SLOPER *by Travelling Lad— Sally in Our Alley*	b. *or* br. g.	6	10–5	Mr. J. R. Anthony	100–8
1916	VERMOUTH *by Barcadaile, dam by Bushey Park*	b. g.	6	11–10	J. M. Reardon	100–8

Year	Horse	Colour and Sex	Age	Weight	Jockey	Odds
1917	BALLYMACAD *by Laveno—Ballymacarney*	b. g.	9	9–12	E. Driscoll	100–9
1918	POETHLYN *by Rydal Head—Fine Champagne*	b. g.	8	11–6	E. Piggot	5–1
1919	POETHLYN *by Rydal Head—Fine Champagne*	b. g.	9	12–7	E. Piggot	11–4
1920	TROYTOWN *by Zria—Diane*	br. g.	7	11–9	Mr. J. R. Anthony	6–1
1921	SHAUN SPADAH *by Easter Prize—Rusialka*	b. g.	10	11–7	F. B. Rees	100–9
1922	MUSIC HALL *by Cliftonhall—Molly*	b. g.	9	11–8	L. B. Rees	100–9
1923	SERGEANT MURPHY *by General Symons—Rose Graft*	ch. g.	13	11–3	Capt. G. N. Bennet	100–6
1924	MASTER ROBERT *by Moorside II—Dodds*	ch. g.	11	10–5	R. Trudgill	25–1
1925	DOUBLE CHANCE *by Roi Herode or Day Comet —Kelibia*	ch. g.	9	10–9	Major Wilson	100–9
1926	JACK HORNER *by Cyllius—Melton's Guide*	ch. g.	9	10–5	W. Watkinson	25–1
1927	SPRIG *by Marco—Spry*	ch. g.	10	12–4	T. Leader	8–1
1928	TIPPERARY TIM *by Cipango—Last Lot*	b. g.	10	10	Mr. Dutton	100–1
1929	GREGALACH *by My Prince—St. Germanie*	ch. g.	7	11–4	R. Everett	100–1
1930	SHAUN GOILIN *sire's pedigree unknown— Golden Day*	ch. g.	10	11–7	T. Cullinan	100–8
1931	GRAKLE *by Jackdaw—Lady Crank*	br. g.	9	11–7	R. Lyall	100–6

F R O M this list of the winners of the Grand National, the following averages have been drawn:

Of the 93 winners, all but 25 have been "aged" horses, *i.e.* eight years old or over. Of the 25 who were not "aged," 5 were five-year-olds, 14 were six-year-olds, and 6 were seven-year-olds. The average age of the winners, taken over the last twenty years of the race, is almost exactly eight years and ten months.

Eleven mares and eleven stallions have won the race—two of these stallions won twice—and all the rest were geldings. It must be remembered, however, that there are five winners during the very early years that are very vaguely described in the records, and it is not known whether they were geldings or stallions.

No horse has won the race more than twice. Those with two victories to their credits are the following:

Peter Simple—1849, 1853.
Abd el Kader—1850-51.
The Lamb—1868, 1871.
The Colonel—1869-70.
Manifesto—1897, 1899.
Poethlyn—1918-19.

The colours of five of the 93 winners are not known definitely; of the remaining 88, there is a remarkable predominance of bays and browns—the two colours being lumped together as is customary in these colour comparisons. 62 winners have been bay or brown, 22 chestnut, 2 black, and 1 grey; this grey, however, was The Lamb, who won twice.

Until 1843, each horse carried the same weight of 12 stone. In 1843 top weight was 12 stone 8 pounds. Bottom weight has fluctuated up and down between 8 stone 7 pounds, and 10 stone. For a long period it was 9 stone 7 pounds, in 1922 it became 10 stone, and in 1931 was raised to 10 stone 7 pounds.

Average weight carried by winners from 1843 to 1931 is 10 stone, 12½ pounds. Dividing the 89 years into 3 periods of approximately the same length, the winners' average weight increases a little, as follows:

1843-1870 winners carried average of 10 stone, 9¾ pounds.
1871-1899 winners carried average of 10 stone, 13½ pounds.
1900-1931 winners carried average of 11 stone.

The average starting price for winners from 1839-1931 is 15—1. Four horses, however, were unquoted in the betting, and thus have not been considered in the computation. If they had been quoted their odds would of course have been very long. The average starting price for winners over the last twenty years is 21—1. This average is high because of the two horses who won in 1928 and 1929 at 100—1. Eliminating these two long shots, the average for the last twenty years drops down to 12—1. The longest price that has ever been quoted against a winner is 100—1; this has occurred twice in the two years mentioned above. The shortest price any horse has won at is 3—1, which was quoted against The Huntsman in 1862.

Only twelve owners have enjoyed the distinction of winning the Grand National more than once. Two of these twelve have won it three times—Captain Machell with Disturbance in 1873, Reugny the year after, and Regal in 1876; Sir Charles Assheton-Smith (while he was still Mr. Duff) with Cloister in 1893, Jerry M. in 1912, and Covertcoat in 1913.

Owners who have won the race twice are:
  Mr. John Elmore: Lottery, 1839; Gaylad, 1842.
  Mr. John Osborne: Abd-el-Kader, 1850, 1851.
  Captain Little: Chandler, 1848; Peter Simple, 1853.
  Mr. J. Mason: Peter Simple, 1849; Miss Mowbray, 1852.
  Mr. C. Capel: Little Charley, 1858; Anatis, 1860.
  Lord Coventry: Emblem, 1863; Emblematic, 1864.
  Lord Poulett: The Lamb, 1868, 1871.
  Mr. Stanley Howard: Eremon, 1907; Jenkinstown, 1910.
  Mr. F. Bibby: Kirkland, 1905; Glenside, 1911.
  Mrs. Hugh Peel: Poethlyn, 1918, 1919.

Jockeys with more than one Grand National victory to their credits are:
  T. Olliver, professional, three winners: 1842, 1843, 1853.
  Mr. A. Goodman, amateur, two winners: 1852, 1866.
  George Stevens, professional, five winners: 1856, 1863, 1864, 1869, 1870.
  Mr. T. F. Pickernell ("Mr. Thomas"), amateur, three winners: 1860, 1871, 1875.
  J. Page, professional, two winners: 1867, 1872.
  Mr. J. M. Richardson, amateur, two winners: 1873, 1874.
  Mr. T. Beasley, amateur, three winners: 1880, 1881, 1889.
  Mr. E. P. Wilson, amateur, two winners: 1884, 1885.
  A. Nightingall, professional, three winners: 1890, 1894, 1901.
  P. Woodland, professional, two winners: 1903, 1913.
  Mr. J. R. Anthony, amateur, three winners: 1911, 1915, 1920.
  E. Piggot, professional, three winners: 1912, 1918, 1919.

Key to Abbreviations

a.	aged	D. S.	dislocated shoulder
B. & R. O.	bolted and ran out	DES.	destroyed
		DIS.	dismounted
B. B.	broke back	F.	fell
B. D.	broke down	F. & D.	fell and died
b. g.	bay gelding	F. & DES.	fell and destroyed
b. h.	bay horse	g.	gelding
B. L.	broke leg	gr. g.	grey gelding
B. L., DES.	broke leg and destroyed	gr. h.	grey horse
		h.	horse
BLUN.	blundered	h. b.	half-bred
b. m.	bay mare	K. O.	knocked over
bl. g.	black gelding	L. S.	lost saddle
bl. h.	black horse	m.	mare
bl. m.	black mare	N. S.	National Stud
br. g.	brown gelding	P. U.	pulled up
br. h.	brown horse	POIS.	poisoned
br. m.	brown mare	R. F. DES.	refused, fell and destroyed
ch. f.	chestnut filly		
ch. g.	chestnut gelding	R. O.	ran out
ch. h.	chestnut horse	REF.	refused
ch. m.	chestnut mare	R. OR REM.	remounted

INDEX

Index

Index

Index

U

Index

Index

Index

Index

Index

Index

Index

Index

Index

Index

Index

Index

Index

Index

Index

Index